Advance Praise for *Value Leadership*

"Peter Cohan has produced a thoughtful and well-written analysis of what it takes to build and sustain a successful business organization. He employs real-life business examples to illustrate his points and he makes a compelling case for the principles which he believes can make or break a company."
—Samuel L. Hayes III, Jacob H. Schiff Professor of Investment Banking, Emeritus, Harvard Business School

"*Value Leadership* is an insightful and inspiring book. It recognizes that restoring trust in corporate America will take more than legislation and compliance with regulations. It will demand a fundamental re-examination of corporate values, cultures, and relationships. Cohan presents a cogent, practical model for this process, which should interest investors, executives, board directors, employees, policy makers, and anyone who wants to see business generate value for society in a sustainable and ethical way."
—W. Michael Hoffman, executive director, Center for Business Ethics, Bentley College

"*Value Leadership* evolves Cohan's earlier paradigms into seven extremely clear principles to help both graduate students and managers in our executive education programs analyze companies in today's hot fields like genomics, bio-informatics, and photonics. I think his principles, cases, and tools will also be quite useful for managers, venture capital investors, board members, and others who have to assess and guide growth businesses."
—Barry Unger, chairman, science and engineering program, division of extended education and faculty of photonics, Boston University

"There are two things every executive should understand about *Value Leadership*. First, the Value Quotient is a strategic assessment and planning tool that is easy to understand and put to work. Second, it actually does work—brilliantly."
—Michael Alan Hamlin, author, *The New Asian Corporation,* and CEO, TeamAsia

"It's so easy to commit conceptually to value leadership, but so hard to implement that commitment in a sustained way and to achieve best-in-class results. Cohan provides guidelines for a systematic approach to both implementation and measurement of value leadership derived from his in-depth studies of companies that demonstrate sustained value leadership. The world needs more value leaders. Peter Cohan can help."
—**Mark P. Rice, Murata Dean, F.W. Olin Graduate School of Business, Babson College**

"*Value Leadership* is an extremely important book because it lays out a clear and navigable road map for companies to restore trust with customers, employees, and investors. It thoroughly integrates uplifting principles with a thoughtful measurement approach to ensure outstanding results, providing a healthy antidote to the cynicism that has grown so pervasive. . . . I recommend this book strongly to boards and management teams, who are almost universally dealing with these issues."
—**Bill Kelvie, CEO, Overture Technologies**

"Peter Cohan takes us back to the future with laser-like focus through the prism of value (based) leadership. Cohan appeals powerfully to our natural instincts to "do the right thing" and reminds us that honesty, integrity, and character in their full splendor are the truly enduring elements of successful American capitalism—and as important and measurable as profits and growth. *Value Leadership* is a much-needed prescription at a unique time in American business and stands apart from its genre by reminding us of the traits that make the pursuit of profits a noble cause."
—**Mahesh Krishnamurti, publisher and CFO, *Worth Magazine***

Value Leadership

Also by Peter S. Cohan

The Technology Leaders: How America's Most Profitable High-Tech Companies Innovate Their Way to Success

Net Profit: How to Invest and Compete in the Real World of Internet Business

e-Profit: High Payoff Strategies for Capturing the E-Commerce Edge

e-Stocks: Finding the Hidden Blue Chips Among the Internet Impostors

Technology Leaders

e-Leaders

Peter S. Cohan

Value Leadership

The 7 Principles That Drive
Corporate Value in Any Economy

JOSSEY-BASS
A Wiley Imprint
www.josseybass.com

Published by Jossey-Bass
A Wiley Imprint
989 Market Street, San Francisco, CA 94103-1741   www.josseybass.com

Jossey-Bass books and products are available through most bookstores. To contact Jossey-Bass
directly call our Customer Care Department within the U.S. at 800-956-7739, outside the U.S. at
317-572-3986, or fax 317-572-4002.

Jossey-Bass also publishes its books in a variety of electronic formats. Some content that appears
in print may not be available in electronic books.

Library of Congress Cataloging-in-Publication Data

Cohan, Peter S., 1957-
  Value leadership : the 7 principles that drive corporate value in any
economy / Peter S. Cohan. — 1st ed.
      p. cm.
Includes bibliographical references and index.
  ISBN 0-7879-6604-5 (alk. paper)
  1. Leadership. 2. Executive ability. 3. Profit. 4. Social
responsibility of business. I. Title: 7 principles that drive corporate value in any economy. II.
Title: Seven principles that drive corporate value in any economy. III. Title.
  HD57.7.C63 2003
  658.4'092 — dc21   2003006810

Printed in the United States of America

FIRST EDITION
HB Printing 10 9 8 7 6 5 4 3 2 1

～ Contents

To the memory of my grandfather,

Joseph B. Cohan (1893–1986).

He was an ethical executive and generous

community benefactor.

I wish he could have read this book.

What Is Value Leadership?

C onsider this statement of corporate values:

OUR VALUES

Communication

We have an obligation to communicate. Here, we take the time to talk with one another . . . and to listen. We believe that information is meant to move and that information moves people.

Respect

We treat others as we would like to be treated ourselves. We do not tolerate abusive or disrespectful treatment.

Integrity

We work with customers and prospects openly, honestly, and sincerely. When we say we will do something, we will do it; when we say we cannot or will not do something, then we won't do it.

Excellence

We are satisfied with nothing less than the very best in everything we do. We will continue to raise the bar for everyone. The great fun here will be for all of us to discover just how good we can really be.[1]

It's hard to imagine a better one. Because this statement comes from Enron's 2000 annual report, it is also hard to imagine a better example of the chasm that separates word and deed in too many companies. As Jeff Skilling, Enron's CEO at the time, would say, the statement of values was "good optics."[2] This was Skilling's shorthand for creating a corporate situation that looked good on the surface while masking its underlying reality. The value of good optics from Skilling's perspective was that if an investment or a job opportunity looked good, Skilling could persuade people to part with their money or their reputation while enriching Skilling's.

Skilling's precollapse departure from Enron—ostensibly "to spend more time with his family"—was his final piece of good optics. By getting out early, Skilling was able to sell his stock and distance himself from Enron. However, the firestorm resulting from Enron's $62 billion bankruptcy in December 2001 eroded the foundation of trust on which our economic system depends.

Although not the largest corporate bankruptcy, Enron's collapse triggered intense scrutiny of corporate misbehavior that accelerated other bankruptcies such as that of the larger WorldCom. The cumulative effect of this exposed misbehavior is a challenge for today's business leaders to restore confidence in American capitalism. If they succeed, a hundred million American households can look forward to the future with greater confidence for themselves and future generations. If they fail, these same families face a future of gnawing economic uncertainty. The purpose of this book is to give executives a framework, based on the value principles of leading companies, to build a bright future for American capitalism.

EXECUTIVES ARE FEELING THE HEAT

This turning point in American capitalism comes as a stunning shock for those flushed with the late 1990s aura of success. Students of economic history, however, predicted the future costs of this and previous eras' excesses. The past couple of decades have witnessed the expansion and subsequent dissolution of many economic bubbles. Between 1980 and 2002 bubbles in oil and gas, thrifts, leveraged buyouts, corporate real estate, hedge funds, and most recently the Internet and telecommunications have made many insiders hundreds of billions of dollars while costing outsiders trillions.

In many of these cases, the industries may initially have generated real profits. As the bubbles progressed, however, they captured the imagination of new investors who demanded ever higher rates of growth to fuel their continued buying. Invariably the source of this growth was debt-fueled acquisitions, which permitted a loosening of investment standards. Although initial investors profited from the second wave's cash, eventually the assets purchased with these new investment dollars became a ticking time bomb. The result was waves of bankruptcies, bailouts, and government investigations. People withdrew from investing until a new investment bubble started to form and caught their attention. And the cycle began anew.

The bursting of the technology bubble has exposed a network of conflicting interests that permeates the holders and seekers of political and economic power. For example, politicians and regulators depend on corporate cash to pay for elections. As a result, government officials are in a weak position to protect society from corporate misbehavior when such protection might jeopardize the corporate cash that fuels their own political ambitions. Similarly auditors hesitate to challenge the accounting practices of deep-pocketed clients out of fear of losing auditing or even more lucrative consulting fees. Investment banks create the illusion that their analysts' stock recommendations are intended for the benefit of the general investing public rather than their real object—investment banking clients. Some CEOs have made public statements to pump up their companies' shares before selling their stock to a gullible public—pitting executives' self-interest against that of small investors, a group that not infrequently includes the company's own employees. And many board members have an incentive not to rock the boat in order to maintain the prestige and pay that goes with their role.

Growing awareness of these conflicts caused the general public to lose faith in American capitalism. For example, a *Wall Street Journal*/NBC survey of 1,005 American adults published in April 2002 revealed a dramatic erosion in respect for corporate leaders. Specifically, the survey found that 57 percent of respondents believed that the standards and values of corporate leaders and executives had *dropped* in the past twenty years. By contrast, in 1998 53 percent of respondents felt business leaders' standards were *the same or higher.*[3]

Over the subsequent months, this distrust of corporate America continued. A Hart-Teeter poll of 1,008 American adults conducted two months later highlighted a leap in distrust for corporate America. From April 2002 to June 2002, the percentage of respondents who believed that what happened at Enron occurs in many companies leaped from 18 percent to 24 percent.[4]

This loss of faith translated into substantial withdrawals of investor funds from the stock market. For example, investors withdrew $11.1 billion from U.S. stock mutual funds in February 2003, continuing a string of monthly withdrawals that started in mid-2002.[5] And this withdrawal of investor funds reflected investor sentiment in the wake of a $7 trillion loss in stock market value between its March 2000 peak, when the Wilshire 5000 index of all U.S. publicly traded stocks was worth $17.4 trillion, to its $10.4 trillion value in July 2002.[6] The erosion of faith and stock market value threatened citizens' confidence in their ability to earn a living and slashed the value of their retirement savings—forcing many to defer planned retirements indefinitely.

These factoids offer glimpses into the pervasive role that faith plays in the effective functioning of our economy. Faith is important because our economy depends on people's willingness to take risks. People will take risks only if they believe they can earn an offsetting return. In some cases these risks are as big as a $100 billion corporate acquisition. In others the risk is as small as a worker who invests a month's effort with hope that her employer will deliver her paycheck at the end of the month.

Loss of faith in our economic system significantly boosts the returns people require in order to take such risks. If workers suspect that a potential employer is cooking its books to boost its stock price, then they may demand higher wages to offset the risk that the company will not survive. If a supplier believes that a corporate customer is shaky, it will demand better financial terms. If investors lose faith in management, they will sell the company's stock or refuse to invest in the company in the first place. If CEOs lose faith in the economic benefits of capital investment in areas such as technology, they will demand higher rates of return from such investments—or stop them altogether. Ultimately, if the fabric of faith on which risk taking depends becomes too frayed, then economic activity grinds to a halt.

As a result, CEOs are under enormous pressure to restore lost faith. In some cases CEOs are so closely tied to the destruction of investor trust that their boards force them to walk the plank. In most cases CEOs were following common practices that began to backfire in an age of intensified scrutiny. And in a few cases, CEOs have avoided misbehaving (because they *were* scathed, as their stock prices fell);

nevertheless an overall mood of investor pessimism holds their companies' stock prices in check.

WHAT IS VALUE LEADERSHIP?

Yet there are amazing examples of companies that have soldiered on to great success despite the gloom. Some leaders can build successful organizations by responding well to scarcity and challenge.

According to John Bachmann, managing director, that's what he helped do when Edward Jones, the privately held St. Louis, Missouri–based securities brokerage that he runs, was perched on the brink of extinction thirty-three years ago.[7]

In 1970 the brokerage industry was in the doldrums. The Dow was down 50 percent, and the equivalent of the NASDAQ had plunged 75 percent. Edward Jones, which had grown to over one hundred offices from its founding in the 1920s, was suffering badly. And it had only $1 million worth of capital left to its name. Furthermore, the industry was about to get worse as the government deregulated fixed commissions for trading securities.

Bachmann, who ran the firm's Columbia, Missouri, office at the time, and Ted Jones, the founder's son, made a crucial decision that propelled Edward Jones to an enviable position in 2003. At that time Edward Jones, with eighty-seven hundred offices, over twenty-five thousand employees, and $2.2 billion in revenue, had sustained double-digit growth in revenues and profits for the previous two decades while the industry saw its fortunes plunge. Edward Jones had topped *Fortune*'s survey of the one hundred best companies to work for in 2002 and 2003. And it had won other awards, including a number one rank in the J. D. Power & Associates customer service survey.

The crucial decision that Bachmann and Jones made over thirty years ago was simple yet profound. With dwindling capital they decided that Edward Jones's survival would depend on focusing on one customer—the long-term individual investor. This decision caused Edward Jones to quit its activities targeted at the institutional investor—such as commodities trading—because the firm lacked the capital and resources to compete for institutional trading business.

For Bachmann and Jones, the focus of Edward Jones would be the Mrs. Ballews of the world. Mrs. Ballew was the proprietor of Centralia, Missouri–based Ballew Funeral Home, and Edward Jones advised her on how to invest the cash that her business generated over the years.

Finding and serving the Mrs. Ballews of the world was Edward Jones's version of the search for the Holy Grail. Ted Jones had an interest in agriculture and told his father that he did not want to spend his career in St. Louis. Instead, Ted went out into the countryside knocking on doors, meeting small businesspeople and farmers, building trust with them, and advising them on long-term investments. In such small communities, word would get around if he did not treat a customer well.

Jones's values fit well with the needs of the market. Because he had no children, he decided not to sell the business as he grew older. Instead, Jones took on partners, giving up his ownership so others could act as stewards of Edward Jones.

And a crucial element of this stewardship was that every investment representative who joined Edward Jones would have to engage in his or her own search for the Holy Grail by spending the first three to four months with the company meeting in person with twenty-five potential customers a day, creating relationships.

Edward Jones is a life-support system for people willing to undertake this quest. Its values are based on respect—for external customers, for long-term relationships, for contributions to the organization, and for generating results. It sells only stocks, bonds, and other investment products that appeal to long-term investors. It provides its customers with statements that aggregate in one place all their accounts from investments, mutual funds, credit cards, bank accounts, and more.

Edward Jones invests an unusual amount of effort into hiring and developing its people. Of the fifteen thousand job inquiries it receives each month, the firm hires only two hundred applicants. It looks for high achievers with a sense of purpose. Interestingly, it discourages people from talking about their own honesty and integrity. According to Bachmann, his mother warned him: "Be careful, John, you could break your arm patting yourself on the back." Once the company hires investment representatives, Edward Jones invests in training them to pass their Series 7 exam.

And if these investment reps take responsibility for their work, demonstrate an aptitude for inventing growth opportunities consistent with the firm's values, and earn the respect of their peers while achieving success, Edward Jones offers them shares in the firm's partnership.

Why do people enjoy working for Edward Jones? People like working in a company that is organized to serve customers and give back to the community. The tight alignment between the organization and its customers' needs emerged from the choices Edward Jones made back in the early 1970s.

What Edward Jones chose not to do is as important as what it does. Each investment representative is a profit center. Edward Jones chose not to create separate profit centers for each product. Everyone at Edward Jones works together to help the investor; they don't compete with each other. Edward Jones reinforces this value by paying its bonuses based mostly on the firm's overall performance above a minimum threshold. Rather than offering incentive travel to, say, the top 10 percent of its investment reps, it offers such travel to anyone who achieves a predetermined level of success. In 2002 thirty-five hundred out of nine thousand total investment reps earned such awards.

Because many industries as of this writing have limited pricing power and very little access to capital, they need to learn how to deal with scarcity in a way that makes them operate more effectively. Bachmann's humbly offered advice to these companies is timeless:

1. Decide who your customer is.
2. Know how your company creates unique value for that customer.
3. Choose not to perform activities that do not create value for that customer.
4. Align all your company's activities to create that value.
5. Recognize that meaningful change takes time, so take the long view.[8]

This inspiring example is intended to highlight an important conclusion: government cannot rebuild confidence in American capitalism. Looking for government to solve the problem is tantamount to expecting a new referee to turn a last-place football team into a Super Bowl contender. The place to look for guidance is a concept of corporate leadership that has helped create value for companies like Edward Jones during good times and bad. This powerful concept—Value Leadership—is supported by seven principles that can help CEOs with the hard work of restoring confidence in American capitalism.

Value Leadership is based on very specific notions of value and leadership. It recognizes that a company cannot survive without the participation of others: employees, customers, investors, and communities. The *value* in Value Leadership alludes to the nature of the relationship between the company and these others. These relationships have value if both the company and the other are better off as a result of forming and sustaining the relationship. The specific details of what would make both parties better off varies by company and by employee, customer, and community. For example, one employee might value the relationship with a company if the company paid a fair wage and gave the employee time off to care for a sick parent; another employee might perceive the relationship as valuable if the company gave the employee sufficient training and career development opportunities to rise quickly within the management ranks. Similar differences emerge from the relationship between a company and individual customers, investors, and communities.

In general, executives seeking to discover these differences should start by listening to individual employees, customers, shareholders, and community members. Although such listening is not a novel concept, it is not something that companies do systematically and open-mindedly. By listening, executives can begin to fashion mutually beneficial value relationships with these groups. If a company hopes to maintain its leadership, it must help such relationships evolve over time rather than allowing them to remain static. Thus the process of listening and forging value relationships is continuous rather than a one-time event.

The *leadership* in Value Leadership suggests a connection between how well a company creates value in its relationships relative to its peers and the relative rate of return that company offers its investors. Companies battle to create competitively superior value for the "best" employees, customers, investors, and communities. Winning these battles yields competitively superior returns for investors because the best people—coordinated effectively—generate the most effective and efficient solutions to customer problems. Through profit sharing and stock ownership, employees and investors share in the gains from these solutions.

In the airline industry, for example, some customers value cheap fares, on-time flight departures and arrivals, and pleasant people. An airline that can satisfy these customer value criteria (CVC) better than competitors is likely to attract more people who share these CVC as regular customers than its peers. An airline can satisfy these CVC in part by hiring the right kinds of employees: those that are service-oriented by nature and able to react quickly and effectively to the unexpected. Such employees may look for an employer that respects their individuality, imbues work with a sense of fun, and lets them share in the profits that result from getting the job done right. An airline that does a better job than competitors of satisfying these employee value criteria (EVC) is more likely to attract and maximize the productivity of such employees. If such employees do a better job than competitors of satisfying customers, then the company is likely to generate better financial results than competitors. A powerful tool for attracting such employees is corporate support of a community cause that has great meaning to the employees. If the company supports an employee-initiated charity, the employee will feel even greater loyalty to the company while the community will benefit from the passionate involvement of that company's employees. Finally, some investors will buy and hold an airline's stock if the company generates consistent profit growth over extended periods of time. If a company does a better job of generating consistent profits than its peers, it will attract such shareholders to buy and hold the stock, which could help drive up the company's stock market value.

Value Leadership means giving a company's employees, customers, investors, and communities a better deal than competitors do. As the airline industry example demonstrates, Value Leadership depends on both providing competitively superior value to individual groups— for example, customers and employees—as well as on orchestrating the relationships among these groups to create a self-sustaining system of value creation. In the airline example, the company started with an understanding of CVC, satisfied the EVC of employees who could do a better job of satisfying these customers, and ended up generating better financial results for buy-and-hold investors.

Although this formula sounds simple, it is difficult to sustain over a long period of time. In some companies creating competitively superior value as long as the founding entrepreneur is CEO is relatively easy. Often sustaining such Value Leadership in subsequent generations of management is difficult. If a company does not sustain Value Leadership, competitors can offer customers, employees, and communities a better deal—ultimately harming the company's financial results, leading buy-and-hold investors to defect to the competitor who grabbed the Value Leadership baton. In order to satisfy the ultimate test of Value Leadership, a company must create a system of value creation that adapts to changes such as fresh customer needs, modified employee interests, upstart competitors, and new technologies.

HOW IS VALUE LEADERSHIP DIFFERENT THAN OTHER MANAGEMENT IDEAS?

Value Leadership differs from management ideas such as reengineering, Six Sigma, the balanced scorecard, and economic value added

(EVA). Although these techniques seek to improve profits through quantitative or engineering analyses, Value Leadership seeks to enhance how a company behaves relative to its employees, customers, and communities.

Reengineering focused on improving a company's business processes. It urged managers to take a "clean sheet of paper" and invent new ways of doing work, stripped of activities that did not add value and handoffs across functions. Value Leadership shares some ideas with reengineering. For example, Value Leadership drives a company to improve the way it interacts with customers. Unlike reengineering, however, Value Leadership places a significant emphasis on the importance of employees and communities. Whereas reengineering depersonalizes business processes, Value Leadership suggests that attracting the right people and encouraging them to work together is a crucial business imperative. Whereas reengineering would simply root out process inefficiencies and discard any pesky people left behind, Value Leadership would create an environment in which people would volunteer to take waste out of the business as a way to preserve the company's long-term value.

Six Sigma brought more statistical rigor to process improvement. It focused managers on measuring the cost of defects in all their business processes so that they could remove the factors that caused those defects. By reducing defects, companies could reduce costs while improving quality. Value Leadership also focuses on measurement; however, rather than counting defects, it assesses how tightly a company's actions accord with its values. Value Leadership is based on the notion that a work environment that creates superior value for employees, customers, and communities will generate higher returns for investors. As we will see when we explore the concept of the Value Quotient (VQ), tools are available to convert this concept into specific activities and processes that lead to better results. Unlike Six Sigma, Value Leadership focuses management attention on adding competitively superior value rather than subtracting waste.

The balanced scorecard suggests that companies that want to implement their strategies should measure factors other than financial ones, such as employee and customer satisfaction and learning. Rather than accepting a company's strategy as the balanced scorecard does, Value Leadership starts with an assessment of a company's strategy, organization, and operations. Value Leadership provides this assessment by guiding a company in the calculation of its VQ, which helps pinpoint opportunities for improvement. Because this assessment process compares a company to others in the Value Leadership database, Value Leadership offers prescriptive activities and tactics that managers can use to achieve superior performance in a highly leveraged manner. Unlike the balanced scorecard, Value Leadership recognizes that a company can accelerate its efforts to improve through an assessment of its strategy, organization, and operations in light of what works best in its industry and relative to the best of breed.

EVA is a form of financial analysis whose object is to increase a company's stock market value. EVA requires managers to quantify the amount of capital allocated to each of its business units and to assess whether that business generates sufficiently high returns to justify the allocated capital. EVA suggests that managers should sell or close businesses that do not justify their cost of capital. Value Leadership suggests that value to investors flows from the way a company behaves toward employees, customers, and communities. Rather than deriving value from financial analysis as EVA does, Value Leadership suggests that value emerges from how well a company manages relationships.

Value Leadership has been ignored during the last two decades, in particular, because of the rising stock market. The bull market that began in 1982 and lasted until 2000 provided executives with tangible rewards for subsuming the principles of Value Leadership to those of shareholder value. CEOs' stock ownership, whether through options or outright grants of stock, enabled CEOs to become extraordinarily wealthy by responding to the demands of stock analysts for consistently exceeding quarterly earnings forecasts. To feed this infinite maw, CEOs slashed payrolls, bought and sold businesses, bought back stock on the open market, and—when all else failed—manipulated their financial reports to make the numbers come out the way the analysts demanded. The rewards for feeding the beast—and the penalties for starving it—were so high that all other CEO activities took a deep backseat. In the process creating value for employees, customers, and communities became niceties occasionally mouthed by highly paid flacks.

WHY IS VALUE LEADERSHIP IMPORTANT NOW?

Value Leadership is intended to help executives address different challenges at different stages of an economic cycle. It offers concepts and methods that can help executives restore faith in their companies during a period when the excesses of the previous boom are being worked out. In future periods of economic contraction, the principles described in *Value Leadership* are intended to be equally useful, although it is possible that not all the companies highlighted will be equally good examples of these principles.

During periods of rapid economic growth and optimism for the future, Value Leadership can help executives from straying too far from the values that produced the success. Human nature suggests that during the periods of greatest success, executives are most likely to become arrogant and insulated from the values that led to that success. Conversely, during periods of economic contraction, executives are most likely to proclaim their willingness to conform to tight management discipline. Because *Value Leadership* analyzes companies that have sustained superior performance through good times and bad, its principles are intended to serve executives throughout the full amplitude of an economic cycle.

Ultimately, Value Leadership works because it meets a deeply held need. People are communal creatures, deriving satisfaction both from achieving their own goals and from helping others in the process. America places significant emphasis on individual accomplishment; that accomplishment is not achieved in isolation. Entrepreneurs feel a strong sense of responsibility for their workers, investors, customers, and communities. They perceive themselves in a virtuous battle against skeptics to convert an idea in their heads into an economic entity that can benefit their stakeholders. Although taking action against competitors is part of the battle, the ultimate benefit of the struggle emerges not so much from beating competitors per se as from convincing a customer that the entrepreneur offers a superior value proposition. This ongoing process of creating higher levels of value in the relationships between a company and its stakeholders meets an economic and psychological need.

HOW SHOULD READERS APPROACH VALUE LEADERSHIP?

Value Leadership can benefit different audiences differently. Investors can use it to identify companies that might be profitable investments and to evaluate their current investments to assess which might be vulnerable. Boards of directors can use it to pinpoint problems with a company's strategy, organization, and operations. For-profit and nonprofit executives can use it to mobilize change that leads to better performance. Workers can use it to evaluate potential employers. And policymakers and regulators can use it to signal to investors the health of the organizations that they oversee.

Let's look at how Value Leadership can accomplish these ends for each group, respectively.

Investors can apply Value Leadership to their current and potential portfolios in several ways. They can develop an information system that enables them to rank the companies in their investment portfolio based on how well they implement the concept. Such an information system would be based on interviews with a company's customers, employees, and communities; as well as detailed analysis of its strategy, capabilities, competitive position, and financial probity. Because maintaining such a system would require substantial effort, it would provide a profit advantage to those few investors who took the time to build and operate it. Such a system could also be used to screen potential investments, with particular value for offering early warning on companies that received public acclamation while hosting deeper problems that might appear later.

Boards of directors can use Value Leadership to help exercise their fiduciary responsibilities. Boards could use the concept to evaluate corporate policies in areas such as financial reporting, succession planning, human resources management, community responsibility, corporate strategy, and executive compensation. Specifically, boards could use Value Leadership as a standard against which to review corporate policies, to pinpoint weaknesses, and to drive improvement. Boards could also use Value Leadership as the concept around which to organize their systems for monitoring corporate compliance with policies and to gather early warning indicators of potential problems. Such a monitoring system could also form the basis for ensuring that the board was fulfilling its fiduciary responsibilities and for signaling the CEO of situations requiring change.

Executives can use Value Leadership to pinpoint opportunities for improvement and to drive the change required to achieve superior performance. As we will soon explore, the VQ is a number that gauges the extent to which an organization embodies Value Leadership principles, to both identify weaknesses and to drive the organization to remedy them. Specifically, executives can, with the assistance of objective outsiders, use the VQ to identify the Value Leadership principles and activities where the organization has the greatest potential for improvement in comparison to Value Leaders. Using the analysis, executives can initiate and execute specific improvement programs. By embedding the VQ into performance evaluation and compensation systems, executives can encourage the persistence and discipline needed to sustain superior performance.

Workers can use Value Leadership to evaluate potential employers. Like investors, workers can develop information about a potential employer to assess career potential and fit. Although time-consuming to develop, information about a potential employer's employee and customer satisfaction, competitiveness, financial probity, and ability to renew itself could repay the investment of time manyfold. Workers who take the time to conduct such an assessment can both avoid the pitfalls of working for a company that does not follow the principles of Value Leadership and increase the chances of enjoying the personal and economic rewards of working for a company that does.

Policymakers and regulators can also benefit from Value Leadership. The concept offers a clear set of principles and ways to assess whether organizations act according to them. Policymakers could encourage leaders to follow the principles by incorporating them into legislation. Regulators could add teeth to such legislation by encouraging organizations, particularly publicly traded companies, to include their VQ in their annual reports along with an analysis of how those scores compared with those of peers, how the scores had changed over time, and what the organizations were doing to improve.

THE SEVEN PRINCIPLES OF VALUE LEADERSHIP

One of the most memorable parts of Plato's *Republic* is the allegory of the cave. Plato described a group of people who had spent their entire lives in a cave, with their legs and necks chained. A lit fire illuminated vessels, statues, and figures of animals in front of a screenlike wall, projecting the objects' shadows onto the wall of the cave. Thus the cave dweller's sole experience of reality was shadows. Later the cave dwellers are released from their chains, leave the cave, and squint as they observe three-dimensional objects, and ultimately the sun and the planets.[9]

According to an interpretation of this allegory, the three-dimensional objects of the allegory represented *platonic solids,* or concepts, and the shadows on the cave wall represented the manifestation of these concepts in the real world. One example of such a platonic solid was the concept of chair-ness. *Chair-ness* was a universal concept of a chair, and the wide array of chair styles and shapes in the real world were analogous to the shadows on the wall of the cave. Just as the different flickers of the flames in the cave could produce different looking shadows from the same object behind the screen, so do we create different real-world interpretations of platonic solids.

The allegory of the cave helps explain the origin of the concept of Value Leadership. The concept emerged from my search for evidence of solid American companies after the bursting of the pre-2000 bubble economy. In light of the widespread desire to fix blame for these problems, numerous culprits were fingered: Wall Street analysts and investment bankers, corrupt corporate executives, unethical accountants, and compromised politicians and regulators. This search for the guilty seems to be a natural way for capitalism to purge its excesses. The search for evidence of solid American companies was based on the belief that such companies could help restore some of the confidence in American capitalism destroyed during the post-2000 collapse.

Here's where the allegory of the cave came into play. Focusing on good companies was like using the shadows flickering on the wall of the cave as exemplars of the best of American capitalism. Although the shadows might create compelling images in one moment, their power to create an inspiring concept could erode in the next. One example that comes to mind is Cisco Systems, which was a beacon of the best of management until the stock market began collapsing in 2000. As Cisco lost $400 billion worth of stock market value, many of its "best practices" began to appear suspect.

Even the eight Value Leaders we'll meet later in this Introduction, although great performers in many respects, had flaws. For example, Wal-Mart had been sued for forcing workers to put in unpaid overtime and for discriminating against women; a Goldman Sachs arbitrage partner, Bob Freeman, was arrested for insider trading in February 1987; and Microsoft was the target of many lawsuits alleging anticompetitive business practices. Thus, making Value Leaders the primary focus of the book would not be the best way to approach the challenge of restoring confidence in American capitalism.

Instead, it made more sense to focus on a platonic solid, or concept, of American capitalism rather than its shadows (the Value Leaders). The concept of Value Leadership emerged from a comparison of the Value Leaders with their peers. Although Value Leaders were not the perfect embodiment of the concept of Value Leadership, their glimmers of greatness seemed to emerge most clearly where their practices follow the concept. Value Leadership focuses on the essence of what makes American capitalism work, the persistent struggle to create ever higher levels of value for a company's stakeholders, in order to inspire executives seeking to reemerge from postboom economic gloom.

Seven Principles of Value Leadership

To make Value Leadership useful, executives need principles. This book explains the following seven principles of Value Leadership:

- **Value human relationships:** treat people with respect so they achieve their full potential consistent with the company's interests.
- **Foster teamwork:** get people, particularly those with different functional skills and responsibilities, to work together to advance the interests of the corporation.
- **Experiment frugally:** harness accidental discoveries to create value for customers and partners.
- **Fulfill your commitments:** say what you intend to do; then do what you say.
- **Fight complacency:** weed out arrogance.
- **Win through multiple means:** use strategy to sustain market leadership.
- **Give to your community:** transfer corporate resources to society.

Eight Value Leaders

To test the concept of Value Leadership and its principles, I sought out companies that seemed to exemplify the concept and principles. Although it would be a mistake to hold out these Value Leaders as timeless exemplars of excellence, it would also be difficult to make Value Leadership a useful concept without examining how real companies used it. To find such Value Leaders, the author started with the fifteen hundred largest publicly traded companies in the United States and screened them based on a blend of eleven quantitative and qualititative factors.

The five qualitative factors were the following:

- Quality of financial reporting and shareholder communications
- Absence of significant legal matters and contingencies
- A high degree of employee satisfaction
- Excellence in customer service
- High level of peer respect

The six quantitative factors were

- Market share
- Ten-year average return on equity
- Revenues and profits per employee
- Balance sheet strength
- Ten-year earnings growth
- Ten-year shareholder return

The principles of Value Leadership appear to correlate quite tightly with the qualitative criteria for selecting Value Leaders. As Table I.1 indicates, the principles of Value Leadership and the five qualitative criteria have many highly positive correlations.

The positive correlations between principles of Value Leadership and the qualitative criteria for picking Value Leaders suggest that Value Leadership can help companies generate important outcomes. For example, executives seeking to enhance employee satisfaction and deliver excellent customer service can benefit most from valuing human relationships and fostering teamwork.

The principles of Value Leadership also appear to correlate quite tightly with the quantitative criteria for selecting Value Leaders. As Table I.2 indicates, many highly positive correlations exist between the principles of Value Leadership and the quantitative criteria.

The positive correlations between principles of Value Leadership and the quantitative criteria for picking Value Leaders also suggest that Value Leadership can help companies improve measures that drive shareholder value. For example, executives seeking to enhance productivity can benefit most from valuing human relationships and fostering teamwork. And executives seeking to improve market share, accelerate earnings growth and return on equity, and enhance shareholder value should embrace the principle "Win through multiple means."

After applying these eleven criteria to the fifteen hundred companies, eight Value Leaders emerged that offer examples of Value Leadership:

- Goldman Sachs, a $23 billion leader in investment banking, known for its blue-chip heritage
- Johnson & Johnson, a $36 billion maker of health care products, famous for Band-Aids and Tylenol

Principle	Link with Criteria for Qualitative Value Leader Selection	Link Strength
Value human relationships	**Financial reporting quality:** Companies that treat employees well treat shareholders well, making sure employees report accurately.	+
	Few legal problems: Fewer employee lawsuits or vendor lawsuits.	+
	High employee satisfaction: Employees treated well are more satisfied.	++
	Excellent customer service: Employees treated well serve customers better.	++
	High peer respect: Peers respect companies that hire the best people.	+
Foster teamwork	**Financial reporting quality:** Teams produce accurate numbers faster.	+
	Few legal problems: Limited correlation.	0
	High employee satisfaction: Team-oriented employees are more satisfied.	++
	Excellent customer service: Teams deliver better customer service.	++
	High peer respect: Teamwork improves performance and earns respect.	+
Experiment frugally	**Financial reporting quality:** No correlation.	0
	Few legal problems: No correlation.	0
	High employee satisfaction: Employees like being encouraged to innovate.	++
	Excellent customer service: No correlation.	0
	High peer respect: Innovative companies earn peer respect.	++
Fulfill your commitments	**Financial reporting quality:** Honest employees report honestly.	++
	Few legal problems: Honest companies have fewer legal problems.	++
	High employee satisfaction: Trusting employees are more satisfied.	+
	Excellent customer service: Honest employees deliver better service.	++
	High peer respect: Peers respect honest companies that perform well.	+
Fight complacency	**Financial reporting quality:** Results-driven company reports better.	+
	Few legal problems: No correlation.	0
	High employee satisfaction: High-performing employees are more satisfied.	+
	Excellent customer service: Enhanced value satisfies customers.	++
	High peer respect: Fighting complacency leads to growth and peer respect.	+

Principle	Link with Criteria for Qualitative Value Leader Selection	Link Strength
Win through multiple means	**Financial reporting quality:** No correlation.	0
	Few legal problems: Possibly more lawsuits from competitors falling behind (leaving a larger number of competitors that can launch lawsuits).	-
	High employee satisfaction: Employees who win are more satisfied.	++
	Excellent customer service: Better service helps companies win.	++
	High peer respect: Winning companies earn peer respect.	++
Give to your community	**Financial reporting quality:** No correlation.	0
	Few legal problems: Fewer lawsuits from community.	+
	High employee satisfaction: Employees who give are more satisfied.	++
	Excellent customer service: Customers like community donations.	+
	High peer respect: Companies that give back to the community earn peer respect.	+

Table I.1. Linkages Between Value Leadership Principles and Criteria for Value Leader Qualitative Selection.

Key: ++ = strong positive correlation; + = moderate positive correlation; 0 = no correlation; – moderate negative correlation.

- J. M. Smucker, a $986 million leader in jams, jellies, and preserves, run by the founders' great grandsons
- MBNA, an $8.8 billion leader in the market for affinity cards (credit cards issued by organizations such as sports teams and universities)
- Microsoft, a $31 billion leader in computer software, whose chairman, Bill Gates, is the world's richest person
- Southwest Airlines, a $5.5 billion low-cost airline, unique in its industry for operating at a profit for thirty consecutive years
- Synopsys, a $907 million leader in semiconductor design software, boldly taking on the challenge of acquiring Avant!, in order to give customers the full product line they demand
- Wal-Mart, a $238 billion retailer with forty-six hundred stores worldwide, known for everyday low prices

Although these eight companies may not be able to keep up their prior performance, CEOs may find it noteworthy that Value Leaders created shareholder wealth four and a half times faster than the

Principle	Link with Criteria for Qualitative Value Leader Selection	Link Strength
Value human relationships	**Market share:** Limited correlation.	0
	Return on equity: Less turnover lowers costs, increases return on equity.	+
	Productivity: Employees treated well produce more.	++
	Balance sheet strength: No correlation.	0
	Earnings growth: Satisfied employees are more productive.	+
	Shareholder return: Earnings growth increases stock price.	+
Foster teamwork	**Market share:** Teamwork helps increase customer value and market share.	+
	Return on equity: Teamwork increases productivity.	+
	Productivity: Employees who work together are more productive.	++
	Balance sheet strength: No correlation.	0
	Earnings growth: High productivity accelerates earnings growth.	+
	Shareholder return: Earnings growth increases stock price.	+
Experiment frugally	**Market share:** Successful new products grab market share.	+
	Return on equity: Profitable new products raise return on equity.	+
	Productivity: New product success enhances revenue per employee.	+
	Balance sheet strength: New product success strengthens cash.	+
	Earnings growth: New product success accelerates earnings growth.	+
	Shareholder return: Earnings growth increases stock price.	+
Fulfill your commitments	**Market share:** Limited correlation.	0
	Return on equity: Lower litigation costs increase return on equity.	+
	Productivity: Honest culture spurs employee happiness and productivity.	+
	Balance sheet strength: No correlation.	0
	Earnings growth: High productivity accelerates earnings growth.	+
	Shareholder return: Earnings growth increases stock price.	+
Fight complacency	**Market share:** Drive to improve raises market share.	+
	Return on equity: Drive to improve enhances earnings and return on equity.	+
	Productivity: Drive to improve enhances productivity.	+
	Balance sheet strength: Drive to improve increases cash generation.	+
	Earnings growth: High productivity accelerates earnings growth.	+
	Shareholder return: Earnings growth increases stock price.	+

Principle	Link with Criteria for Qualitative Value Leader Selection	Link Strength
Win through multiple means	**Market share:** Winning is measured by market share leadership.	++
	Return on equity: Winning increases pricing power and return on equity.	++
	Productivity: Winning motivates employees to produce more.	+
	Balance sheet strength: Winning can increase cash generation.	+
	Earnings growth: Winning accelerates earnings growth.	++
	Shareholder return: Winning increases stock price.	++
Give to your community	**Market share:** Giving to community spurs higher customer loyalty.	+
	Return on equity: Higher customer loyalty increases return on equity.	+
	Productivity: Employees who give are happier and produce more.	+
	Balance sheet strength: Higher customer loyalty increases cash.	+
	Earnings growth: Higher customer loyalty spurs earnings growth.	+
	Shareholder return: Higher customer loyalty increases stock price.	+

Table I.2. Linkages Between Value Leadership Principles and Criteria for Value Leader Quantitative Selection

Key: ++ = strong positive correlation; + = moderate positive correlation; 0 = no correlation.

average company. In fact, $1,000 invested in each of these eight companies ten years ago, or at the time of their initial public offerings, would be worth $47,240, a 491 percent increase. This rate greatly exceeds the growth of $8,000 invested in the Standard & Poor 500 at the same time, which would have been worth $16,500, a 106 percent improvement. An investment of $8,000 in the Value Leaders' peer companies would have generated $26,050, a 226 percent increase.[10]

THE VQ

A basic axiom of management is that what you cannot measure, you cannot manage. One of the biggest benefits of this book is that it offers a way to quantify and manage the amorphous topic of values. Earlier we mentioned how executives could use a tool, the VQ, to assess where their companies stand with respect to the seven principles of Value Leadership.

Even though we will examine the VQ in greater detail in Chapter One, let's explore the underlying logic for it here. The VQ is a percentage between 0 and 100 that is based on specific evidence of how closely a company's actions follow the principles of Value Leadership. Specifically, the VQ is predicated on a set of three or four activities that companies can perform within each of the seven Value Leadership principles. For example, within the principle "Experiment frugally" are four activities: grow organically, manage development risk, partner internally, and partner externally. We developed these activities by comparing the practices of Value Leaders with their peers. To develop the VQ, we scored the companies based on whether they perform each of the activities, and if so, how well they perform them.

We will explore the mechanics of the process further in Chapter One; however, for purposes of illustration, let's compare the VQs of two retailers: Wal-Mart and J. C. Penney. Wal-Mart's VQ is 91 percent whereas J. C. Penney's is 53 percent. The VQs were developed through a four-step process:

1. Score each company on how well it performs the activities within each of the seven principles. The scores for each activity range from 5, excellent, to 1, poor.

2. Total the scores for each activity and multiply the sum by a weight that enables each principle to contribute equally to the overall score. For principles with four activities, the multiplier is three; for principles with three activities, the multiplier is four. As a result, the maximum possible score for each principle is 60.

3. Sum the weighted scores for each of the seven principles.

4. Divide the result by the maximum possible score of 420.

Figure I.1 illustrates the results of performing step 2 for Wal-Mart and J. C. Penney.

The key to the value of VQ as a change management tool is its ability to quantify corporate behavior relative to the seven principles. To illustrate how to perform step 1, let's examine how the activity scores for Wal-Mart and J. C. Penney were developed for the principle "Value human relationships" (see Table I.3).

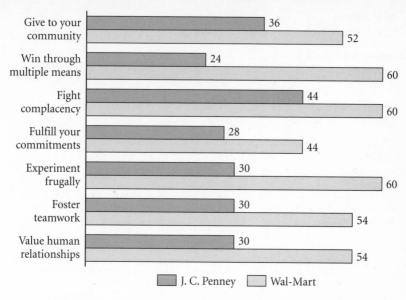

Figure I.1.   Wal-Mart and J. C. Penney Value Quotients.

This example demonstrates how to calculate the VQ components to develop the overall VQ for a company. We develop the "Value human relationships" component by assessing how well a company performs four activities related to valuing human relationships. I analyzed the differences between Value Leaders and their peers to extract the essential activities that enabled companies to realize each of the seven principles. By using these companies as a database of best practices, I calibrated how well each company performed the activities to develop their scores. Wal-Mart's score of 54 reflects its very strong performance in hiring, training, and measuring employee performance. Wal-Mart's reputation for low pay and long working hours results in a lower score in the area of pay.

The VQ helps executives identify specific activities that their organization may seek to improve. By comparing their firm to the activities supporting Value Leadership, executives can use the VQ as a basis for driving organizational improvement.

ORGANIZATION OF THIS BOOK

Value Leadership continues with a more detailed description of the VQ in Chapter One. Chapters Two through Eight expand on each of

Value Human Relationships: Activity	Score	Comment
Commit to core values		
Wal-Mart	5	Wal-Mart cheer epitomizes cultlike culture.
J. C. Penney	3	Tradition of hiring for low ambition and talent.
Hire for values		
Wal-Mart	5	Saturday morning meeting and training.
J. C. Penney	3	Cost-cutting initiatives limit training.
Balance performance measurement		
Wal-Mart	3	Stronger emphasis on results.
J. C. Penney	2	Measures customer service and item turns.
Reward employees intelligently		
Wal-Mart	5	Profit sharing, stock ownership, and low wages.
J. C. Penney	2	Late offering 401(k) options.
*Total**		
Wal-Mart	54	
J. C. Penney	30	

Table I.3.   Value Human Relationships: Wal-Mart and J. C. Penney.
Note: Maximum total score: 20. Key to component scores: 5 = excellent; 4 = very good; 3 = good; 2 = fair; 1 = poor. *Multiplied by weight of 3.

the seven principles of Value Leadership, offering case studies to illustrate the importance of the activities and tactics that enable Value Leaders to bring the principles to life in their daily work. Chapter Nine shows how readers can use Value Leadership. The Appendix offers supporting details on how I chose Value Leaders and calculated their VQs.

CONCLUSION

Executives must restore confidence in American capitalism. Although the challenge may appear overwhelming, Value Leadership gives executives the inspiration and tools to overcome it. To begin this journey of leadership renewal, read on.

CHAPTER ONE

Where Do You Stand?

(Start with the Value Quotient)

───❦───

Value Leadership is a beacon that executives can use to navigate their companies in the often turbulent waters of business. Chapter One offers a tool, the Value Quotient (VQ), that can help a company maintain its heading on that beacon by helping executives assess how well their company follows the concept of Value Leadership. To achieve this the remainder of this chapter answers the following questions: How does the VQ work? Why is the VQ useful? How can the VQ help your business?

HOW DOES THE VQ WORK?

The VQ transforms an abstraction into specific actions that one can measure and thus quantify. The VQ is based on four levels of analysis: concept, principles, activities, and tactics. The concept of Value Leadership is supported by seven principles (for example, "Value human relationships") that prescribe the way an organization should put value into practice. Each of the seven principles has three to four activities (such as "Adhere to core values") that broadly help an executive realize the principle. Each activity has between five and eight tactics (such as "Define core values") or specific action steps that managers and their employees take to incorporate these activities into the company's daily work.

I based these four levels of analysis on comparing the Value Leaders with their peers as well as my observations from twenty-two years as a management consultant. In many companies change flows from the top down. If the CEO is intrigued by a new concept, there is often a danger that the benefits the CEO expects to flow from the new concept will be blocked by the perceived costs of changing the organization. By focusing on four levels of analysis, I hope that executives will see clearly the full costs—and benefits—of adopting Value Leadership before initiating its adoption.

The four levels of analysis are intended to infuse Value Leadership with meaning by converting it into an organization's daily actions. To do so the concept is made up of *principles*. The principles help executives and managers communicate values to a company's shareholders, employees, customers, and communities. To translate the principles into daily action are specific *activities*. The activities are outwardly focused processes that generally require the cooperation of workers in different departments. I developed the activities by analyzing how Value Leaders conduct their business to realize each of the principles. To incorporate these activities into employee's daily efforts, I have disaggregated them into *tactics*. The tactics are specific action steps assigned to particular workers who agree to complete specific deliverables by deadlines. By articulating these four levels of analysis up front, we provide executives tools for better assessing whether the benefits of adopting Value Leadership outweigh its costs.

As we will see, the VQ is calculated by adding up the scores for the activities and tactics. Later in this chapter, we will discuss how you can estimate your company's VQ at the activity level. Although calculating the VQ at the activity level is less precise, executives can generate useful results relatively quickly. An activity-level analysis can help the executive identify which Value Leadership principles the company does well and which it needs to improve. Should the executive subsequently focus attention on improving the company's performance of these principles, he or she should calculate the VQ at the more detailed, tactic level. Chapters Two through Eight provide worksheets for the tactic-level VQ analysis.

WHY IS THE VQ USEFUL?

The VQ is useful because it melds two critical perspectives on business that are often pursued independently. Management consultants help executives improve corporate performance by evaluating issues of strategy, organization, and operations. Financial analysts evaluate companies for investment based on quantitative analysis of factors likely to influence companies' prospects for profit. Both perspectives are powerful in their own right. By combining the two perspectives, however, investors can gain deeper insights into a company's economic prospects, and executives gain a perspective on how their actions influence investor perceptions.

My business experience combines both perspectives. As a consultant to managers of some of the world's largest companies since 1981, the perspective I've developed on the characteristics that distinguish leading companies from their peers has influenced the development of the VQ.

Based on my consulting experience, I know that leading companies

- Hire and motivate the smartest and most ambitious people
- Offer employees an intense combination of on-the-job and classroom training
- Win by giving customers more value than competitors
- Avoid resting on their laurels, instead maintaining strict standards for growth, profits, and conduct that drive the organization forward
- Invest in pragmatic solutions to customer problems that could become big new sources of revenue, regardless of who came up with them
- Spend shareholders' money frugally

I've observed peer companies that

- Hire and promote people who put their career interests ahead of the teams'
- Shun tying employee evaluation to market leadership and customer satisfaction

- Adapt slowly to changes in their industry
- Encourage competition for resources among functions
- Exercise power from the top down

Beginning in 1995, I applied my management consulting experience to investment analysis. Specifically, I invested in private companies and evaluated investments for TV, print, and online media. Two Web sites, bigtipper.com and validea.com,[1] tracked the change in the value of my recommendations for publicly traded stock investments. As Figure 1.1 illustrates, from 1998 to the first half of 2000, the return on my publicly traded stock recommendations exceeded those of the S&P 500.

Beginning in 2001, I publicly predicted (on TV and in online and print publications such as BusinessWeek Online, TheStreet.com, and others) price declines in several securities. Investors could have profited from these predictions by selling short. In a short sale, investors borrow securities from a broker who sells the shares and holds onto the proceeds. The short seller then has an obligation to repay the broker's loan of the shares, or cover, by buying back the shares on the open market. The short seller bets that the price of the shares will drop; the short seller can then repay the loan with cheaper shares, pocketing the difference. Short selling is very risky because if the share value rises, the short sellers' theoretical losses could exceed the amount of the original investment.

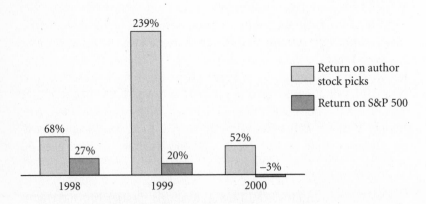

Figure 1.1.   Peter S. Cohan Public Stock Pick Returns vs. S&P 500.
Sources: bigtipper.com, valididea.com.
Note: For 1998, 1999, and six months following 2000 pick dates.

My predictions of stock price declines between January 2001 and July 2002 could have generated significant profits for investors. For example, individuals who had sold short the securities of four companies that I had publicly questioned on the date of the following articles' publication and then covered their position on July 25, 2002, would have earned a return of 1,161 percent.[2] Examples include the following:

• *Williams Communications Group.* I recommended shorting this company in March 2001 in an article in the *Oklahoman,* a few weeks prior to its spin-off by Williams Energy (WMB) because it appeared to have too much debt and large net losses in an industry that had too much capacity, leading to substantial price cuts. Furthermore, its management consistently issued public statements that emphasized positive developments while glossing over negatives, denying it would file for bankruptcy almost up until the day in April 2002 when it filed for Chapter 11. In March 2001 Williams Communications Group traded at $9.85. Although the company was bankrupt, its stock still traded at 3 cents a share on July 25, 2002, yielding a 3,273 percent return for those who covered their position that day.

• *VeriSign (VRSN).* I suggested that this stock could tumble in a *Business Week Online* article on March 12, 2002, when it was trading at $32.38. The article argued that VeriSign had overpaid for acquisitions, lacked a clear corporate strategy, was shrinking in its core business, and had dwindling cash. On July 25, 2002, VeriSign stock was trading at $5.64. If readers had covered their position on July 25, 2002, their return would have totaled 474 percent.

• *AOL Time Warner (AOL).* I argued that this stock was overvalued in a June 29, 2002, e-mail newsletter when it was trading at $15. I believed that the value of AOL Time Warner's assets was overstated because approximately 75 percent of the assets were goodwill and intangibles that would need to be written down. I also believed that AOL Time Warner's $28 billion in debt was high relative to its equity. By July 26, 2002, AOL was trading at $9.35 a share. If readers had covered their position on July 25, 2002, their return would have been 60 percent.

• *WMB.* In an article in TheStreet.com on June 5, 2002, I questioned management's credibility based on its actions in driving Williams Communications Group into bankruptcy. I was further concerned about WMB's liquidity and its exposure to the merchant energy sector, which seemed to have diminished profit prospects. At that time WMB was trading at $9.12 a share. On July 25, 2002, WMB traded at 97 cents. If readers had covered their position on July 25, 2002, their return would have been 840 percent.[3]

The approach I used to forecast the direction of specific stock prices also informed the development of the Value Leadership concept and the VQ. The stock picks were intended to take advantage of broader stock market trends. I recommended buying certain stocks when the overall markets were rising and selling specific stocks when the overall markets were tumbling. I used the following criteria to pick companies whose stocks I believed would rise during the period when the overall market was rising:

- They did business in a fast-growing market segment.
- They were more profitable than other companies in their market segment.
- Their executive team was very talented.
- They were market leaders.

I used the following criteria to pick companies whose stock prices I thought would decline during the period when markets were dropping:

- Their accounting was complex and difficult to understand.
- Their accounting appeared to overstate the health of the company given deterioration in the profit potential of its industry.
- Their management declined to answer questions attempting to clarify the complexity of the accounting or the variance between the financial statements and the condition of the industry.

The management and stock selection criteria I derived from my experience contributed to the formulations of the principles of Value Leadership. As Table 1.1 illustrates, referring to the lists of criteria just described, some of the Value Leadership principles were consistent with leading management and rising-market stock selection criteria. Other principles were the opposite of management criteria for peer companies and down-market stock selection criteria. For example, the principle "Value human relationships" is consistent with these leading

Principle	Linkage with Author's Management and Stock Selection Criteria
Value human relationships	**Agree:** They hire and motivate the smartest and most ambitious people. They offer employees an intense combination of on-the-job and classroom training. Their executive team is very talented. **Oppose:** They hire and promote people who put their career interests ahead of the team's.
Foster teamwork	**Agree:** They offer employees an intense combination of on-the-job and classroom training. They invest in pragmatic solutions to customer problems that could become big new sources of revenue, regardless of who came up with them. Their executive team is very talented. **Oppose:** They hire and promote people who put their career interests ahead of the team's. They encourage competition for resources among functions.
Experiment frugally	**Agree:** They invest in pragmatic solutions to customer problems that could become big new sources of revenue, regardless of who came up with them. They spend shareholders' money frugally. They are more profitable than other companies in their market segment. They are market leaders. **Oppose:** They adapt slowly to changes in their industry, encourage competition for resources among functions, and exercise power from the top down.
Fulfill your commitments	**Agree:** They win by giving customers more value than do competitors and spend shareholders' money frugally. **Oppose:** They shun tying employee evaluation to market leadership and customer satisfaction. They exercise power from the top down. Their accounting is complex and difficult to understand. Their accounting appears to overstate the health of the company given deterioration in the profit potential of its industry. Management declines to answer questions attempting to clarify the complexity of the accounting or the variance between the financial statements and the condition of the industry.
Fight complacency	**Agree:** They avoid resting on their laurels, maintaining strict standard for growth, profits, and conduct that drive the organization forward. They do business in a fast-growing market segment. They are more profitable than other companies in their market segment. Their executive team is very talented. They are market leaders. **Oppose:** They adapt slowly to changes in their industry. They encourage competition for resources among functions. They exercise power from the top down.

Table 1.1.   Linkages Between Value Leadership Principles and Peter S. Cohan's Management and Stock Selection Criteria.   *(Continues)*

Principle	Linkage with Author's Management and Stock Selection Criteria
Win through multiple means	**Agree:** They win by giving customers more value than competitors. They invest in pragmatic solutions to customer problems that could become big new sources of revenue, regardless of who came up with them. They spend shareholders' money frugally. They are market leaders. **Oppose:** They shun tying employee evaluation to market leadership and customer satisfaction. They adapt slowly to changes in their industry.
Give to your community	**Agree:** Their market leadership extends to their role in the community. **Oppose:** They shun tying employee evaluation to community participation.

Table 1.1. Continued.

Note: Companies that perform the activities after "Agree" support the specific Value Leadership principle; companies that perform the activities following "Oppose" undermine the Value Leadership principle.

company criteria: "Hire and motivate the smartest and most ambitious people" and "Offer employees an intense combination of on-the-job and classroom training." It is also the opposite of peer company criterion "Hire and promote people who put their career interests ahead of the team's." And it is consistent with the rising-market stock selection criterion "Their executive team was very talented."

As we noted in the Introduction, Value Leaders can offer examples that illuminate the concept of Value Leadership. The introduction also clarified the connection between the principles of Value Leadership and the qualitative and quantitative criteria used to select the Value Leaders. Although Value Leaders have performed well in the past, readers should not infer that the specific Value Leaders discussed in this book will continue to perform well in the future. As long as these eight Value Leaders continue to follow the seven principles of Value Leadership, they should continue to perform well. If they diverge from these principles, their performance could deteriorate. Just as the shadows on the cave wall depicted reality of the cave dwellers in Plato's allegory of the cave, the Value Leaders represent a useful way to perceive how the concept of Value Leadership manifests itself in the world.

With that as a caveat, it is worth noting that the eight Value Leaders significantly outperformed their peers in shareholder value, sales growth, and profitability. As Figure 1.2 indicates, Value Leaders increased their stock prices at almost *five times* the rate of the S&P 500 index between 1992 and 2002. This period began with a recession that ended in 1993, was followed by an economic boom from 1993 to 2000, and ended with a recession that began in 2001 and is still under way at this writing. Figure 1.3 shows that Value Leaders grew their revenues 33 percent faster and earned 109 percent higher profit margins than their industries between 1997 and 2002.

As we discussed in the Introduction, the VQ helps executives gauge how well their companies use the seven principles of Value Leadership that have contributed to the Value Leader's excellent track record. The VQ takes the concept of Value Leadership down to the level of principles, activities, and tactics. It helps executives quantify how well their companies follow Value Leadership by comparing their company's

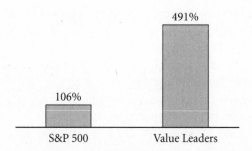

Figure 1.2.   Percentage Change in Share Price of S&P 500 and Eight Value Leaders.

Note: Average, June 1992 to June 2002.

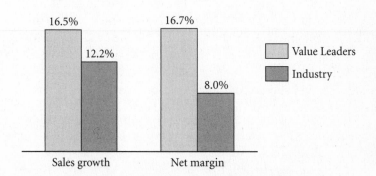

Figure 1.3.   Sales Growth and Net Margins of Eight Value Leaders vs. Industry.

Note: 1997 to 2002.

activities and tactics to those of companies that come closest to realizing the concept.

The VQ can be used at two levels. First, it can help executives conduct a relatively quick activity-level diagnostic analysis that pinpoints specific Value Leadership areas in which a company most needs to improve. Second, the VQ can be the focus of a more detailed tactical change initiative designed to develop an organization so that it achieves and sustains superior performance.

HOW CAN THE VQ HELP YOUR BUSINESS?

The VQ can help you make your business more successful by pinpointing opportunities for improvement that have been shown to enhance performance. To demonstrate how the VQ can help, this section first provides an example of how the VQ is applied to Synopsys, a Silicon Valley company. Second, it offers benchmarks of VQ scoring based on a Value Leadership database (as detailed in the Appendix). Third, it describes a process that you can use to apply the VQ to your company. It concludes by showing which chapters of this book can help most, depending on the outcome of your company's VQ.

Gathering data to provide meaningful VQ results requires primary research. In general, the more care and time a company invests in gathering information to generate the VQ scores, the more accurate the results and the more valuable the resulting insights will be. To gather data carefully, executives may seek outside assistance to develop interview guides and conduct interviews with relevant employees, customers, shareholders, and community members. Although internal and external interviews represent a good first step for quickly identifying key opportunities for improvement, more in-depth interviewing and analysis may be required to gain a thorough understanding of how well a company follows specific Value Leadership principles. If an initial VQ analysis makes clear that a company needs to enhance how it follows, say, the principle "Win through multiple means," then more in-depth organizational analysis is recommended as detailed in Chapter Nine. More details about how best to collect and analyze this data are available in the Appendix.

Investors can also benefit from conducting a VQ analysis. Investors place their bets based on an assessment of the likely future value of a company. Although investors can attempt to build such forecasts by extrapolating from the past into the future, it is not uncommon for unpredictable events to throw off such forecasts, making them less reliable for estimating the future value of a company. One way investors can sidestep this problem is to think of a company as a collection of people dedicated to getting and keeping customers. The better the company is at performing this function, the more likely it is to adapt effectively as it is buffeted by such unpredictable events. And the better a company adapts to such changes, the more likely it is to grow profitably and predictably, thus making the company more valuable than its less adaptable peers.

Investors can use the VQ as a tool for seeking value by helping them to assess how well a company in which they might invest adapts to change. They must overcome significant hurdles to develop meaningful data from which to calculate a company's VQ. Rather than dismissing the VQ because of these challenges, investors may wish to look at the challenges as a barrier to entry. Those willing to do their homework can sustain a competitive advantage over those who are not.

Given these challenges, some thoughts on VQ methodology may be helpful. Often the quality of the results is improved by hiring an objective third party to gather the data and to conduct the analysis required to develop the VQ scores. Whether you decide to work with or without outside assistance, to calculate a company's VQ you should take the following four steps:

- *Identify which employees within a company can offer a comprehensive assessment of how closely a company follows the principles of Value Leadership.* Similarly, pick a set of sample customers, shareholders, and community members who can offer their perspectives on the company. Clearly, the CEO of a company will have an easier time tapping into these relationships than an investor. However, because some resourceful investors—particularly investors who sell stocks short—are known for cultivating such relationships within an industry, the challenge for investors is not insurmountable.
- *Develop interview guides for each interviewee along the lines we will detail later.* The interview guides help structure the conversations with key stakeholders. Providing the interviewee with a guide beforehand enables that person to prepare for the conversation, making for a more effective interview.
- *Conduct interviews and summarize results.* The number and scope of the interviews is likely to vary depending on the size of the company. For a very large company, for example, it might make sense to conduct as many as fifty interviews, consisting of a cross section of fifteen to twenty individuals from among the company's employees,

customers, shareholders, and community members. A smaller company might benefit from twenty interviews, similarly distributed among the four groups.

• *Prepare the company's VQ using the worksheet that appears later in this chapter.* To assign the scores, you should assess how well your company conducts each of the twenty-four activities relative to the Value Leaders highlighted in the Appendix. Although the scores are based on judgments, the use of the Value Leaders' scores can be effective benchmarks for calibrating the company's VQ.

VQ for Synopsys

To demonstrate how to apply the VQ, let's review the process followed to analyze Synopsys. As we noted in the Introduction, Synopsys is a leading provider of chip design software. After the company agreed to participate, the author conducted interviews with its CEO, president, and CFO.

For example, the interview guide for Synopsys CEO Aart de Geus included the following questions organized by topic:

CEO Background

- What was your background prior to working at Synopsys?
- Why did you join Synopsys?

Value Human Relationships

- What are the core values of Synopsys?
- How were these values developed?
- How widely and how frequently are these values communicated within Synopsys?
- How do these values influence the way the company hires, evaluates, and rewards employees?

Foster Teamwork

- How does Synopsys encourage teamwork among different departments within the company?
- How does Synopsys manage partnerships within its industry?
- What steps, if any, is Synopsys taking to enhance teamwork?

- How does Synopsys use its performance measurement and compensation systems to influence manager and employee behavior?

Experiment Frugally

- How does Synopsys develop new products and services?
- How does Synopsys measure the effectiveness of its new product development process?

Fight Complacency

- Is Synopsys worried about becoming complacent? If so, how does Synopsys fight complacency?
- What performance measurement and reward processes encourage the company's self-renewal?
- Why does Synopsys make acquisitions, and how does it manage their financial risks and integration issues?
- How is Synopsys developing its next generation of managers and executives? How confident is Synopsys of its executive "bench strength"?

Win Through Multiple Means

- What capabilities contribute most to the company's market leadership?
- How does Synopsys keep competitors from copying these capabilities? How, in general, does Synopsys keep ahead of its competitors?
- What are the two or three most significant risks facing Synopsys, and what processes are in place to manage these risks?

Give to Your Community

- How does Synopsys give to its communities?
- Why is such giving important?

Synopsys CEO de Geus addressed the principle "Fulfill your commitments" in part during his discussion of core values.[4] (A more extensive discussion of the principle occurred during the author interview with Brad Henske, the company's former CFO.)[5]

Based on these interviews, I concluded that Synopsys closely follows the principles of Value Leadership. To support this conclusion, let's first analyze the interviews and then illustrate how to use them to develop a VQ for Synopsys.

CEO BACKGROUND. The core values of Synopsys were clear at its inception. According to chairman and CEO Aart de Geus, prior to founding Synopsys, de Geus worked at General Electric's (GE's) semiconductor R&D unit in Research Park Triangle, North Carolina. De Geus was working to develop tools to improve the semiconductor design process, called synthesis design tools. In 1987 GE decided it would exit the semiconductor business. So de Geus began interviewing for a job with semiconductor companies. In many of his interviews, the companies seemed so interested in synthesis that de Geus decided that he and his GE team should build a business around it. De Geus developed a proposal in which GE would let go of its synthesis technology and provide the initial investment in Synopsys.[6]

The way Synopsys was started reflected its integrity. In de Geus's view, GE was a high-integrity company, which had treated de Geus and his colleagues fairly. De Geus approached GE with the Synopsys business proposal without a second thought; it was the right thing to do and he did it. Although he might have approached other investors to finance the licensing of GE's intellectual property, this option was inconsistent with the value that de Geus placed on dealing straightforwardly with GE. In the end GE's contributions of intellectual property and seed capital, combined with de Geus's ability to turn these resources into a profitable business, transformed what would have been a loss for GE into a big profit after the successful IPO of Synopsys.

VALUE HUMAN RELATIONSHIPS. Synopsys was founded with the intent that it would prosper for a long time rather than being "built to flip." (During the dot-com era, companies with limited revenues and profits often formed very quickly with the intention of "flipping" or being acquired by bigger firms, enabling their investors to realize a quick return on their investment.) With longevity in mind, the Synopsys founders discussed its core values before the company began operating. They asked themselves which companies they wanted to emulate and began by patterning the company after Sun Microsystems and Hewlett-Packard. De Geus attracted a team of people who shared his core values. In light of the often difficult challenges facing a start-up company, such shared values helped determine how well the team would fare when Synopsys was fighting for its survival.

The company's values have been particularly useful in its many acquisitions. During the process of evaluating acquisition candidates, its core values have helped determine whether the process should continue. If an acquisition candidate does not fit with the values, discussions end. On the other hand, Synopsys believes that it must "refresh its DNA," according to de Geus, and that acquisitions offer it new products and new approaches to management that achieve this objective.

To illustrate how Synopsys refreshes its DNA, it is useful to understand the values at the company's core. Synopsys thinks of its core values in the form of a pyramid with a flag on top. At the base of the pyramid is *integrity,* which de Geus says means that "you do what you say and say what you do." As people make verbal commitments and subsequently meet those commitments, they gradually build trust. In the middle of the pyramid is *customer success through execution excellence,* which means finding ever better ways of performing business activities. Execution excellence means that Synopsys is never satisfied with its efforts. It strives to become "best in class" in the way it works; and when it achieves its goal, it sets the bar higher. For example, once Synopsys achieved the highest market share in the electronic design automation market, it set a higher goal of becoming the best $1 billion software company. At the top of the pyramid is *leadership,* which aims at making Synopsys first in its industry by anticipating where the industry is going and meeting the future needs of customers ahead of the competition. In de Geus's view, a great leader can see and grasp the future, and a great manager can execute on how to get there. The flag on the top of the Synopsys pyramid of values is *passion,* which de Geus defines as a sense of caring about work, an inner energy to achieve results. When Synopsys makes an acquisition, he says, its "DNA adapts" as it adds to the capabilities subject to execution excellence.

Synopsys has put in place specific processes for embedding its values into its workforce. Since its founding in 1987, Synopsys has communicated its values throughout the organization, a process that de Geus believes is critical for aligning the organization, and Synopsys has acted according to its values. After Synopsys completed its acquisition of Avant! in 2002, it required all of its managers to attend an internally run two-day management development program. The course, which featured seven or eight different modules, included a two-and-a-half-hour session that de Geus taught, addressing the values and culture of Synopsys.

One of the key themes of de Geus's session was to give managers guidance on how to behave in what he calls "the gray zone." If employees are categorized by the extent to which they embody the Synopsys values and their ability to achieve desired results, de Geus noted that the least desirable managers are the ones who do not agree with the company's values and fail to achieve results. On the other end of the spectrum, managers who agree with Synopsys values and meet their performance targets are the most valuable to the company. He defines the *gray zone* as the awkward challenge facing executives who must decide what to do about managers who either achieve results but behave unethically in some way or who are truthful but get poor results.

The Synopsys hiring process also aligns its organization with its values. By communicating its values to potential employees through the media, Synopsys hopes potential employees will self-select. More specifically, de Geus anticipates that if more potential Synopsys job applicants read about the company and decide that they want to work there, then the company's hiring process will operate more effectively.

To interview candidates Synopsys conducts behavioral interviews. Instead of asking an applicant "Are you good at conflict management?" the Synopsys interviewer says, "Tell me about a situation when you did not do well managing a conflict." If the candidate responds with a story that suggests he does not take responsibility or is not self-aware, the interviewer may have legitimate grounds to reject the candidate. Before making a hiring decision, Synopsys conducts a roundtable discussion with all staff who interviewed the candidate. One might say, "He looked good, but I'm not sure how far he got on the project." This comment might amplify a weak signal that other interviewers had noticed, leading the roundtable to conclude "This guy never finishes anything on time."

The company's employee organizational review process also aligns its organization with its values. Every six months Synopsys senior management meets with business unit general managers and reviews their list of top and bottom performers. Managers base their ranking on behavioral criteria, cultural fit, and financial performance. Management decides which employees have upward mobility within the organization and promotes and trains these select individuals.

FOSTER TEAMWORK. Teamwork is important at Synopsys because its products are complex and must work in different semiconductor design functions and global office locations. In very few situations can an individual working alone solve an important product development problem. Synopsys employs many incredibly talented individuals who generally work in teams. The company has two career tracks: the management track, which takes teamwork into account in evaluating performance; and the individual contributor track, which tends to reward individual technical contribution up to the vice presidential level of Synopsys Fellow. However, even successful individual contributors must be team players, serving as role models within the Synopsys culture. Every year Synopsys management gives out excellence awards intended to promote successful group behavior. As de Geus points out, workers who receive countless bonus payments throughout their career are far more likely to reflect back warmly on receiving an excellence award, because they place such a high value on peer recognition. De Geus has found that employees have a deeper and more positive emotional reaction to peer recognition than to receiving a stream of bonus payments.

Synopsys also has formal processes to encourage strong external partnering, applying the same values to internal teamwork as it does to external teamwork. For example, as de Geus notes, when a customer is making a $10 million purchase, the customer must trust the supplier. Specifically, the customer wants to be confident that the supplier will survive for the long term and that the customer has a personalized relationship with the supplier. Synopsys dedicates an executive sponsor to each of its largest customers. These executive sponsors include Synopsys senior vice presidents, vice presidents, and directors. If a customer has a problem with a Synopsys product or service, the customer calls his or her executive sponsor.

Synopsys pays money for hard results and offers psychological rewards for role-model behavior. Synopsys has found that offering extra monetary rewards for less tangible outcomes, such as doing a great job on a project, tends to create a perception of unfairness. Because the basis of such an award might be seen as subjective, people who thought they did a good job on a project but did not receive such an award would feel that the company was somehow being arbitrary in its rewards, which could generate resentment. To avoid these unintentional side effects, Synopsys pays additional compensation only to those who meet or exceed quantitative targets. Individuals who behave in a way that promotes the company's values get rewarded by being praised for their accomplishment in an all-company voice mail or e-mail from the CEO. The employee gets a memorable and satisfying psychological reward, and Synopsys encourages all its employees to emulate the praised behavior.

EXPERIMENT FRUGALLY. Synopsys develops new product ideas through a process that links customers with a core product development team. According to de Geus, if a company listens to customers the wrong way, it can miss out on important opportunities. Specifically, Synopsys does not come up with new product ideas by listening to customers complain about their current products. Focusing on such complaints may lead a company to make incremental improvements to products whose best years have already passed. Instead, Synopsys works with customers to anticipate their future needs. By getting customers to discuss capabilities that might help them do their jobs better in the future, Synopsys product development teams can better apply their knowledge of cutting-edge technology to inventing products that these customers will value.

Synopsys assesses new product ideas through a core team consisting of representatives from R&D, applications engineering, and marketing. Each function brings a different perspective: R&D is inclined to work on the latest hot technology; applications engineers may look for a more practical solution using more proven technology; and marketing may push for a single product feature that will make it easy to sell.

Synopsys has a novel approach for blending these three perspectives into a prioritized list of new product development projects. Each core team member scores each proposed product development project. Instead of offering a quantitative score or a detailed analysis, the team members summarize their conclusion with a color: red means do not proceed with the project; orange means potentially proceed with the project pending the resolution of open issues; and green means definitely pursue the project. The benefit of this color-scoring approach is that the teams can prioritize the projects quickly without arguing extensively about the rationale for the scoring.

Despite the simplicity of the color scheme, Synopsys has a more complex method of arriving at the answer. First, the teams estimate the approximate value of each project, assigning so-called lucky bucks.

Second, the teams estimate the cost to turn the idea into a marketable product. The first two criteria are combined into a single number, the ratio of lucky bucks to cost. Third, the teams assess whether Synopsys has the capabilities needed to succeed with the development of the product. In addition, Synopsys senior managers review the priorities to make sure they fit with the company's overall product strategy. This review might lead Synopsys to cut projects that might make good individual products but do not fit within its broader product portfolio.

FIGHT COMPLACENCY. De Geus cites the title of Intel chairman Andrew Grove's book, *Only the Paranoid Survive,* to explain how Synopsys fights complacency. Because it sells software to help chip designers, Synopsys sees itself as being at the heart of high technology. The company pays close attention to the industry trade press, specifically *EE Times,* very frequently finding new competitors or new technologies that could be threatening to it. Synopsys structures its staff meetings and its strategic planning discussions to include discussions of new competitors. This structure supplements the natural tendency of Synopsys people to remain constantly paranoid about the competition.

WIN THROUGH MULTIPLE MEANS. Synopsys has made many acquisitions to enhance its competitiveness. De Geus notes that it is hard to make acquisitions succeed and that acquirers know the true risks of the deal only after the transaction has closed. Synopsys needs strategic reasons to justify undertaking these risks, such as the target's technology, positioning, people, or ability to help Synopsys sell more products through its existing distribution channels. In general, acquisition candidates that satisfy these criteria come at a high price.

In order to justify paying high prices, Synopsys must integrate the acquired company successfully. Because of its relatively extensive experience with acquisitions, Synopsys has developed very detailed procedures for managing them. The key step in its methodology is to focus first on integrating the sales and distribution forces. This means that Synopsys decides whether the two companies' sales forces overlap; if so, it eliminates the overlap immediately so that customers are not confused. Second, Synopsys analyzes the acquired company's product line and eliminates overlap. In doing so, Synopsys anticipates and tries to address the annoyance of customers who are currently using the terminated products. Finally, Synopsys assembles a management structure that retains the best managers from the acquired company.

GIVE TO YOUR COMMUNITY. Finally, Synopsys gives to its communities by leveraging its core competencies. Initially, the company's community activities were ad hoc. Its employees cleaned nature trails and led food, blood, and toy drives. As Synopsys became larger, it received requests for money and employee time. After some internal discussion, Synopsys decided it should pick themes that were consistent with what de Geus calls its "corporate DNA," such as learning and education. To that end Synopsys began to sponsor science fairs at schools in the Silicon Valley area. The benefit of such sponsorships was that they inspired students who might not ordinarily have been interested in science to participate in the fairs.

Synopsys employees benefit significantly from community service. For example, at a Safeway in California, a Synopsys vice president was wearing a T-shirt with the company's logo. A woman approached the vice president and asked him if he worked for Synopsys. She described to him how her son had been a poor student. Then her son won a prize at a Synopsys-sponsored science fair. This motivated him to start studying, and he subsequently became an A+ student. The vice president reacted to the woman's story with a great feeling of pride in Synopsys. Although this is just one story, it illustrates how good the company's community activities can make its employees feel.[7]

The purpose of including the case study of Synopsys management practices is to offer executives an example of the information needed to calculate a company's VQ. As Table 1.2 indicates, the VQ for Synopsys is a solid 87 percent.

The Synopsys VQ reveals significant variation in how closely the company follows the different principles of Value Leadership. For example, Synopsys scored highest in valuing human relationships and in fulfilling its commitments. Given the clear way it articulated its core values and the way it applies these values in hiring, its use of the first principle makes sense. In light of the tremendous importance that talented people and long-term customer relationships play in its industry, Synopsys's strong score on the second principle is also expected. By contrast, Synopsys scores less well in the principles "Give to your community" and "Foster teamwork." In the company's defense, the first principle may be less important to its overall success because many Synopsys customers live outside its community. Nevertheless, the company seems to have made a difference in the areas on which it has focused. Synopsys also appears to have done well in promoting teamwork; however, it could enhance its formal processes somewhat.

Principle	Activity: Evaluation	Score
Value human relationships	**Commit to core values:** Core values are clearly communicated.	5
	Hire for values: Hiring approach selects employees who share values.	5
	Balance performance measurement: Balances results and values.	5
	Reward employees intelligently: Money for results, praise for values.	5
	Weighted total (sum times 3)	60
Foster teamwork	**Team training:** Management training reinforces team behavior.	4
	Job rotation: High-potential employees choose job rotations.	4
	Team decision making: Teams drive product development and sales.	4
	Team rewards: Rewards hard results and team behavior.	5
	Weighted total (sum times 3)	51
Experiment frugally	**Grow organically:** Grows by leveraging capabilities to new markets.	4
	Manage development risk: Green/orange/red–light process manages risk.	5
	Partner internally: Core product development teams work well.	5
	Partner externally: Executive sponsors partner with customer.	4
	Weighted total (sum times 3)	54
Fulfill your commitments	**Hire and promote honest people:** Integrity tested by interviews.	5
	Account honestly: Conservative revenue accounting.	5
	Treat employees, customers, and communities fairly: Rewards hard results with cash, model behavior with peer recognition.	4
	Weighted total (sum times 4)	56
Fight complacency	**Plan CEO succession:** Promoted long-time employee to president.	4
	Sustain a healthy paranoia: Believes only paranoid survive.	5
	Attack new markets: Acquisition strategy has been effective.	4
	Weighted total (sum times 4)	52

Table 1.2.   Value Quotient Analysis: Synopsys.   *(Continues)*

Principle	Activity: Evaluation	Score
Win through multiple means	**Understand the customer:** Executive sponsors know customers.	5
	Build diverse capabilities: Acquisitions add to capabilities.	3
	Sustain competitive superiority: Ambition raises performance bar.	5
	Weighted total (sum times 4)	52
Give to your community	**Inspire employees:** Safeway story demonstrates high inspiration.	4
	Enrich the community: Encourages local interest in science.	3
	Better society: More science interest helps regional economy.	3
	Weighted total (sum times 4)	40
Value Quotient	**(Sum divided by 420)**	87%

Table 1.2. Continued.

Key: 5 = excellent; 4 = very good; 3 = good; 2 = fair; 1 = poor. Weighted scores for each principle are calculated by multiplying the activity scores by 3 for four-activity principles and by 4 for three-activity principles.

VQ Benchmarks

The Synopsys analysis offers a useful starting point for thinking about how to apply the VQ to your company. To provide further guidance, we now examine a range of VQ principle–level scores from the eight Value Leaders. As Table 1.3 illustrates, the range of principle-level scores among the eight Value Leaders varies significantly. For example, the range between the highest score and the lowest score on the principle "Value human relationships" is six. The highest scorers, at sixty, include Southwest Airlines and six others that all have very clearly defined core values and that hire, measure, and reward people in a manner very consistent with their core values. By contrast, the lowest scorer, Wal-Mart, at fifty-four, had clearly defined values; however, it allegedly underpaid some employees by allegedly asking them to work hours "off the clock."

VQ Worksheet

The foregoing VQ analysis of Synopsys and the VQ benchmark should help indicate how to apply the VQ analysis to your company. As noted

Principle	Benchmark and Evaluation	Score
Value human relationships	**High:** Clear core values and tight link to hiring, training, and pay (all other Value Leaders).	60
	Low: Strong core values and link to hiring and training, but pay is low given alleged off-book work hours (Wal-Mart).	54
	Range	6
Foster teamwork	**High:** Trains teams, rotates jobs, extensive team decision making, rewards results with values (Southwest, Smucker, Goldman Sachs).	60
	Low: Encourages teamwork in product development, does some training and job rotation, some pay for results and values (Microsoft).	42
	Range	18
Experiment frugally	**High:** Builds off core capabilities, tight risk management, and strong internal and external partnering (MBNA, Wal-Mart).	60
	Low: Internal new product development generated some revenue growth, but big acquisition required for big shift (Smucker).	42
	Range	18
Fulfill your commitments	**High:** Hire for integrity; do conservative accounting; and treat employees, customers, and communities fairly (Goldman Sachs, Johnson & Johnson, Smucker, Southwest).	60
	Low: Evolving value placed on integrity, quality, and information security (Microsoft).	40
	Range	20
Fight complacency	**High:** Effective CEO succession, intense paranoia, growth from new market entry (Wal-Mart, Goldman Sachs, and Johnson & Johnson).	60
	Low: Promoted long-time family member, somewhat comfortable, big growth from acquisition in core market (Smucker, MBNA).	52
	Range	8
Win through multiple means	**High:** Deep customer knowledge, top capabilities, and clear market leadership (Goldman Sachs, Wal-Mart, Southwest, Microsoft, MBNA).	60
	Low: Deep customer knowledge, strong capabilities, and top in many markets (Johnson & Johnson, Smucker, Synopsys).	52
	Range	8

Table 1.3. Value Quotient Benchmarks.   *(Continues)*

Principle	Benchmark and Evaluation	Score
Give to your community	**High:** Lets employees choose charity, gives significantly to local community, and attacks big societal problems (MBNA, Johnson & Johnson, Microsoft).	60
	Low: Employees participate in local high school science competition, moderate community enrichment (Synopsys).	40
	Range	20
Value Quotient	**High:** Goldman Sachs	98%
	Low: Synopsys	87%
	Range	11%

Table 1.3. Continued.

Key: 5 = excellent; 4 = very good; 3 = good; 2 = fair; 1 = poor.

More details on the development of this benchmark information are available in the Appendix.

earlier, often the quality of the results is improved by hiring an objective third party to gather the data and to conduct the analysis required to develop the VQ scores. To calculate your company's VQ, you should take the following four steps:

1. *Identify which employees within your company can offer a comprehensive assessment of how closely your company follows the principles of Value Leadership.* Similarly, pick a set of sample customers, shareholders, and community members who can offer their perspectives on your company.

2. *Develop interview guides for each interviewee along the lines detailed in the previous section.* The interview guides help structure the conversation with key stakeholders and, when provided to interviewees beforehand, enable the interviewees to prepare for the interviews, making them more effective.

3. *Conduct interviews and summarize results. The number and scope of the interviews is likely to vary depending on the size of the company.* For a very large company, for example, it might make sense to conduct as many as fifty interviews, consisting of a cross section of fifteen to twenty individuals from among your company's employees, customers, shareholders, and community members. A smaller company might benefit from twenty interviews, similarly distributed among the four groups.

4. *Prepare your company's VQ using the worksheet in Exhibit 1.1.* To assign the scores, you should assess how well your company conducts each of the twenty-four activities relative to the Value Leaders highlighted in the Appendix. Although the scores are based on judgments, the use of the Value Leaders' scores can be effective benchmarks for calibrating your company's VQ.

Depending on your VQ results, you may find that your company is particularly in need of improvement in specific principles and stronger in other principles. You may wish to read this book based on these results, focusing initially on the chapters that discuss principles that your company's VQ indicates the greatest need for improvement. To assist with that process, the following list summarizes which chapters address which principles:

Principle	*Chapter*
Value human relationships	Two
Foster teamwork	Three
Experiment frugally	Four
Fulfill your commitments	Five
Fight complacency	Six
Win through multiple means	Seven
Give to your community	Eight

These chapters discuss each of the principles in depth. The chapters define the principles and show how they support the concept of Value Leadership. They then provide quantitative evidence that companies that adhere to the principles generate superior economic performance. Each chapter presents three or four specific activities that support the principle, listing a set of effective tactics for putting each activity to work in an organization. Each chapter also presents case studies that illustrate the benefit of each activity, often providing a contrasting example of a company that does not perform the activity, and draws from these case studies a set of general principles. Each chapter also includes a longer case study illustrating how a company transformed itself in an effort to follow the principle highlighted in the chapter. Every chapter concludes with a more detailed VQ worksheet to enable the reader to assess his or her company's use of the principle at the activity and tactical levels.

Principle	Activity: Evaluation	Score
Value human relationships	Commit to core values Hire for values Balance performance measurement Reward employees intelligently Weighted total (sum times 3)	_____
Foster teamwork	Train teams Rotate jobs Make team decisions Reward team behavior Weighted total (sum times 3)	_____
Experiment frugally	Grow organically Manage development risk Partner internally Partner externally Weighted total (sum times 3)	_____
Fulfill your commitments	Hire and promote honest people Account honestly Treat employees, customers, and communities fairly Weighted total (sum times 4)	_____
Fight complacency	Plan CEO succession Sustain a healthy paranoia Attack new markets Weighted total (sum times 4)	_____
Win through multiple means	Understand the customer Build diverse capabilities Sustain competitive superiority Weighted total (sum times 4)	_____
Give to your community	Inspire employees Enrich the community Attack big societal problems Weighted total (sum times 4)	_____
Value Quotient	(Sum divided by 420)	

Exhibit 1.1.   Value Quotient Worksheet.

Key: 5 = excellent; 4 = very good; 3 = good; 2 = fair; 1 = poor; 0 = not applicable.

CONCLUSION

The VQ can help your organization assess how well it adheres to the concept of Value Leadership. As this chapter has shown, Value Leadership is a concept that helps companies generate performance measurably superior to their peers. Value Leadership's underlying principles and activities have strong conceptual linkages to eleven criteria used to pinpoint the best-performing companies. Therefore, how well a company adheres to the concept of Value Leadership determines not only how much good it does for employees, customers, and the community but how well it performs for shareholders. The VQ is a valuable way to gauge how closely a company follows the concept of Value Leadership. As such, it can guide executives to focus on improving their organizations by adopting the principles likely to generate the greatest performance improvement.

To take your first step on the road to Value Leadership, read on!

CHAPTER TWO

People Matter
(Value Human Relationships)

V aluing human relationships means treating people with respect so that they achieve their full potential consistent with the company's interests. When a business is expanding, treating people with respect is important because the business needs to attract and encourage the productivity of the right kinds of people. When a business contracts and must cut employees, treating people with respect is important in order to maintain the productivity of the employees who remain and to maintain the company's reputation as one that values human relationships in the minds of potential employees, customers, and communities.

Treating people with respect would seem to some—perhaps naively—to be a natural outgrowth of an executive's upbringing. The notion here is that business leaders emerge from a process by which investors choose an individual to run a company because they believe that individual has earned their respect; is capable of earning the respect of workers, customers, and communities; and can use that respect to generate a return on thir investment. In many cases this view reflects reality.

In other cases investors choose the wrong leader because the individual has tremendous technical skills, is an extremely persuasive salesperson, or has extraordinary financial or analytical skills that can make a significant contribution to the company's survival and growth. In short, companies often choose executives who lack basic people skills. As a result, these companies fail to sustain market leadership because they value people only to the extent that they can perform specific business functions efficiently. These leaders tend to ignore people's needs for self-actualization and peer recognition; thus, the best people leave the company for an organization that meets these needs. Such poorly led companies tend to have higher turnover, which is costly, and to be less effective at developing new products and providing good service. The result is higher costs, more sluggish sales growth, and declining market share.

Treating people with respect is thus a powerful source of competitive advantage. Although many companies print "people are our most valuable asset" in their annual reports, far fewer companies actually treat people with respect. Every industry has a finite pool of workers who can perform work that affects a company's customers. Within this pool a subset is likely to perform this work far more effectively than the rest. The market leaders in any given industry are likely to be the ones that can attract and motivate the top performing subset of workers. And as we will see in this chapter, the best workers are highly motivated by a work environment that treats them with respect, helps them self-actualize, and gives them opportunities for peer recognition.

Thus, valuing human relationships is not a feel-good philosophy; it is an economic imperative. Companies that attract and motivate the best people are able to develop new products that keep existing customers buying from the company and attract new customers. When workers feel respected, they radiate that respect to their coworkers, customers, and the surrounding community. This feeling of respect reinforces the relationships that sustain a company's flow of profits. And it creates a virtuous cycle in which great workers draw in other great workers who are attracted to the company's growing reputation for sustaining a desirable work environment.

LINK WITH VALUE LEADERSHIP

"Value human relationships" is a critical principle supporting the concept of Value Leadership. It enhances the lives of employees. In some companies employees feel as if they are off-the-shelf parts in an economic machine. Their managers expect the employees to perform specific functions; however, the managers appear indifferent to the employees beyond their specific function. As a result, such employees feel as though management does not respect them. Employees in these companies tend to transmit the same lack of respect to their customers, suppliers, and communities.

By contrast, companies that value human relationships treat their employees with respect, taking great care to hire people who fit with clearly defined corporate values. Because these employees share the corporate values, they feel genuine enthusiasm about their work. This enthusiasm leads them to do a better job of creating value for customers, suppliers, and communities. During economic contractions companies that value human relationships elicit ideas from employees on ways to cut costs without sacrificing employees. And should employee cuts ultimately be required, companies that conform with this principle treat employees in such a way that the remaining employees continue to feel good about the company.

ECONOMIC BENEFITS

Valuing human relationships creates economic benefits as well. For example, Value Leaders are 39 percent more productive than their industries. Specifically, in 2002 the average Value Leader generated $398,750 in revenue per employee, while the average revenue per employee for Value Leaders' industries was $286,625. Furthermore, Value Leaders are over twice as profitable as their peers. For example, the average Value Leader had a 1997 to 2002 average net profit margin of 16.7 percent compared to an industry average of 8.0 percent over the period. The principle of valuing human relationships contributes to these economic benefits by creating an environment that makes employees want to produce more and to offer better service to customers, which may extend the customer relationship and thereby increase revenue and profit per customer.

CASES

This chapter illustrates these points with examples, principles, and tactics. It compares J. M. Smucker's strong corporate values with those of Hansen Natural. The chapter contrasts Southwest Airlines' tendency to hire for attitude with that of American Airlines' practice of hiring for skills. This chapter illustrates how Goldman Sachs has instituted formal processes to measure and reward those who embody its clearly articulated values, contrasting the approach with Merrill Lynch's virtuous-sounding values whose measurement can be clouded with bureacratic infighting. It contrasts Smucker's and Southwest's linking of rewards to values with United's harsher work environment. The chapter offers an example of how Gordon Bethune helped turn Continental Airlines around by applying the principle "Value human relationships" and presents management levers for executives seeking similarly to transform their companies. The chapter concludes with a Value Quotient (VQ) worksheet for executives seeking to assess how well their companies value human relationships.

ACTIVITY ANALYSIS

To value human relationships, an organization must perform four activities well:

- **Commit to core values:** act according to values that start at the top and permeate the company.
- **Hire for values:** hire and promote individuals who embody these values.
- **Balance performance measurement:** measure performance through both quantitative and nonquantitative factors.
- **Reward employees intelligently:** offer employees the rewards they value most, such as a blend of respect and high compensation.

Commit to Core Values

Many successful entrepreneurs bring a strong set of personal values to their role as CEO. These entrepreneurs then infuse their companies with these values: articulating them clearly, surrounding themselves with executives who share these values, and evangelizing the values to employees. The ultimate test of these values is whether the company continues to live by them after the founder leaves the company. In general, the CEO can have the most significant influence on a company's values. The founding CEO tends to have the most impact on these values; if the founder chooses a successor, the successor will likely preserve them. If the board ousts the founder, the chosen successor

may need to change the company's values. And subsequent generations of CEOs may be able to operate the company effectively without changing its values, particularly if those values help create a work
environment that keeps the company performing well for customers
and shareholders. If companies commit to the right values and live
these values each day, then the companies can truly be said to commit
to core values.

Executives who believe that their organization should do a better
job of committing to core values may consider the following tactics:

• *Assemble a team of leading executives to develop a core value statement.* This team should include all key operating executives. Although
the team must be balanced to assure broad representation, it should
not be so large that it is difficult to manage.

• *Assess each executive's core values and study core values of admired
companies.* The assessment process should include intensive interviews with key executives and should be supplemented with the results
of reviews of the executives by superiors, peers, subordinates, and key
outsiders such as customers, shareholders, or board members, as
appropriate.

• *Brainstorm an exhaustive list of core values; then select the top three
or four values.* The initial list of values should include all the values
emerging from the previous step as well as others developed through
discussion among team members. The team may also wish to consider
the core values of admired companies. To select the top three or four
values, the team may consider an exercise in which each team member votes on the top four choices.

• *Define the values clearly and develop stories that illustrate each
value.* Once the team agrees on the core values, it should develop a
sentence or two that clearly defines the value and describes why it is
so important to the company. The team should also agree on a story
or two from the experience of company employees that it will use to
convey the meaning of the value within the company.

• *Communicate values repeatedly throughout the organization in
many forums and media.* Despite the perceived tedium of repetition,
the management team should announce the new values in an all-
company meeting. The company should post the values and the
related stories on its Web site and reinforce them through the internal company newsletter, marketing literature, reward ceremonies,
training programs, performance evaluation, pay, and promotions.

Orville, Ohio–based J. M. Smucker has very strong values that emanated from its founder over a century ago. These values, based on the Mennonite religion, emphasize the importance of respecting the individual and contributing to the community. Smucker's values permeate its hiring practices, plant locations, and role in the community.

J. M. Smucker commits to core values and has sustained that commitment through several generations of management. According to *Small Business Network,* J. M. Smucker still operates according to the values and principles of Jerome Monroe Smucker, a devout Swiss-German Mennonite who founded the company in 1897. His great-grandson Tim, now co-CEO, suggested that his great-grandfather was inspired by the quote from Galatians, "Whatsoever a man soweth, that shall he also reap." Tim believes that the company's "Basic Beliefs" concerning quality, people, ethics, growth, and independence are responsible for Smucker's market leadership.[1]

Smucker has spent over one hundred years putting these values into practice. According to the *Akron (Ohio) Beacon Journal,* Smucker locates its operations in small towns where many potential employees share Smucker's values. For example, Smucker has 650 employees in its headquarters town of Orville, Ohio. According to former CEO Paul Smucker, Smucker employees have good family lives, contribute to the local community, and possess a strong work ethic. And as we will explore more in Chapter Nine, Smucker invests in the local communities in which it operates.

This value congruence between Smucker and the communities in which it operates is not limited to rural American Mennonite towns. For example, when Smucker sought a location for a fruit jelly plant in Australia, it picked Kyabram, population four thousand, largely because Paul Smucker realized that Kyabram shared the values of Orville, Ohio, in the 1950s.[2] As we will explore later in this chapter, Smucker's careful selection of plant locations engenders very strong worker loyalty, a trait that enhances Smucker's productivity.

Contrast Smucker's commitment to core values with its beverage competitor, Hansen Natural. Hansen Natural makes "alternative beverages" such as natural sodas in cans, apple juice, and children's multivitamin juice. Similar to Smucker, Hansen Natural has a homey-sounding heritage, having begun as a family business selling apple juice. However, an examination of Hansen's history and culture reveals that an important value at Hansen is to increase sales of a popular product by rapidly expanding production and distribution. Regrettably for

Hansen's owners, the premium placed on earning quick returns contributed to a 33 percent decline in its stock price following a debt-fueled acquisition spree.

Like many companies, Hansen grew without a clearly articulated set of core values. Its development followed the interests of its founder. According to the *Orange County Business Journal*, Hansen Natural was founded in 1980, when Tim Hansen expanded the Hansen family apple juice business, launching Hansen's Natural Sodas. Hansen came up with several exotic flavors and starred in advertising campaigns as an adventurer who traveled the world to find new flavors. His eagerness to pounce on the opportunity—and the ego boost of his successful advertising campaign—reflects the value Tim Hansen placed on short-term growth. As a result, the company grew quickly and borrowed too much to expand its plant capacity, resulting in a 1990 bankruptcy filing. Ultimately, Rodney Sacks, a South African lawyer, acquired Hansen Natural in a $14 million reverse merger in 1992. Sacks was attracted to Hansen Natural because its growth potential was not limited by the regional distribution of the packaging business that Sacks initially hoped to start.[3] Sacks's packaging industry background and his choice to buy Hansen due to its apparent growth potential reflected his interest in earning an investment profit from the company.

Hansen's growth goals proved difficult to achieve. After the company emerged from bankruptcy, things looked rosy for a short while. For example, its stock price rose from $1.40 in 1996 to $6 in 1999. Soon thereafter, the trouble started. In 2000 Hansen decided to increase its debt tenfold to finance acquisitions such as its $6.5 million purchase of Blue Sky, a soda and seltzer company. Sales increased from $72 million in 1999 to $92 million in 2001; as a result of this debt-fueled acquisition strategy, however, its net income dropped from $4.5 million to $3 million, causing its stock to dip back to $4 by 2002.

Under Sacks's guidance, Hansen operated without committing to core values. This absence of values may have contributed to Hansen's problems with employee relations. According to *Hansen Natural's 2001 Annual Report*, Hansen had several disputes with a contractor and a potential employee. In March 2002 Hansen paid $60,000 to settle a suit charging that sexual harassment caused her to be denied employment. And in January 2002 Hansen settled a dispute over a $175,000 payment to Chicago White Sox homerun slugger Sammy Sosa.[4] As these incidents suggest, the failure to commit to core values can contribute to a work environment that inhibits productivity.

The comparison of Smucker and Hansen Natural reveals general principles for committing to core values. First, core values emerge from a company's founder. Many companies are like Hansen Natural, with a founder or owner primarily interested in earning a relatively quick return on investment. Such companies may be better off not articulating a set of core values because to do so might be an exercise in hypocrisy. Companies like Smucker, whose founders have strong beliefs, tend to commit to core values without much introspection because the values are so deeply ingrained that the founders do not separate their business behavior from their behavior in other aspects of their lives.

Second, companies that commit to core values tend to last longer because their purpose transcends making a profit. Companies with clearly articulated values tend to do a better job of attracting and motivating people to work productively to further the company's mission. When workers believe that their efforts contribute to an organization that has meaning to which they can relate, the workers tend to transmit that meaning to customers and communities as well. If the company's specific values are aligned with the customers' demands, then they guide companies through many generations of managers.

Third, companies that commit to core values must communicate the values frequently and through many media. Communicating core values is important because it sets expectations, thereby creating an implicit contract between management and employees. The obvious risk of such public commitment to core values is that management may not fulfill the terms of the contract. Of course, if management is not willing to act according to its values, employees will become less productive and are more likely to seek out employment with companies that do act in accordance with their core values. Executives who communicate their values and act accordingly are likely to create a self-reinforcing internal pressure for people throughout the organization to follow that lead. This pressure is a powerful tool for motivating employees to commit to core values in their daily actions. And once employees make that commitment, customers and communities view the company in a more favorable light.

Hire for Values

Many companies have value statements; however, very few actually use them to make hiring decisions. Hiring for values leads to an intense focus on screening in only those potential employees who will use those values in their job. Companies that hire for values interview far more individuals with the basic skills to do a job because they must screen out so many who lack the right values. Such companies hire for attitude and train for skills—an approach that contrasts with other companies, which tend to hire for skills and disregard attitude. The investment in screening for all but the best-fitting employees pays off in several ways: through higher productivity, because employees who fit work more effectively with their peers; better customer service, because happier employees convey that happiness to customers; and lower turnover, because more satisfied workers are more likely to want to keep their jobs.

Executives who seek to do a better job of hiring for values may consider the following tactics:

• *Communicate core values in media likely to reach potential employees.* To reach potential employees, the company should identify the media that the most desirable employees use to learn about employment opportunities. The company should try to encourage stories in these media that will communicate these values to the potential employees.

• *Interview candidates with managers and employees who are "culture carriers."* The managers and employees who conduct interviews should be selected for their insights into the company's culture. They should have a reputation for having hired top-performing employees and for having been mentored by company executives with a deep-seated understanding of the company's values.

• *Conduct behavioral interviews that will lower traditional interview defenses and expose the candidate's true colors.* Interviews should require candidates to think on their feet rather than giving them an opportunity to regurgitate rote answers to typical interview questions. Such tests should be specifically focused on candidate personality traits that are particularly salient to the company's culture.

• *Debrief all interviewers together after candidate interviews.* The team conducting interviews should debrief after the round of interviews and comment on each candidate. This debriefing process can help amplify subtle signals of problems with a candidate who may superficially appear to be strong. Such debriefing may help the interview team to decide whether to reject a candidate who might otherwise have passed to the next round of interviews, or it might help to focus questions the next round of interviews on a point of apparent vulnerability or strength.

• *Analyze the effectiveness of the interview process, making improvements based on the successes and failures of new employees.* The company should measure the effectiveness of the interview process by tracking how employees hired by specific individuals performed in the months and years after they were hired. The company could attempt to spread the techniques used by the best-performing hiring teams and try to evaluate the sources of failure for the teams that hired the less successful employees.

Southwest Airlines considers its ability to hire for values to be among its chief sources of competitive advantage. Southwest looks for people who, as team players, do not take themselves too seriously and are extremely customer-oriented. Of these qualities the most important one that Southwest seeks is the ability to work effectively with other people.

Southwest fills most jobs through a hiring process that begins with a group interview of twenty people to determine how they interact with each other. According to the *Boston Globe,* Southwest searches with religious devotion to find people with the right attitude. In group interviews Southwest officials ask individuals to talk about themselves for five minutes. The officials watch what other applicants are doing as the talks begin. Officials pass over those who work on their own presentations; applicants who cheer on the speaker tend to get hired.[5] According to the *Globe and Mail,* one pilot was eliminated as a job candidate after he declined to model a pair of shorts during the job interview. Southwest used this as a test to determine whether pilots had a sense of humor. Another potential candidate had to leave after being rude to a receptionist.[6] Southwest's interview approach is designed to screen out candidates who will not work well with others. Southwest believes that this team-oriented outlook is a source of competitive advantage that enables the airline to provide a better customer experience than do the more internally competitive employees of some of its peers, such as American Airlines.

Southwest is so strict about its hiring process that it puts employees on a six-month probationary period to make sure that they fit with its culture. According to Colleen Barrett, chief operating officer, Southwest scrutinizes an employee's performance very closely during this probationary period. If Southwest identifies an employee who does not fit with its notions of teamwork or attitude, it will counsel him or her once or twice and then dismiss the employee.[7]

Southwest hires employees who embody its values and can convert them into action. A single person who does not fit with those values will distract others from their jobs as they expel what we might call the foreign body from the corporate immune system. Given the difficulty of both defining an adaptive set of values and hiring people who embody these values, companies like Southwest enjoy an advantage over peers that is very difficult to replicate.

Southwest's peer, American Airlines, highlights the nature of this advantage. According to the *California Management Review,* hiring at American is based on very different criteria than at Southwest. For example, American focuses primarily on a potential employee's technical skills. To a lesser extent, American screens for an employee's interpersonal skills, particularly for employees who interact directly with customers. However, American does not hire based on a potential employee's ability to work with people in different departments.

Unlike Southwest, American's hiring officials would not likely ask a potential pilot to try on a pair of shorts during an interview. For example, American seeks to recruit the most self-assured, arrogant pilots it can find because it believes that such pilots do the best job of flying airplanes. Not surprisingly, American's pilot-selection criteria generate problems. American pilots often demonstrate arrogance bordering on hostility toward employees in other functional groups.[8] This hostility annoys flight attendants who interact with these pilots and may treat passengers more brusquely to take out their frustrations with the hostile pilots.

The comparison of American and Southwest reveals general principles about hiring for values. First, hiring for values can contribute to superior financial performance. Compared to American, Southwest grew twelve times faster (with five-year average sales growth of 9.9 percent) and is four times more profitable (with a five-year net profit margin of 10 percent). Although hiring for values does not explain all of this superior performance, Southwest clearly believes that its people constitute an important source of competitive advantage.

Second, customers get better service from employees who enjoy their jobs. Therefore, companies such as Southwest invest significantly in identifying the characteristics of people who will enjoy serving customers. Their core values incorporate these characteristics. While adhering closely to their values, these executives consistently improve their ability to hire people who are best able to live these values on the job (and exclude those who are not).

By contrast, peer companies hire workers who they believe will perform well a specific set of tasks. This task orientation reflects peer companies' philosophy that employees are useful as long as they do a good job performing a particular function that the business requires in order to operate. Management's view of workers as performing specific functions leads to hiring individuals who they expect will perform their functions independently of how well they work with others. In short, many peer companies approach management as a scientific process. The science has side effects, however, on employees and customers who feel that management does not care about their concerns and who would prefer to do business with companies that treat them with greater respect.

Balance Performance Measurement

These differences in hiring practices also show up in performance measurement. Most companies tend to measure employee performance rigorously. They differ fundamentally, however, in *what* they measure. Whereas Value Leaders balance quantitative and qualitative factors in evaluating employee performance, peer companies tend to focus on quantitative factors alone, without regard to the process by which employees achieve results. To survive, companies need profits and they need to measure the extent to which employees contribute to the profits. Nevertheless, if a company does not also reward behavior consistent with its values, it runs the risk of creating a culture in which the ends justify the means, one that could threaten its long-term survival.

Ultimately, the difference comes down to whether a company looks at itself as cutting transactions or building relationships. A transaction-oriented firm tends to look at employees and customers as useful only to the extent that they can generate short-term revenues; it sees them as dispensable thereafter. Transaction-oriented companies tend to measure financial outcomes only. By contrast, relationship builders take a longer-term orientation. They invest in employees because they believe that such investment will encourage employees to create value for customers over a longer period by offering them good service and by developing new products that meet their evolving needs. Relationship builders tend to measure financial and nonfinancial variables in order to encourage a healthy balance among employees between the urge for financial results and the desire to act according to the company's core values.

There are no universal rules about how to strike the right balance between quantitative and qualitative measures. In general, however, successful performance measurement systems are based on a deep understanding of the qualitative factors that drive quantitative results. For example, some companies, such as Cisco Systems, have found that higher customer satisfaction leads to greater customer loyalty and higher customer profitability. Furthermore, these companies have found that linking a substantial proportion of employee bonuses to improved customer satisfaction motivates the spirit of teamwork that raises revenue and profit growth. This kind of insight into the relationships between qualitative factors and financial results should inform the development of balanced performance measurement systems.

Executives seeking to do a better job of balancing performance measurement should consider the following tactics:

• *Form a team of executives to develop balanced performance measures.* The ideas applied to team formation would be the same as for the core values team. In addition, it would be particularly important for the team to include financial and information technology executives.

• *Agree on key financial and nonfinancial indicators that determine the health of the business.* The financial indicators might include cash flow, revenue growth, profit margins, and balance sheet strength. The nonfinancial indicators might include customer and employee satisfaction, product development effectiveness, community perception, and others.

• *Develop specific measures of these indicators that are meaningful at different levels of the company.* The same indicator might be broken down into pieces that could be managed at different levels of the organization. For example, a division general manager might be responsible for meeting a specific gross margin goal, whereas a production line worker might be required to meet specific manufacturing yield rates for the worker's stage in the production process.

• *Communicate the balanced performance measures to all employees.* Senior management would introduce the balanced performance measures in an all-company meeting. The company's performance on all the measures would be reported quarterly throughout the company. All-company ceremonies would occur periodically to reward top performers.

• *Incorporate the measures into employee performance objectives and performance reviews.* Each executive would meet with the managers he or she supervises to agree on how to measure the manager's performance. Similarly, each manager would negotiate with employees to agree on how the employee would achieve specific goals related to the performance measures.

• *Develop systems to track the measures, if necessary.* In order to incorporate the balanced performance measures into the management process, the company might need to build new performance measurement systems.

Goldman Sachs exemplifies the tight linkage between Value Leaders' values and the way they evaluate people. Specifically, Goldman Sachs has developed an exceptionally effective process for finding very bright, ambitious employees and systematically subsuming their drive for personal success to tireless pursuit of the interests of Goldman Sachs. Somewhat ironically, the individuals who achieve the greatest professional success at the company are the ones who are most effective at achieving business objectives while harmonizing with the firm's interests.

According to TheVault.com, Goldman Sachs is intense and goal-driven, a place where success is taken for granted. Although others perceive Goldman employees as industry leaders, Goldman prides itself on cutting individual egos down to size, subordinating individual interests to those of the firm. For example, a newly hired Goldman Sachs employee observed that some colleagues hired from "top schools" conveyed an arrogant tone that was inappropriate at Goldman.[9]

Goldman's performance evaluation process starts as soon as a new employee begins work. Newly hired employees find it difficult to adjust to the careful scrutiny to which coworkers subject them. Employees feel as though their activities are under constant surveillance. On a positive note, Goldman analysts and associates consider their colleagues to be intelligent, perceptive, and willing to sacrifice to help the team succeed. Working as part of a Goldman Sachs team can be challenging because employees feel constant pressure to live up to coworkers' high standards.[10]

In order to climb the ladder at Goldman Sachs, obvious politicking limits a career, whereas accomplishments dictate success. According to *Fast Company,* the career of Goldman's cohead of investment banking, Bob Higgins, helps illustrate what it takes to get ahead at Goldman.[11]

Given Goldman's emphasis on teamwork, Higgins believes that success comes from excelling at the work a manager gives an employee and having faith that management will notice achievements eventually. By contrast, Higgins noted that politicking for promotions at Goldman sticks out "like a polyester suit in a crowd of pinstripes."

In 1975 Higgins got a valuable lesson about how Goldman values teamwork in its employees. Higgins had been working as a securities analyst at Goldman for a few months when Robert Rubin, then head of Goldman's arbitrage trading department, contacted him. Rubin wanted to understand the fit between a manufacturer of diamond drill bits and the company it offered to acquire, Hughes Tool. Higgins nervously met with Rubin for an hour, presented Rubin his analysis, and returned to his desk. A few minutes later, Higgins got a call from the head of research, who told Higgins that Rubin had called him to say how helpful Higgins had been. Although Higgins noted that this kind of response typifies Goldman, it was his first experience with how Goldman puts teamwork into practice.

Goldman takes a very rigorous approach to evaluating people, balancing quantitative and nonquantitative factors. In the investment-banking division, for example, Higgins evaluates his peers and junior people, and they evaluate Higgins. This 360-degree process leads each person to produce thirty written evaluations. The evaluation forms solicit feedback in eleven categories, including an assessment of overall performance as well as teamwork. In the case of teamwork, managers judge people by whether they avoid politicking, whether they share information and credit, and whether they are a resource to others. The goal of the 360-degree evaluation process is to learn the business, not to get career advice. Higgins advised Goldman employees that to get ahead, they must produce at a level that puts them among the top people at Goldman. However, he suggests that the employee's contribution within the team framework determines whether or not the employee will rise to the senior level.[12]

Although Goldman Sachs institutionalized a tight linkage between its values and the way it judges performance, others tend to forgo such linkages. For example, although Merrill Lynch's shared values of client focus, respect for the individual, teamwork, responsible citizenship, and integrity may sound virtuous,[13] employees report that their rise or fall within the company depends to a great extent on their skill at internal politics. This gap between stated values and actual behavior breeds employee cynicism.

Employees agree that the most significant drawback of working at Merrill Lynch is its "horrendous bureaucracy," which pits its supposed "shared values" against the way it treats employees. According to The-Vault.com, Merrill Lynch's bureaucracy can combine with office politics to make employee's lives miserable and incomprehensible. Sometimes, for no apparent reason, employees take the blame for things they did not do and they receive assignments that do not fit with their job descriptions. Furthermore, employees suggest that when these problems occur, no manager is available to rectify them. One employee went so far as to compare life at Merrill Lynch to "a page from a Kafka novel."[14]

Based on the way employees feel about Merrill Lynch, we see that its "shared values" are primarily for external marketing purposes. Unlike Goldman Sachs, Merrill does not appreciate the connection between its values and the way it measures employee performance. For example, one Merrill financial consultant says he tells people he is proud to be working for Merrill, but he knows that bureaucracy and politics can make life at the company pretty miserable.[15]

The comparison of the performance measures used at Goldman Sachs and Merrill Lynch reveal general principles. First, companies cannot expect to attract the best people or earn their loyalty unless they consistently align the values they state with the way they actually measure people's performance. For example, some Merrill Lynch employees must snicker cynically when they read Merrill's statement of values and compare it to the way that some of them get bounced around within its bureaucracy. By contrast, Goldman Sachs operates with a very tight alignment between its values—which employees must be able to recite in pop quizzes—and its many formal processes for measuring employee performance. Thus, Goldman Sachs tends to get and keep the best people in the industry, increasingly rewarding those who meet its high standards.

Second, companies must make formal processes for measuring performance consistent with their values and apply them rigorously. Such attention to detail infuses the balanced performance measures with meaning. These companies' employees believe that they cannot escape the pressure to meet the company's performance standards. By using 360-degree evaluations, employees realize that they will be judged on every interaction with others in the company and with customers. This tight scrutiny forces employees to apply the company's values in their every interaction, knowing that their future within the organization depends on it. Although such tight performance measurement may seem oppressive to some, it helps communicate clearly to all employees what they are supposed to be doing. Such clarity frees employees from worrying about corporate politics so that they can focus all their attention and energy on doing the job.

Reward Employees Intelligently

Many companies recognize the importance of weeding out employees who don't fit their culture before they can cause damage to the company's competitive position. These companies realize that sustaining employee trust in management depends heavily on rewarding good performers and helping poor performers to improve or, if this is not possible, to depart the company with dignity. As a result, such companies' longer-tenured employees tend to perform well and receive rewards that they perceive as valuable.

Other companies tend to be less concerned with maintaining a long-term relationship with employees. As a result, they may offer higher base salaries while feeling no qualms about terminating these higher-paid employees in the event of a short-term need to cut costs in order to satisfy financial targets. Companies with a longer-term outlook tend to invest in employees; more short-term-focused companies tend to hire and fire employees with less concern about employee morale.

Some companies reward employees with a pyramid of pay, at the top of which is an intangible and rare commodity—mutual respect. Other companies make employees feel they must check their humanity at the door when they report to work. Treating employees with respect is an intangible (and inexpensive) currency that motivates them. Typically, such companies offer base pay that is lower than that of their competitors. However, when profit sharing and other pay components are added, these companies' best-performing employees receive higher total compensation than do their peers. Furthermore, by linking a higher proportion of their pay to the achievement of corporate goals, the best-performing companies reinforce the importance of looking out for the interests of the team rather than the department or an individual.

Executives seeking to do a better job of rewarding employees intelligently may use the following tactics:

• *Agree on which behaviors to link to financial rewards and which to psychological rewards.* For example, objectively measurable outcomes such as sales targets or product profit margins might receive financial rewards, whereas acting on behalf of the team might be rewarded through peer recognition.

• *Develop specific performance standards for giving the financial and psychological rewards and link the specific rewards to the standards.* For example, the standards by which a worker might receive peer recognition for teamwork might be based on the standards used to reward previous winners, such as working very long hours to help out a team member who was working part-time due to an injury.

• *Communicate the standards clearly to employees when they agree on performance objectives with their managers.* To ensure that managers and employees clearly understand the standards, hold meetings at the beginning of the performance evaluation period and have both individuals sign off.

• *Distribute rewards fairly.* Although fairness is often subjective, executives should be aware that employees who perceive that rewards are not being allocated fairly can lose motivation. Thus, the costs to the company from unfair distribution of rewards in the form of negative productivity can be substantial.

Smucker rewards employees intelligently. According to the *Akron (Ohio) Beacon Journal,* Smucker does not offer stock options, all-expense-paid vacations, or on-site day care. Rather, it offers employees such as fruit processors and office workers a work environment in which they feel respected and valued. In a sense Smucker turns conventional wisdom about linking pay to performance on its side: rather than using performance measurement as a way to make distinctions among employees, it offers employees a basket of rewards, consisting of good pay and the psychic rewards of feeling respected by management and peers, that makes them all feel affection for their employer, thereby raising corporate productivity.[16]

Employee comments reveal the motivational power of Smucker's approach, according to the *Akron (Ohio) Beacon Journal.* John Nicholas, a Smucker staffing manager, enthused about the positive nature of the work environment: Smucker people are friendly; they want to work at Smucker; they feel challenged, respected, and valued. Jeff Seibert, who has unloaded juice tanks in a Smucker warehouse since 1985, respects the Smucker family. Seibert believes that the Smuckers have been fair to employees in the plant. He finds the Smuckers willing to talk with employees, listen to their problems, and give employees positive solutions to them.

Other employees cited Smucker's promise to treat others the way they wanted to be treated, Smucker's career opportunities, and its respect for workers.

Smucker also compensates employees by giving them the time and support they need to handle family matters. For example, Ernestine Wilson, who stacks trays of restaurant jellies onto pallets, gushed about Smucker's generosity to her when her husband had cancer. Wilson, who started working at Smucker in 1968, was allowed to come to work when she could and to park close to her shop so that she could leave quickly if she needed.

And Smucker provides tangible incentives as well. Every employee gets an annual 2 percent bonus at the holidays. But employees seem to value the intangibles more. Brenda Dempsey, corporate communications manager for Smucker, appreciates the Christmas bonus and the flex time. However, she finds that Smucker's unquantifiable intangibles make it a special workplace. A senior project leader in Smucker's information technology group feels good about working twelve hours a day because he doesn't worry about losing his job (due to steady demand for Smucker's products throughout the economic cycle) and doesn't fear that someone will ask him to lie.

Its respect for employees does not mean that Smucker has lost sight of financial results. In fact, Smucker's compensation approach translates into higher productivity. According to Moneycentral.msn.com, Smucker generates 50 percent higher sales per employee ($305,000) and 133 percent higher net income per employee ($14,000) than the processed and packaged goods industry average.[17]

In addition to the high productivity resulting from its work environment, Smucker's employee turnover rate is a relatively low 5 percent. Many Smucker jelly workers work as many as three and four decades on its production line. And some employees work with their parents, husbands, and wives. Although problems occasionally arise, such as during contract negotiations, workers believe that Smucker's respect for employees is sincere, springing from a determination to sustain its family's good name.[18]

Smucker has superior insight into what motivates people and uses that insight to structure reward systems that generate higher productivity. For example, intangible benefits, such as treating people with respect or making work fun, are simultaneously inexpensive and difficult for competitors to copy because delivering these benefits requires changes in rhetoric, values, and behavior. Other companies simply find it too difficult to make these changes, thus leaving companies like Smucker with a powerful competitive weapon.

Southwest's approach to employee incentives is very similar to Smucker's. Therefore, the contrast between Southwest and a peer, United Airlines, provides valuable insight into the way peer companies approach employee incentives. According to the *Washington Post*, at least two former United flight attendants who switched to Southwest saw a significant difference between the two airlines. United furloughed flight attendants Rochelle Weber and Cathy Sims after September 11, 2001; by April 2002 Weber and Sims had participated in Southwest's four-and-a-half-week unpaid training sessions.[19]

Both estimated that they would earn 30 percent to 40 percent less money as full-time Southwest flight attendants then they did at United. The possible pay cuts did not seem to bother Weber and Sims because they noticed that their future colleagues at Southwest seemed happier. Unlike their experience at United, no one at Southwest complained about management, their immediate superiors, or their coworkers.

Another United worker, pilot Steve Dereby, who has been working at United since 1986, believes that Southwest takes a unique approach to employee relations. Dereby points out with some frustration that Southwest has done a superb job of motivating employees to serve customers, whereas other airlines—including United—have failed to inspire their employees.[20]

Companies that reward employees intelligently design their compensation systems with a deep understanding of what motivates their people. Remarkably, they demonstrate that employees will give up base pay if in the bargain their employer treats them with respect and gives them a chance to participate in the profits they generate for the company. This respectful attitude motivates employees to act like owners, looking for ways to make the company operate more effectively and efficiently.

By contrast, other companies treat workers more as parts of an economic machine. When management needs employees to produce during periods of high demand, the employees work longer hours and receive higher pay. When demand declines, management dismisses employees based on their relative skill at internal politics. Employees with the most political skill tend to lose their jobs only if management needs to cut costs greater than the amount it can recover by cutting the jobs of politically weaker employees.

TRANSFORMING CONTINENTAL AIRLINES

Gordon Bethune's transformation of Continental Airlines ranks among the most remarkable instances of tightening a company's conformance to the principle "Value human relationships." Bethune's success resulted from changes that extend beyond the way Continental treats employees. Nevertheless, a brief review of the key elements of Bethune's transformation strategy could help executives seeking to transform their own organizations.

When Gordon Bethune took over the CEO slot in 1994, Continental Airlines was about to enter bankruptcy for the third time. According to *Fortune,* Bethune turned Continental into one of the most admired and financially strong airlines. Before Bethune, Continental offered miserable service, late flights, and bad meals. Under Bethune, Continental earned the top slot in J. D. Power's overall satisfaction survey in all but one of the years between 1995 and 2000.[21]

Due to the airline industry's very low profit margins, Bethune joked that it attracts masochists. Bethune argues that the airline industry is a people business. By 2002 Continental employed 42,900 people, most of whom Bethune was able to get going in the same direction through a series of change initiatives. For example, Bethune was able to motivate Continental people to improve on-time performance.

Before Bethune, late plane arrivals cost Continental $6 million a month. So he offered to give half of this money to employees when Continental reached the top half of the ten top-ranked on-time airlines in America. Bethune's bargain cost Continental only $65 a month because employees, including managers and below, would get part of that $6 million (the $65 per month represented half of the $130 in cost savings that he would pay as a bonus if the 46,154 eligible Continental employees met their end of the bargain). Although one of Bethune's associates doubted this figure would be sufficient to get employees' attention, Bethune believed it would work. In February 1995 Continental was ranked fourth, and Bethune issued checks for his employees. In March 1995 Continental came in first place, a victory that the airline had not achieved since 1935. And in April 1995, Continental came in first again.

The airline achieved this dramatic improvement by giving its employees the power and incentive to cut waste out of the flying process. Airlines hold "late meetings" to review why flights did not arrive on time the previous day. Before Bethune, the object of these meetings was to blame other departments for the late arrival. As a result, a flight attendant would blame the caterer for not delivering twenty meals. The caterer would have five meals and tell the flight attendant that he would get the other fifteen from the kitchen in twenty minutes. The flight attendant would hold the flight until the other fifteen meals arrived; the plane would be twenty minutes late; and she could blame the caterer.

Once Bethune started rewarding employees for beating the competition in on-time performance, employee behavior changed. Now when the caterer does not have all twenty meals, the flight attendant demands that the caterer makes sure that he never misses his full meal delivery, and he now has an incentive to comply with her request. Now the flight attendant closes the door so that the flight can leave on time, despite the missing meals, and finds some passengers willing to trade food for alcohol in order to get the airplane to leave on time. Because the flight attendant is paid for on-time performance, all Continental employees are better off and customers get more of what they value.

Bethune used a similarly effective approach to fix a problem of employee "sick outs." He realized that Continental people called in sick for work because they didn't like their jobs. Bethune changed many aspects of Continental to make people like their jobs more. And he found a simple and effective way to cut absenteeism: Continental gives away eight free cars to employees every six months through a lottery. Only employees who don't miss work for six months running are eligible for the drawings. In December, if an employee does not feel like going to work, she decides to go anyway because she has only one more month to go before the car drawing. Bethune reasons that because Continental's cost of absenteeism has dropped so much, the cars cost the airline nothing.[22]

These examples of Bethune's transformation of Continental help illustrate the change process we discussed earlier. Bethune changed Continental's values. Before he came on the scene, Continental was indifferent to on-time performance, absenteeism, and productivity; since his arrival, Continental has improved dramatically in all these areas. Bethune achieved the transformation by understanding the linkages between what customers want from an airline and how

Continental employees do their job. By changing Continental's values and offering self-financing incentives to motivate employees to achieve these values, Bethune engineered a successful turnaround.

MANAGEMENT LEVERS

Executives aspiring to achieve a transformation in the way they manage employees along the lines of Bethune's accomplishments at Continental can take the following five steps:

- Build a change team.
- Develop new values.
- Screen staff for fit with the new values.
- Close the value-fit gap.
- Train, measure, and compensate.

We briefly explore the key activities required to exercise these management levers effectively.

Build a Change Team

The CEO cannot hope to achieve change without gaining the support of the company's stakeholders. Thus, the CEO should form a change team consisting of participants from key internal line and staff functions as well as external participants such as money managers, customers, suppliers, and government regulators. The CEO should get input from the board on the change team's charter and should keep the board informed regarding the team's progress. The CEO should define the change team's objectives and set a schedule including specific deliverables and a time frame for their completion.

Develop New Values

As we will explore in greater depth in Chapter Nine, developing values can be a powerful competitive weapon. The change team can create this weapon by researching customers' unmet needs, analyzing competitor strengths and weaknesses, identifying the company's current "values in action," and involving employees at all levels.

The change team can then develop a new set of corporate values at the intersection of these three bodies of analysis. It should develop values that enable the company to satisfy unmet customer needs better than the competition can. In striving to develop such values, the firm must know how the behaviors resulting from these values will affect how well the company can satisfy unmet customer needs relative to competitors.

Screen Staff for Fit with the New Values

Once the change team has developed its set of values, it must check how well the company's people embody them. If none of the company's people feel that they can work in accordance with the change team's values, then the values will likely need to be modified. In extreme cases the complete lack of alignment between the new values and the company's current organization could spur the board to replace management, a not uncommon outcome during the early 2000s.

Having agreed on the new values, the change team faces the delicate task of assessing which employees embody the new values and which do not. If the values are fundamentally new, many of the organization's current leaders will likely not fit so well with them. The change team may also find individuals at lower levels of the organizational hierarchy who fit better with the new values.

Close the Value-Fit Gap

The change team must then use the foregoing analysis to make decisions about people in order to assure that the company's key roles are occupied by people who embody the new values. In some cases the CEO may need to replace some people who can't act according to the new values with those who can. In many cases the CEO may decide that some individuals will require training in order to sensitize them to the new values. In other cases the change team may be able to promote certain individuals within the firm to fill key leadership roles or fill the roles with people from the outside.

Train, Measure, and Compensate

Ultimately, the CEO must embed the new values into the organization by instituting a set of ongoing processes. In most cases the change team will recommend changes to the existing processes for training, measuring, and compensating people. For example, it might recommend training all employees in the new values. Such a program could include a discussion of the new values, reviews of case studies illustrating how such values can alter an employee's work approach, role playing with the new and old values, and the development of personal value statements that show how individuals would behave differently based on their understanding of the new values. Similarly, the change team might recommend a new emphasis on balanced performance measures and compensation designed to encourage cooperation between functions and across networks of suppliers, partners, and customers.

VALUE QUOTIENT

Tactical-level analysis can help executives pinpoint opportunities for improvement. If you perceive that your organization can improve in the way it applies the principle "Value human relationships," such analysis can help identify how best to improve the way your organization performs targeted activities.

Exhibit 2.1 can help you calculate your company's VQ through two levels of analysis. The first level of analysis is binary, meaning that you can use the worksheet as a checklist to determine whether or not your company performs the specific tactics on the list. If your company does not perform any of the tactics within a specific activity, then it should consider initiating such tactics. The second level of analysis is analog, meaning that the worksheet can help pinpoint opportunities to improve how well your company performs a specific tactic that it has already been performing. To raise your company's score on a particular tactic, you may wish to initiate an in-depth process to change the way your organization performs that tactic along the lines developed in Chapter Nine.

To conduct the binary and analog levels of analysis, your company should gather data through interviews with employees. Ideally, your company should use objective third parties to identify an appropriate sample of interviewees, develop interview guides, conduct the interviews, and analyze the results. The outcome of collecting and analyzing the data will be specific scores for each tactic. Although assigning these scores requires judgment, they should be calibrated by comparing the scores with the Value Leaders and other best-of-breed competitors.

Value Human Relationships: Activity and Tactics	Score

Commit to core values

☐ Assemble a team of leading executives to develop core value statement. _____

☐ Assess each executives' core values and study core values of admired companies. _____

☐ Brainstorm exhaustive list of core values then select top three or four values. _____

☐ Define the values clearly and develop stories that illustrate each value. _____

☐ Communicate values repeatedly throughout the organization in many forums and media. _____

☐ Link selected incentives to employee behavior consistent with the values. _____

Hire for values

☐ Communicate core values in media likely to reach potential employees. _____

☐ Interview candidates with managers and employees who are culture carriers. _____

☐ Conduct behavioral interviews that will lower traditional interview defenses and expose the candidates' true colors. _____

☐ Analyze the effectiveness of the interview process, making improvements based on new employee outcomes. _____

☐ Communicate program success to all employees. _____

Balance performance measurement

☐ Form a team of executives to develop balanced performance measures. _____

☐ Agree on key financial and nonfinancial indicators that determine the health of the business. _____

☐ Develop specific measures of these indicators that are meaningful at different levels of the company. _____

☐ Communicate the balanced performance measures to all employees. _____

☐ Incorporate the measures into employee performance objectives and performance reviews. _____

☐ Develop systems to track the measures, if necessary. _____

Reward employees intelligently

☐ Agree on which behaviors should be linked to financial rewards and which to psychological rewards. _____

☐ Develop specific performance standards for giving the financial and psychological rewards and link the specific rewards to the standards. _____

☐ Communicate the standards clearly to employees when they agree on performance objectives with their managers. _____

☐ Distribute rewards fairly. _____

Total _____

Exhibit 2.1.   Value Quotient Worksheet: Value Human Relationships.
Key: 5 = excellent; 4 = very good; 3 = good; 2 = fair; 1 = poor; 0 = not applicable.

Scores for each tactic range from excellent (five) to poor (one). If an organization does not perform the tactic at all, it receives a score of zero. To calculate the activity scores, the analyst can average the scores for the tactics supporting that activity and round the average to the nearest whole number. To illustrate how a score might be assigned for a specific tactic, consider the tactic "Assemble a team of leading executives to develop core value statement." If your company has not assembled such a team, it would receive a score of zero. On the other hand, if your company has recently completed intensive senior management team development to prepare itself to forge a consensus on your company's core values, it would receive a score of five for this tactic.

Once you have completed the scoring process, read Chapter Nine to find out how best to use the scores to lead a change process.

CONCLUSION

The principle of valuing human relationships extends the definition of value beyond its traditional borders. Companies that value human relationships embrace a set of core values, and their activities emanate from this core. Such companies hire people who believe in their core values; they measure employees based on their embodiment of the core values; and they compensate in a way that motivates employees to achieve more. As a result, customers receive better service and often lower prices; managers get higher productivity and deeper market penetration; and shareholders get higher returns.

CHAPTER THREE

Two Heads Are Better Than One

(Foster Teamwork)

Fostering teamwork means getting people—particularly those with different functional skills and responsibilities—to work together to advance the interests of the corporation. A corollary to this definition is that teamwork also demands that individuals who patently advance their own interests ahead of the corporation's will not survive. Rather, individual advancement depends on sublimating individual wants to the group's shared interest. In this sense companies that foster teamwork use a tinge of socialist ethics to achieve very capitalist results. Teamwork succeeds only when a company's departments show mutual respect, which can yield insights that generate better products and more efficient and effective business processes. Furthermore, a willingness to work with others creates a more satisfying work environment and helps keep a company from becoming complacent.

LINK WITH VALUE LEADERSHIP

Fostering teamwork contributes significantly to a company's conformance with Value Leadership. When employees work in teams, they develop more effective solutions for customers. For example, an engineer's new product idea at the cutting edge of technology may be too expensive to manufacture at a cost that will provide value for the customer and a profit for shareholders. But if the engineer develops that new product idea in a team with employees from manufacturing, purchasing, finance, and marketing, then the team is much more likely to work out such kinks before the customer gets ready to buy the new product. Fostering teamwork thus makes an important contribution to a company's ability to create new products and services that customers are eager to buy.

ECONOMIC BENEFITS

Fostering teamwork can contribute to a company's economic performance. Specifically, it accelerates growth and heightens productivity and profit margins. Value Leaders' five-year average revenues grew 35 percent faster, were 39 percent more productive, and earned five-year average profit margins 109 percent higher than their industries. Specifically, Value Leaders' five-year revenues grew at an average 16.5 percent rate compared to a 12.2 percent rate for their industries; their revenues per employee averaged $398,750 compared to $286,625 for their industries; and their five-year net margins were 16.7 percent compared to 8.0 percent for their industries. Although Value Leaders' ability to foster teamwork does not explain all of this superior performance, such teamwork contributes to these results. Teamwork helps with the development of new products that customers are eager to buy; it helps cut the cost of developing and building these products; and it streamlines the duplication of work that often flows from interdepartmental handoffs.

CASES

This chapter shows how these dynamics work in companies, drawing general principles from a comparison of the team-training practices of Southwest and American Airlines. It describes the CEO development practices at Wal-Mart and J. C. Penney and points out the benefits of creating an effective process for developing new CEOs internally instead of hiring "turnaround" CEOs from outside. The chapter draws out general principles emerging from a comparison of team decision-making practices at Southwest and American Airlines.

It continues by evaluating the team rewards that Goldman Sachs and Merrill Lynch offer. It presents a case of the turnaround at Johnson & Johnson's (J&J's) Critikon division with the help of the Kaizen method of process improvement. The chapter then describes management levers for achieving such a turnaround and concludes with a Value Quotient (VQ) worksheet that can help executives assess how well their companies follow the principle "Foster teamwork."

ACTIVITY ANALYSIS

Beyond hiring team players, which we discussed in Chapter Two, fostering teamwork depends on a company's performing four activities well:

- **Train teams.** After hiring employees, companies expose them to the values and practices that will guide their work.
- **Rotate jobs.** By exposing employees to new functions, companies help these employees understand the challenges that other functions face. Value Leaders rotate people through different jobs in order to enhance teamwork and to test potential senior executives.
- **Make team decisions.** To accomplish a group initiative, such as manufacturing a car or "turning around" an airplane at a gate, different functions must interact and make joint decisions. Value Leaders establish shared goals for these initiatives and encourage different functions to cooperate in order to achieve better results.
- **Reward team behavior.** As we noted in Chapter Two, Value Leaders reward people differently than do peer companies. Value Leaders offer psychic and financial incentives for effective team behavior.

Train Teams

Teamwork begins with hiring team players, and training defines its rules and practices. Companies that train teams use training to inculcate people with the values and practices they'll need to succeed in a teamwork culture. By contrast, other companies use employee training to instill functional skills. Although companies that train teams also provide skill-related training, say, for pilots, such companies outperform their peer companies by teaching people how to work together to win.

Executives seeking to enhance their approach to training teams might consider the following tactics:

• *Hire a training director with experience developing and implementing team training.* Although finding training directors who can manage training to deliver specific skills may be common, the ability to deliver team training is one that can sustain competitive advantage. Because firms often find it difficult to work effectively in teams, a training director who can improve team performance can help his or her employer compete more effectively.

• *Interview "culture carriers" at different levels of the organization to identify the specific behaviors that generate the most effective teamwork.* Individuals who epitomize the company's culture are a useful source of specific behaviors that should be encouraged through team training. Such culture carriers can provide ideas about the values to be reinforced by the training as well as memorable stories that can help bring these values to life.

• *Develop fun, experiential training exercises to illustrate the effectiveness of these behaviors.* If training is enjoyable, it develops a better reputation throughout the company. This enthusiasm becomes contagious and makes employees more eager to learn and to apply the lessons.

• *Introduce these exercises to employees at the different levels of the organization.* As employees advance through their careers, they should be exposed to team training that is most appropriate for the level that they are entering. For example, manufacturing line employees should learn to work effectively with others in the manufacturing process, whereas general managers should receive training that will enable them to work more effectively with peers both inside and outside the company.

• *Assess and improve the effectiveness of the exercises.* Evaluating training effectiveness is the only way to identify what aspects of the training are working well and which need to be eliminated or improved.

Southwest Airlines' training program combines fun with values. According to *Personnel Journal*, Southwest Airlines' University of People teaches teamwork at both the entry and managerial levels.[1]

New hires participate in an exercise to spur creativity through teamwork. An eight-person team receives twelve straws, four strips of masking tape, and a raw egg. The team gets seven minutes to construct a device that keeps the egg from cracking when dropped onto a plastic sheet from a height of ten feet. Liz Simmons, director of corporate learning and development, suggests that team emotions span the range from exhilaration to disappointment. After the exercise, each team describes to the others how it conceived its egg shelter. The teams' success depends on how creative they were in generating ideas, how they depersonalized the ideas (for example, by writing them on a blackboard without listing the name of the originator), objectively selected the best one, and embraced it as a team. Simmons noted that at least one team always succeeds as a result of its ability to build teamwork fast.

Southwest's Frontline Leadership training program has a different team-building exercise called Oz. Managers journey to unearth the mysteries behind an effective employee and leader at Southwest. The employees in the training program seek out experienced employees who can enlighten them on what it takes to be an effective Southwest employee and leader. In the process of seeking out and getting to know these employees, the new employees build their own understanding of what they will need to do to succeed at the company. The new employees also develop a network of advisors who can help them make key decisions during their career at Southwest. Participants in the Crocodile River exercise use two-by-fours to cross a simulated river, thus enhancing teamwork in dangerous circumstances.[2]

Southwest trains teams by creating fun group exercises for all employees, from entry level to executive. It builds a shared experience base that helps employees communicate and solve problems as they perform their jobs. Southwest's team training attempts to capture the genius of its best employees, or culture carriers, and infuse the entire organization with this spirit. Through fun group exercises and systematic networking, Southwest uses its training programs to build and nurture a culture of teamwork.

Other airlines, such as American Airlines, train for functional skills, not teamwork. For example, American decided that its ticket-counter employees were not performing customer service well enough. Its approach to the problem was typically analytical: breaking customer service into functional components and developing skills training in each component.

The airline developed a training program in customer service for its ticket-counter employees. American believed that as a result of this program, customers would notice an enhanced level of service from employees at the ticket counter. According to its Web site, all

American's ticket-counter employees received customer skills training in 2000. Specifically, employees received training in functions such as how to better communicate, how to be more attentive to the people who are talking to them, how to handle problems better, how to use eye contact, and how to remember to use the customer's name.[3] To an extent, the skills that American tried to train its people to develop are natural reactions for people who enjoy serving others.

But American's efforts did not translate into greater customer satisfaction. According to the American Customer Satisfaction Index, American's efforts to improve customer satisfaction were less than successful. Between 1995 and 2002, the airline's level of customer satisfaction declined 10 percent, ranking it one notch above bottom relative to its peers.[4] This suggests that American may need to supplement its highly touted training programs if American is to approach Southwest's industry-leading levels of customer satisfaction.

The comparison of Southwest and American's approaches to training reveal two general principles. First, training teams is only one part of an effort to foster teamwork. If a company decides to foster teamwork through training alone—without changing its core values and supporting processes to reflect that change—then employees are likely to react to a new training program with some cynicism. Nevertheless, training teams in the context of a culture that fosters teamwork can be very useful because it helps employees learn behaviors that the company values and because it introduces employees to culture carriers, who can offer employees guidance during their careers. Culture carriers act as role models for new employees. Because senior management selects the culture carriers after observing their behavior in crucial corporate roles, the culture carriers are the living embodiment of corporate values. New employees who seek out and learn from these culture carriers can learn how to function most effectively within the company, thereby enhancing their own careers and ultimately increasing the chances that they too may someday be selected as culture carriers for the next generation of new employees.

Second, training teams must instill openness to seeing how other team members view a situation. Although different companies will try to encourage different behaviors to foster teamwork, a universal requirement of effective team training is to make employees more able to perceive how team members might view a situation differently than they do. A critical prerequisite of effective teamwork is to appreciate its members' different perspectives so that the team can develop an effective team solution. For example, team training can help employees responsible for turning around an airplane at a gate do their job faster. With a deeper appreciation of each team member's responsibilities, the team members can make split-second decisions that cut down on inefficiencies resulting from confusion among members of the team. The food service example from Continental Airlines in Chapter Two is a good example of this. At Continental, the catering staff learned how important timely delivery of meals was for flight attendants striving for on-time flight departures. As a result, the catering staff was more likely to take actions required to deliver their meals on time.

Rotate Jobs

Developing leaders internally depends on giving potential leaders responsibility for managing key parts of the business. Companies that rotate jobs tend to develop senior executives by exposing internal candidates to different parts of the operation. By offering potential leadership candidates such exposure, the board gets better data on which to base succession plans. Just as importantly, job rotation gives these companies more leaders with a deeper appreciation of different parts of the company, thus making them better able to lead teams of people from across the company due to their deeper understanding of different departments. Other companies tend to encourage more functional specialization, an approach that often requires them to bring in more well-rounded leadership from outside the company.

Executives seeking to improve the way they rotate jobs to foster teamwork might consider the following tactics:

• *Analyze the characteristics of the most successful executives both inside the company and at best-of-breed companies.* The company might target the skills needed for, say, an effective general manager. To understand effective general management skills, it might interview the most successful general manager in the company and perhaps in companies that lead other industries facing similar challenges.

• *Use these characteristics to select a set of high-potential managers and employees.* Once it has identified the characteristics of effective managers, the company can assess its current general managers and those in training. With the assessment, the company can determine whether it needs to replace the current general managers and those it is developing.

• *Evaluate these executive candidates individually, identifying strengths and opportunities for development.* If the current general managers are strong, the company can assess developmental opportunities in order to help these managers improve their effectiveness.

• *Give the executive candidates job opportunities and training to bolster their skills for promotion.* The company should have in place a structured process for comparing high-potential candidates' developmental needs with the training programs and new jobs that will enable these candidates to fulfill their potential within the company.

• *Evaluate executive candidates as they rise within the organization, promoting the top candidate to CEO when needed.* The company should also reassess high-potential candidates after each developmental milestone and rank them. As the number of potential upward opportunities narrow, candidates lower on the list should consider finding new career opportunities outside the company and the highest potential candidates should continue to receive greater career challenges.

Lee Scott's ascent to CEO of Wal-Mart exemplifies the use of job rotation to test and develop team leaders. According to *Fortune,* Scott's rise to the top accelerated in 1996 as Wal-Mart tried to recover from a rocky diversification effort that led to the departure of Bill Fields, who had run Wal-Mart's stores division. Rather than replace him, Wal-Mart decided to challenge the two who reported to Fields to fix the stores. Specifically, Wal-Mart asked Lee Scott, who ran merchandising (buying and promoting goods), to work with Tom Coughlin, who ran the stores as head of operations.[5]

Because he previously ran trucking and logistics at Wal-Mart, Scott's move into merchandising came as a shock. He learned of the merchandising post in October 1995. At the time he had been scouting logistics opportunities for Wal-Mart in Europe and was asked to call in to a board meeting. Standing at a pay phone in Paris, Scott listened in on a conference call in which former CEO David Glass; board member Rob Walton; William Fields, the former head of Wal-Mart's stores divisions; and Don Soderquist, Wal-Mart's senior vice chairman, asked Scott to take the merchandising role the following Monday. Although Glass believed that Scott could become an effective CEO right away, he knew that to be truly top-notch, Scott would have to gain cross-functional experience, both for the added insights it would provide him and for the increased acceptance it would earn him from his colleagues.

Wal-Mart was able to overcome the traditional retailing conflict between operations and merchandising. In fact, Scott and Coughlin worked together to solve problems they had identified. The two made the most progress by using Wal-Mart's technology to reduce inventory of items that sold poorly and meeting the demand for more popular items. Scott and Coughlin pressured their divisions to use existing technology so that stores could track inventory accurately and let buyers purchase the right quantity. Coughlin pushed store managers to eliminate unsold inventory. Scott made buyers account for all their purchases and the reasons behind them. The result: between 1996 and 1999, sales rose by 78 percent, and inventory climbed only 24 percent.[6]

Job rotation also helped Scott develop a new skill that sustained Wal-Mart's market leadership. According to *WWD* (formerly *Women's Wear Daily*), Scott demonstrated a surprisingly strong ability to collaborate with Wal-Mart's key suppliers. Immediately prior to Scott's appointment as CEO, he was vice chairman and chief operating officer, and before that he'd served as president and CEO of the core Wal-Mart discount division. While in charge of merchandising, Scott was known for helping general merchandising managers (GMMs) do their jobs. Rather than trying to be an expert, Scott built a team and removed barriers inhibiting the GMMs' performance. He empowered merchandisers and let them take some risks. As we noted earlier, Scott replaced the traditional competition between stores with merchandising teamwork and camaraderie.[7]

Scott also encouraged teamwork between Wal-Mart and its suppliers by creating supplier councils. Suppliers believe that these councils are mutually beneficial. Jay Diamond is president and CEO of the Halmode division of Kellwood, which owns the master license for the Kathy Lee apparel collection, a $200 million business sold exclusively at Wal-Mart. Diamond believes that Wal-Mart became far more fashionable between 1995 and 2000, improving the pricing and value of its apparel. Halmode provided brand manager teams to help Wal-Mart in its fashion presentation. Halmode worked with Wal-Mart buyers, and merchandise managers traveled overseas with Wal-Mart and helped them with colors and styles. Diamond believed that Wal-Mart's goal was to partner with suppliers.[8]

Other suppliers also recognized Lee Scott as an excellent leader of multifunctional teams. Gil Harrison, chairman of Financo, believed that Scott understood the customer and could work with all members of the Wal-Mart team. Harrison saw Scott as a leader, a strategic thinker, and a profit-oriented executive who understood all the pieces of the Wal-Mart organization. Finally, Harrison perceived Scott as more accessible than Glass, making him a better leader.[9]

Wal-Mart's approach to developing leaders has proven effective. Scott rose from his initial job in trucking because he demonstrated a willingness to listen to colleagues and partners and to build teams. Companies that rotate jobs develop and promote executives who demonstrate the ability to place the interests of the company above the interests of the specific department in which they operate. By rotating potential leaders through different operating units, such companies develop their own executive talent and communicate the importance of teamwork throughout the organization.

By contrast, other companies tend to encourage greater functional specialization, which makes it more difficult to develop executive talent internally. Because these companies' functional executives tend to rise by optimizing the resources in their specific departments, they fail to develop a corporate perspective. As a result, these companies tend to earn lower profits and to seek an executive from outside the company to rescue it if times get tough.

Wal-Mart's peer, J. C. Penney, sought the assistance of retailing guru Allen Questrom when its business began to hit the skids. According to TheStreet.com, hiring Questrom, who turned around bankrupt Federated Department Stores in the 1990s, did not deliver J. C. Penney from all its problems. For example, in January 2002 anonymous hedge funds issued rumors of billing irregularities at Penney's Eckard drugstore unit. In July 2001 Eckard entered a plea deal with the Department of Justice and agreed to pay $1.7 million for overcharging on Medicaid prescriptions. The government also filed a related civil case in 1998, which was pending in 2002.

J. C. Penney has been trying to turn itself around since 2000, when it hired Allen Questrom. A large part of Questrom's plan for reviving J. C. Penney was the potential of Eckerd, which J. C. Penney bought in 1996, and believed it had managed poorly. The Eckerd division, which operated twenty-six hundred stores, lost $600,000 in 2001 on revenue of $13 billion. At a Lehman Brothers institutional client conference, Questrom bragged that Eckerd could be worth between $9 billion and $11 billion by 2004, almost twice J. C. Penney's July 2002 market capitalization of $5 billion.[10]

J. C. Penney's decision to hire an outsider such as Questrom springs from its inability to develop a strong CEO internally. According to *Business History Review,* J. C. Penney was founded and operated by men from small-town America. The company grew rapidly and by 1929 its sales had reached $210 million. In a move that would come to haunt it in later years, J. C. Penney shunned potential employees with ambition and ability. Its personnel director, who had worked as a salesman in small-town stores for eleven years before becoming an assistant store manager, suggested that Penney's was built with average men, and it did not look for exceptional men or need geniuses.[11]

The rapid growth of cities populated with ethnically diverse veterans and their growing families presented J. C. Penney with a challenge that its homogeneous, small-town, mediocre minds could not solve. Unlike Wal-Mart, Penney was unable to produce the kind of team leader needed to compete in such a different marketplace. Whether outsider Questrom can do so in the twenty-first century remains to be seen.

Job rotation practices sharply differentiate the Value Leaders from their peers. The CEOs of all eight Value Leaders are either founders or were developed internally in cultures that encouraged job rotation:

- Goldman Sachs: Hank Paulson, internally developed
- J. M. Smucker: Tim Smucker, internally developed
- Johnson & Johnson (J&J): William Weldon, internally developed
- MBNA: Chuck Cawley, cofounder
- Microsoft: Steve Ballmer, internally developed
- Southwest Airlines: James Parker, internally developed
- Synopsys: Aart de Geus, cofounder
- Wal-Mart: Lee Scott, internally developed

By contrast, half of the eight peer companies paired with the Value Leaders are led by a CEO brought in from outside:

- Goldman Sachs peer Merrill Lynch: David Komansky, internally developed
- J. M. Smucker peer Hansen Natural: Rodney Sacks, came from outside
- J&J peer Merck: Ray Gilmartin, recruited from outside
- MBNA peer Capital One: Richard Fairbank, internally developed
- Microsoft peer Computer Associates: Sanjay Kumar, internally developed

- Southwest peer American Airlines: Donald Carty, internally developed
- Synopsys peer Cadence: Ray Bingham, recruited from outside
- Wal-Mart peer J. C. Penney: Allen Questrom, recruited from outside

The examples explored here reveal general principles about rotating jobs. First, an effective program of job rotation depends on a corporate culture that values teamwork. Companies in which functional fiefdoms prevail will view job rotation as a waste of time. For companies that do value teamwork, job rotation is the best way to give high-potential employees a chance to truly understand the work of different functions. This understanding helps these employees to appreciate the trade-offs among different functions that need to be made to optimize the company's overall performance.

Second, effective job rotation depends on a CEO who puts the company's interests ahead of his or her own. If a CEO views the job as a lifetime sinecure, the CEO will develop the next generation of management only as a way to silence directors who ask about succession planning. When it comes time to actually promote the next generation to a senior executive position, the CEO will find reasons that the candidate is not good enough. By contrast, a CEO who puts the interest of the company first will recognize that the ultimate judge of his or her success is the strength of the CEO's successor and the depth of management left to work with that successor.

Third, effective job rotation depends on a carefully planned and executed strategy for developing the next generation of managers. An important contributor to a company's long-term survival is its ability to develop executives who will be able to lead it effectively into the future. Therefore, an incumbent CEO must devote significant time to designing and implementing the development of the next generation. Incumbent CEOs must monitor closely the careers of high-potential executives, participate in decisions about who is prepared for additional responsibility, and balance the needs of the company against the developmental requirements of the candidate to determine what the new responsibilities should be. CEOs must also scrutinize the effectiveness of the job rotation process, analyzing whether it produces the best candidates and modifying the process accordingly.

Make Team Decisions

Team decisions contribute to superior performance. When each functional representative on a team cares deeply about an external outcome, such as customer satisfaction, the team operates more effectively. Ineffective "teams" are really a collection of functional representatives defending their turf against the other team members. The functional representatives in effective teams care more about how the team's work affects an external outcome than they do about how that work affects their department's interests. Although the difference may be subtle, it is crucially important to the external outcome. Ineffective teams waste time deflecting blame onto other team members, making customers suffer. Effective teams find creative solutions to problems, subsuming their departmental interests to those of the customer. Effective teams strive to resolve their disputes internally rather than escalating them to upper management.

Executives who want to improve their approach to making team decisions may use the following tactics:

• *Agree on important team performance outcomes.* Teams should agree with their managers on how the teams will be measured. Agreeing on team goals is far more effective than measuring the role of individual department representatives of the team.

• *Develop objective ways to measure these outcomes.* If performance measurement is subject to interpretation, then the team will take the objectives less seriously and will not be able to focus as clearly on ways to improve the process to achieve better performance.

• *Make teams, rather than individual team members, accountable for achieving these outcomes.* If teams are responsible for achieving objectives, the team members will have a greater incentive to solve their own problems and overcome team impediments. By contrast, if individual team members have different goals, they will tend to blame other team members for problems rather than solving them.

• *Encourage teams to learn from problems; discourage affixing blame.* Consistent with the goal of creating a work environment that encourages mutual respect, companies should look at problems as learning opportunities that can lead to better ways of working. If companies encourage the affixing of blame, they seriously diminish the chances of achieving ever higher levels of performance.

Southwest Airlines makes team decisions. By assigning account-ability for results to teams rather than to functions and by emphasiz-ing learning instead of measurement, Southwest achieves far faster gate turnaround than American Airlines. Most airlines hold delay meetings in which airline employees assess the cause of delays in order to minimize future ones. According to the *California Management Review,* in the early 1990s Southwest instituted the concept of "team delays," which allowed less precise reporting of the cause of flight delays. Before the change, determining the cause of flight delays led to conflict as different groups of employees, such as flight atten-dants and gate agents, tried to shift responsibility to other functions rather than to solve problems. A chief Southwest pilot pointed out that the team delay concept identified problems between two or three dif-ferent employee groups in working together. By placing responsibil-ity on a team, different functions felt compelled to solve the team's problem rather than to blame each other.[12]

At Southwest supervisors coach employees rather than issue orders. In fact, its supervisors strive to help the people who report to them do their jobs better. Because one supervisor found disciplining an employee somewhat inconsistent with Southwest's family atmosphere, he tried to provide that discipline respectfully. Moreover, Southwest supervisors believe that their primary role is to create an environment that makes it easier for line employees to function, arguing that at Southwest peer pressure generally solves discipline problems such as that of the worker who takes a three-hour lunch. Supervisors at the airline encourage employees to identify the causes of delay and develop ways to do their jobs better the next time. If a flight is delayed ten minutes due to excess freight, a Southwest supervisor encourages employees to develop a solution—for example by rerouting the freight—rather than screaming at other employees.

Southwest also acknowledges that conflict is inevitable and there-fore should be explicitly managed. Its line employees know how activ-ities, such as turning a plane around at the gate, should proceed. If things do not go as they should, Southwest encourages the line employees to solve the problems themselves, even if the people involved work in different cities. When employees escalate conflicts to higher levels, Southwest managers encourage employees to act as a team to solve problems rather than getting the managers to resolve the problem. According to Southwest President Colleen Barrett, South-west is delighted when employees suddenly recognize the perspective of the other person with whom they had been arguing.[13]

By contrast, peer companies encourage conflict between functions, rewarding functions that do the most effective job of deflecting responsibility for problems onto other departments. According to *FW*, American Airlines' long-time CEO, Robert Crandall, was driven by "competitive anger."[14] According to *California Management Review*, American's employees are naturally competitive and need to know where they stand. Because the airline's field managers scrutinize every delay, different functions make sure that they are not blamed for delays. Each time a delay occurs, managers figure out which function caused it. With each delay supervisors penalize employees immediately by forcing them to explain what happened in a very contentious meeting. If a delay occurs on a flight scheduled to make connections elsewhere, American's response is "management by intimidation." One field manager notes that in such situations, "Crandall wants to see the corpse."[15]

American's management style causes employees to look out for their own functions in order to avoid becoming a Crandall corpse. As a result, shared goals such as on-time performance, accurate baggage handling, and satisfied customers take a back seat. Furthermore, American spends so much time debating, reporting, and meeting about the cause of delays that passengers get short shrift. The airline also has a system of codes to explain the source of delays. Quite frequently, the source of delay is a communication breakdown—a contingency for which American does not have a code. Rather than creating a new code, the airline blames the delay on the last group off the plane. American's effort to minimize delays encourages employees to spend their time avoiding blame for delays rather than taking steps to minimize them.

The company's focus on measurement and accountability uses statistics as a substitute for delegation and organizational learning. For example, its field managers receive performance standards, called minimum acceptable performance standards (MAPS), for on-time performance, baggage handling, and customer complaints. American headquarters monitors MAPS each day and punishes field managers who miss them. The MAPS measurement routine makes field managers afraid to delegate. Yet American's field managers recognize that the only way to develop people is to let them make mistakes and learn from them. In essence the MAPS measurement routine inhibits delegation and organizational learning.

American's field managers also feel caught between their desire to develop their employees and the demands of a headquarters that cares only about numbers. Field managers advance by meeting quantitative targets from headquarters without regard to how they achieve the targets. American's culture of fear discourages discussion between the field and headquarters and inhibits learning. Somewhat ironically, American includes "supporting good working relationships" in field managers' job descriptions but allocates zero weight to this item in field managers' performance measurement system.[16]

The comparison of American and Southwest highlights general principles of making team decisions. First, making team decisions depends on understanding the distinction between effective and ineffective teams. Organizations need to hire people who specialize in specific functions. Team members consist of individuals from different functions. Effective teams work harder on achieving external outcomes than they do on defending the interests of their departments. Ineffective teams operate more as if the team members were protecting their departmental interests from the attacks of the other team members. The CEO creates the incentives that determine whether or not teams are effective.

Second, teams must make decisions with the right objectives in mind. In the Southwest Airlines example, it was clear that the teams were trying to minimize the amount of time it would take to turn an airplane around at the gate. The Southwest team members understood how critically important fast gate turnaround was for Southwest's profitability. By contrast, American Airlines, faced with the same desire for profitability, focused different departments on achieving objectives that had the unintended consequence of getting people to optimize the efficiency of their own departments at the expense of corporate performance.

Third, making team decisions depends heavily on how teams resolve problems. Every team can be judged on the basis of which problems they can solve quickly and routinely and which problems consume much more time to solve. If teams take a long time to solve commonly occurring problems, they will perform less effectively than teams that can solve common problems rapidly. The real test of an effective team, however, is how it approaches the solution of uncommon problems. An effective team will try to solve such problems within the team itself, only involving higher-level executives if the team cannot identify a solution. A less effective team will approach uncommon problems by seeking to deflect blame for the problem rather than trying to solve it.

Reward Team Behavior

Rewarding team behavior can "personality-proof" a company, whereas rewarding functional excellence creates a star system. In some ways companies that reward team behavior seem more consistent with Japanese values than American ones. Such companies seem to follow the Japanese proverb that the nail that sticks out gets hammered down. By contrast, companies that use the star system appear to follow the American saying that the squeaky wheel gets the grease.

Executives seeking to improve the way they reward team behavior should use the following tactics:

• *Monitor employee behavior closely to find the true team players.* Managers must be wary of team members who appear to be team players when the managers are present and resort to political behavior when managers are absent.

• *Give promotions and higher pay to team players.* Managers should create clear distinctions between team players and others so that the others will understand how they need to change if they want to advance within the organization.

• *Encourage team players to promote the role of the team rather than their individual contribution.* Managers should encourage people to discuss their accomplishments in the context of the others who contributed to the outcome rather than taking all the responsibility for success and assigning all the blame for failure on others.

Goldman Sachs created a culture that rewards teamwork in many ways. According to the *Plain Dealer,* Goldman rewards people who put the company's interests ahead of their individual ones. The search for such individuals begins with recruitment. According to former Goldman co-CEO Stephen Friedman, Goldman sometimes interviews classmates and professors of business-school prospects. If those interviewed do not view the prospects as team players, Goldman rejects even top candidates who might become stars elsewhere.

Goldman partners use compensation to reinforce the importance of teamwork. Instead of linking pay exclusively to profits, the company pays a bonus based on a worker's teamwork. Individuals who play politics, say, by working harder for some powerful partners than for others, get less of a bonus than they had anticipated.[17]

Achieving partnership at Goldman depends heavily on teamwork. According to the *Washington Post,* people who delivered "the numbers" but put individual interests ahead of the firm's were denied the ultimate sinecure—a Goldman partnership. For example, former co-CEO Friedman has told potential partners they did not make the cut, arguing that despite their basic abilities, intelligence, and energy, they were perceived as pursuing their own agendas rather than Goldman's broader interests. Unlike its peers that heap money and praise on star performers, Goldman pays senior traders as much as investment banking "rainmakers." An employee whose department generated large profits can earn a relatively small bonus if the rest of Goldman does not perform well. Because Goldman partners evaluate each other, colleagues' perception that a Goldman banker is "not a team player" can result in a far smaller bonus.[18]

Goldman partners must leave their equity in the firm until they retire. Even then they can't sell all at once. As a result, most partners' net worth rises and falls depending on the company's overall performance. As a result, Goldman partners are skilled and fearless in going after new business, attacking as teams.[19]

In its daily operations as well, Goldman uses specific procedures to measure and reward teamwork. According to the *Wall Street Journal,* Goldman's computers score the performance of the bankers who start up and maintain relationships with blue-chip clients. The computers monitor bankers' performance, tracking business won versus lost and clients visited or neglected. When Goldman finishes a deal, memos are sent around listing everyone involved. When Goldman goes after a new client, everyone working on the project, even first-year associates, meets with Goldman's management committee. In annual compensation reviews, departments get equal credit for every transaction in which they participated, regardless of the time they actually spent on it.[20]

Goldman is not the only company that pays for teamwork. Southwest and Smucker issue profit-sharing checks, and Wal-Mart pays stock to all its employees. These companies pay employees to work together in the corporation's best interests. Although they typically pay lower base salaries and encourage employees to keep expenses low, they use incentives to align workers' actions with the interests of customers and shareholders. By subsuming employees' individual interests to those of the firm, these companies reward such employees more highly than peers.

Merrill Lynch typifies the star system so common at peer companies. Whereas Goldman actively hammers down the nail that sticks out, often before that nail is hired, Merrill tends to give the most grease to the squeakiest wheels. Battles over pay and power, particularly in Merrill's investment banking operations, have led to significant turnover. According to *Investment Dealers' Digest,* in 1995 Deutsche Bank raided several of Merrill's top performing executives, exposing the flaws in Merrill's efforts to reward teamwork. That year, Herb Allison, the newly named head of Merrill's institutional division, was seeking to keep one of its star traders, Grant Kvalheim, cohead of debt capital markets, from bolting to Deutsche Bank.[21]

Allison was a cerebral and somewhat cool personality who had previously served as Merrill's chief administrative officer. He hoped that retaining Kvalheim would strengthen Merrill's perception of Allison's interpersonal skills and better his odds to win the company's presidency in 1997. On June 8, 1995, Allison expected Kvalheim, who had been offered a much broader role at Merrill and a higher salary, to show up for work, signifying that Allison had sealed the deal to keep this debt market star at Merrill.

Rather than show up for work that day, Kvalheim met with Edson Mitchell, Merrill's former head of debt capital markets, who had joined Deutsche Bank in April 1995. Mitchell had promptly jumped to Deutsche Bank in London. Deutsche Bank's Mitchell had flown to New York on a moment's notice to make a last pitch to Kvalheim, whom he had hired at Merrill nine years earlier and wanted to work with again. Mitchell's pitch to Kvalheim worked, revealing significant flaws in Merrill's efforts to reward team behavior. Kvalheim promptly jumped to Deutsche Bank in London. What swayed him to join Deutsche Bank was the opportunity to work with Mitchell, the chance to lead a debt market team that could work together to build a bigger business, and a compensation package reportedly in excess of $2 million a year for two and a half years.

Although Merrill prided itself on teamwork, striving to keep Merrill's salaries manageable, Allison's efforts to build teamwork backfired. Due to low compensation and limited advancement opportunities, many of Merrill's best people left in 1995. Fearing the threat of Mitchell at Deutsche Bank, Merrill responded by increasing the salaries of people it was afraid could be swayed to join Mitchell. Ultimately, some saw Allison's reputation as being cool and calculating as the biggest challenge to his efforts to keep his team together.[22] Although Allison did rise to the president's slot in 1997, he left in July 1999 after it became clear that he would not be taking over the CEO slot.

The comparison of Goldman Sachs and Merrill Lynch reveals general principles about rewarding team behavior. First, team-oriented compensation represents the natural outcome of a culture that fosters teamwork throughout an employee's career. Grafting team rewards onto a culture that reveres star performers is impossible. Companies that reward team behavior also infuse the concept of teamwork into the way they hire, train, develop, operate, and compensate employees.

Second, rewarding team behavior requires a process for monitoring employees closely. In order to avoid rewarding individuals who only appear to be team players, it is important to gather information on employee performance from many different sources. Other employees find it demoralizing if an employee can "game" the system. However, when employees believe that the company administers the reward system fairly, it frees employees from internal politicking and allows them to focus all their attention on doing the job. Although such close monitoring of employee behavior may appear oppressive to some, it is liberating for employees who prefer to work on solving customer problems.

Third, even in a team culture, not all team members perform equally well, nor are all team members equally rewarded. Thus, companies must find ways to promote and reward the best employees without discouraging the others. The best way to achieve this is to communicate persistently and clearly the criteria used to distribute rewards. If a disappointed employee understands why he or she did not receive the promotion, then that employee will have a clearer picture of how to modify behavior to improve the chance of getting the next promotion.

KAIZEN AT J&J

Although transforming a corporate culture is a significant challenge, such transformations have taken place, generating compelling results.

J&J's Critikon division achieved just that through the use of a Japanese process called Kaizen. Because Critikon tapped into the insights of employees from all its key functions, J&J's use of Kaizen offers an excellent example of the value of teamwork. According to *National Productivity Review,* in early 1991 J&J Medical's Critikon Vascular Access plant in Southington, Connecticut, was in trouble—with long lead times, flat productivity, and excess inventory. Competitors were meeting the demands of Critikon's customers with more innovative products. In June 1991 Critikon began turning the corner, generating half-a-million dollars in savings in just four-and-one-half days.[23]

These quick wins and subsequent increases in productivity resulted from Critikon's use of Kaizen: just-in-time continuous improvement. *Kaizen* is a Japanese word meaning gradual, orderly, and continuous improvement. The Kaizen business strategy involves everyone in an organization working together to make improvements without large capital investments.

In April 1991 Herb Brown joined the Southington facility as director of manufacturing. Brown met with his management team: three manufacturing business unit managers; the plant controller; and managers of engineering and technical services, quality assurance, and human resources. They discussed Critikon's business challenges and Brown's experiences with Kaizen. Brown discussed Critikon's need to cut costs, improve service, cut lead times, and increase flexibility.

In June 1991 the division launched a Kaizen strategy with a five-day "Kaizen breakthrough" workshop. This workshop involved Brown's management team, production associates, and headquarters personnel in four project teams that produced half-a-million dollars in savings in four-and-one-half days. The quick wins gave Kaizen tremendous momentum and helped Critikon cut operating costs.

Critikon's results were so remarkable that the Stonington, Connecticut, facility won a 1994 Shingo Prize for Excellence in Manufacturing. In recognizing Critikon, the Shingo Prize committee noted achievements in ten categories including quality (for example, 68 percent reductions in customer complaints), customer service (60 percent reduction in response time to process complaints), and productivity (50 percent increase in output per employee since 1990).

Critikon followed the four steps of the Kaizen process as follows:

• *Secure top management commitment and set ambitious goals.* Brown's previous success with Kaizen helped him gain top management support. He created teams from human resources, accounting, management information systems, planning, suppliers, headquarters, and J&J corporate offices. Each team had specific goals, such as 70 percent reduction in changeover time for machine X, 50 percent reduction in work in process at machine Y, or 25 percent reduction in staffing for work cell number four. The goals were jointly developed by the Kaizen team leader, the business unit manager, and the Critikon production system manager. People supported the goals because they were told at the beginning that no layoffs would result from Kaizen activities. If the process became so efficient as to eliminate a position, the employee "Kaizened" out was redeployed to a comparable open position.

• *Combine condensed learning with immediate application.* Between 1991 and 1994, units per employee increased 50 percent without a layoff. "Breakthrough" Kaizen events of two to three days were initially scheduled every four to six weeks. After several years these events occurred every two months. Teams learned key terms such as *waste* (excess inventories, walking, rework, unnecessary motion, inspection, and all other nonvalue-adding work). The teams also received tools to assess the speed of production against the demand for product, the analysis of the machine's and operator's work, and time- and motion-study observations.

• *Change the process.* Every day Kaizen team members visited the manufacturing floor with clipboards and stopwatches. Based on the data they thus collected, Critikon made decisions to reduce staffing, eliminate inventories, move equipment, reduce walk time, link machines, and modify tooling. Every two to three hours, the team reviewed progress and returned to the floor. Critikon conducted trial runs, collected quantitative results, and modified processes accordingly.

• *Present results and reward participants.* Finally, Critikon teams presented results and rewarded participants. Teams presented sketches of modified tooling, actual changeover carts, and before-and-after videos. Pride in accomplishment and mutual admiration among team members fostered good-natured boasting. After the last team presented results, management shared observations, expressed its pleasure with the results, and encouraged the teams to continue. Each team member received a certificate of graduation.

Critikon liked the results so much that J&J took steps to embed Kaizen into its culture. In January 1993 it converted all production associates to salaried employees and provided them with the same benefits as all other salaried employees. It eliminated across-the-board wage increases and implemented a performance evaluation and pay-for-performance system. This system encouraged departments to work together to enhance business unit performance. J&J's business unit organizational structure and the Kaizen process substantially reduced competition among departments.

At a more philosophical level, Kaizen helped J&J foster teamwork. Now, Critikon's employees have the power to take action, obtain resources, ask questions, and learn. Critikon's management trusts employees to analyze and change the way work gets done. Its workers function as industrial engineers in an environment of learning and improvement.

Critikon's biggest obstacle in its Kaizen process was fear of job loss. As noted earlier, Brown addressed this concern through his pledge that Kaizen would not result in layoffs. Although employees were naturally skeptical at first, Brown kept his word. And as workers saw that eliminating wasteful work actually improved the quality of people's jobs, their enthusiasm for Kaizen grew.[24]

MANAGEMENT LEVERS

J&J enjoyed significant benefits from fostering teamwork at Critikon. Companies seeking to transform themselves by fostering teamwork as J&J did must be prepared to change all elements of their organizational culture. Here are five management levers for fostering teamwork:

• *Build teamwork team.* As we noted in Chapter Two, changing a company's culture begins by forming a team of people that fairly represents its key stakeholders. Fostering teamwork will ultimately change the way all functions and business units interact with each other. To foster teamwork, management should assemble a broad group without making the team so large that it is unwieldy. Having selected the team members, executives should establish clear goals, including expected short-term wins, to build enthusiasm. The team should also study companies that do an effective job of fostering teamwork, with a particular focus on companies that have achieved a successful transformation from a star system to a teamwork culture.

• *Analyze the teamwork-values gap.* The team should then analyze its own values and the organizational processes that support them. Specifically, the team should analyze the characteristics of the most successful people in the company and those who advance the most rapidly. The team should also study the processes for selecting new employees, evaluating performance, choosing high-potential individuals, and providing pay and other incentives. Out of this analysis, the team should identify the gaps between the current values and teamwork values.

• *Close the teamwork-values gap.* To close this teamwork-values gap, the team should develop a vision for how the company can foster teamwork. This vision might include a new values statement; new hiring standards and processes; new training and job rotation process; and a new way of making group decisions, performing activities, evaluating performance, and providing compensation and other incentives.

• *Prototype the vision.* Rather than try to change the entire company at once, the team should prototype the vision within a department or division where it can expect relatively rapid results. Senior management must choose this prototyping site with care to maximize the chances of success.

• *Institute the vision.* Once the prototype has generated positive results, the team should spread the vision across the entire company. Although setbacks are expected, the team should be willing to learn from these setbacks rather than use them as an opportunity to shut down the change process.

VALUE QUOTIENT

Tactical-level analysis can help executives pinpoint opportunities for improvement. If you perceive that your organization can improve in the way it applies the principle "Foster teamwork," such analysis can help identify how best to improve the way your organization performs targeted activities.

Exhibit 3.1 can help you calculate your company's VQ through two levels of analysis. The first level of analysis is binary, meaning that you can use the worksheet as a checklist to determine whether or not your company performs the specific tactics on the list. If your company does not perform any of the tactics within a specific activity, then it should consider initiating such tactics. The second level of analysis is analog, meaning that the worksheet can help pinpoint opportunities to improve how well your company performs a specific tactic that it has already been performing. To raise your company's score on a particular tactic, you may wish to initiate an in-depth process to change the way your organization performs that tactic along the lines developed in Chapter Nine.

To conduct the binary and analog levels of analysis, your company should gather data through interviews with employees. Ideally, your company should use objective third parties to identify an appropriate sample of interviewees, develop interview guides, conduct the interviews,

Foster Teamwork: Activity and Tactics	Score

Train teams

☐ Hire a training director with experience developing and implementing team training. _____

☐ Interview culture carriers at different levels of the organization to identify the specific behaviors that generate the most effective teamwork. _____

☐ Develop fun, experiential training exercises to illustrate the effectiveness of these behaviors. _____

☐ Introduce these exercises to employees at the different levels of the organization. _____

☐ Assess and improve the effectiveness of the exercises. _____

Rotate jobs

☐ Analyze the characteristics of the most successful executives, both inside the company and at best-of-breed companies. _____

☐ Use these characteristics to select a set of high-potential managers and employees. _____

☐ Evaluate these executive candidates individually, identifying strengths and opportunities for development. _____

☐ Give the executive candidates job opportunities and training to bolster their skills for promotion. _____

☐ Evaluate executive candidates as they rise within the organization, promoting the top candidate to CEO when needed. _____

Make team decisions

☐ Agree on important team performance outcomes. _____

☐ Develop objective ways to measure these outcomes. _____

☐ Make teams, rather than individual team members, accountable for achieving these outcomes. _____

☐ Encourage teams to learn from problems and discourage affixing blame. _____

Reward team behavior

☐ Monitor employee behavior closely to find the true team players. _____

☐ Give promotions and higher pay to team players. _____

☐ Encourage team players to promote the role of the team, rather than their individual contribution. _____

☐ Distribute rewards fairly. _____

Total _____

Exhibit 3.1. Value Quotient Worksheet: Foster Teamwork.

Key: 5 = excellent; 4 = very good; 3 = good; 2 = fair; 1= poor; 0 = not applicable.

and analyze the results. The outcome of collecting and analyzing the data will be specific scores for each tactic. Although assigning these scores requires judgment, they should be calibrated by comparing the scores with the Value Leaders and other best-of-breed competitors.

Scores for each tactic range from excellent (five) to poor (one). If an organization does not perform the tactic at all, it receives a score of zero. To calculate the activity scores, the analyst can average the scores for the tactics supporting that activity and round the average to the nearest whole number. To illustrate how a score might be assigned for a specific tactic, consider the tactic "Develop fun, experiential training exercises to illustrate the effectiveness of these behaviors." If your company has not developed such exercises, it cannot apply them and therefore receives a score of zero. On the other hand, if your company has recently introduced a battery of such exercises based on studying best practices and detailed interviews of senior executives and key employees, it would receive a score of five.

CONCLUSION

Fostering teamwork offers companies enormous benefits. By hiring team players and reinforcing team values through a series of corporate processes, companies are more productive; their customers are more satisfied; and their cadre of executive talent is significantly wiser and more experienced. Other companies function less effectively because their people tend to compete individually and departmentally. These companies' inside game becomes so all-consuming that they have little energy left over for serving customers. And often the most talented individual performers rise as far as they can at peer companies only to jump ship to whichever company will give them the best deal. The competitive dynamics between teamwork and star-system companies let Value Leaders gain market share through many executive generations.

CHAPTER FOUR

Growth Matters
(Experiment Frugally)

F rugal experimentation is a management discipline that harnesses accidental discoveries to create value for customers and partners. By experimenting frugally, executives create a Darwinian process in which ideas live or die on the willingness of customers to pay for them. Frugal experimentation lets employees develop ideas for new products and better processes rather than backing only the ideas that spring from the CEO's forehead. Such experimentation bases growth on a company's strengths rather than on the latest business fad. It kills unworkable ideas before the company spends too much money rather than overfunding the ideas of powerful executives until the market rejects them. And frugal experimentation celebrates the success of those whose ideas win in the marketplace while avoiding the temptation to publicly humiliate the advocates of ideas that fail.

LINK WITH VALUE LEADERSHIP

Frugal experimentation is an integral component of Value Leadership. It benefits employees and partners by letting them create new products and services whose profit contributions benefit shareholders. Employees value frugal experimentation because it gives them a chance to contribute to the company in a way that they find meaningful. Partners value it because it lowers their costs, increases their revenues, or helps their business in other valuable ways. Through the value that frugal experimentation creates for employees and partners, shareowners benefit as well. Customers buy the new products that they had a hand in developing, contributing new profits to shareholders. Lower costs result from the operation of new processes that companies develop jointly with partners. Furthermore, because they are quick to shift resources from losing projects to winning ones, frugal experimenters lower the cost of failure that successful new products must bear. These lower costs also flow to the shareowners.

ECONOMIC BENEFITS

A comparison of eight Value Leaders with eight industry peers reveals that frugal experimentation pays off. Specifically, the Value Leaders grew 56 percent faster than their peers and enjoy significant net profit margins, while their peers lost money. The eight value leaders grew revenues 16.5 percent between 1997 and 2002, while their eight peers grew 10.6 percent. Furthermore, eight Value Leaders' 2002 net profit margins averaged 9.4 percent compared to -0.2 percent for the eight peers. Although frugal experimentation alone does not explain these differences, it is a contributing factor.

CASES

This chapter demonstrates how frugal experimentation works in practice. It shows how Wal-Mart built on its strengths to establish a $6 billion pharmacy retailing business through an initial failure that led to subsequent victory. It contrasts Wal-Mart's profitable diversification with J. C. Penney's (Penney's) $100 million loss doing the opposite in a failed home shopping venture. The chapter also examines how J. M. Smucker's Appleseed Project generated profitable new product ideas such as its Uncrustables crust-free peanut butter and jelly sandwiches by working closely with employees and customers. It contrasts Smucker's success with Capital One's top-down approach to innovation that resulted in $250 million worth of losses from a wireless reselling venture that was the brainchild of its CEO, Richard Fairbanks. It contrasts Microsoft's profitable fast-follower approach to managing development risk with the acquire-and-crush strategy of Computer Associates (CA), which locked CA into the moribund mainframe software market. And it shows how Merck-Medco partnered externally to cap the rate of drug price increases. The chapter concludes with the remarkable story of 3M, which emerged debt-free after its first fourteen years in business to profit from the happy accidents of its employees' technical prowess in solving its customers' business problems.

ACTIVITY ANALYSIS

To experiment frugally, executives must perform four activities:

- **Grow organically.** Frugal experimentation builds on a firm's strengths, identifying new products and better processes that extend naturally from what a firm does well.

- **Manage development risk.** Frugal experimentation demands executives who can try many possible avenues for growth without spending too much money on dead ends. To make this balance work, executives must identify the major risks that could keep them from turning the idea into profitable growth. Moreover, executives should monitor ongoing projects rigorously to ensure that they are still worthwhile. They then must terminate underperforming projects quickly rather than let them absorb any more funds than they already have.

- **Partner internally.** Companies can experiment frugally by encouraging different functions to work together. Sharing ideas across departments makes ideas more robust. Such cross-functional development also kills ideas that may seem great to one department, say, engineering, while looking infeasible to manufacturing. As a result, unworkable ideas get killed before the company spends too much money.

- **Partner externally.** All companies participate in value-creating networks. Frugal experimentation demands that new products and better processes help lower the costs or enhance the market position of a firm's partners. To achieve this goal, executives must work effectively with suppliers, customers, and other partners.

External partnering enables a firm to achieve bigger returns from new products and better processes because it creates a bigger pie for the entire value-creating network.

Grow Organically

Growing organically enables firms to experiment with new products and processes that emerge from strengths. By contrast, growth through acquisition creates the perception of rapid growth. Because acquired companies tend to be difficult to integrate, companies very rarely can grow profitably through a persistent strategy of acquisitions. Ultimately, the failure of one or more acquisitions can lead to costly write-offs and consume so much management time that the initial objective of the acquisition gets lost.

Growing organically is difficult to achieve. Executives who do it well usually have specific capabilities that the company can use to gain share in several different markets. These executives can look at their capabilities objectively. By contrast, many executives' judgment is clouded by their strong sense of their own self-worth or by their ambition to be perceived as participating in an exciting new business opportunity. Such clouded judgment can lead executives to invest heavily in new areas only to discover that the size of the market opportunity is not as significant as they had anticipated or that the firm can't compete as it had anticipated.

Moreover, discovering through analysis that an exciting growth opportunity is less profitable than anticipated is invariably cheaper than making that same discovery after investing tens of millions of dollars in a new facility. Furthermore, growing organically tends to give firms a deeper understanding of their true strengths and weaknesses, thus raising the chances for profitable new products or processes.

The benefits of growing organically do not preclude selective acquisitions. However, in order for these acquisitions to work, they must pass three difficult tests. First, the acquired company must offer access to a large and attractive market. Second, the acquirer must possess capabilities needed to compete in that market. Relying exclusively on the target company to provide all the necessary capabilities is dangerous because then the acquirer becomes too dependent on the target's executives. Third, the acquirer must pay a reasonable price for the acquired company; otherwise, the benefits of the acquisition will not flow to the acquired company's shareholders.

Executives seeking to grow organically may use the following tactics:

• *Identify rapidly growing markets that could benefit from the company's strengths.* Accomplishing this is challenging because executives must not only find fast growing markets, but they must quickly assess whether they have a reasonable chance of competing effectively in them.

• *Evaluate the size, growth rate, and profit potential of these markets.* Although in principle this kind of analysis is straightforward, in practice knowing whether growth forecasts are reliable is difficult. Thus, understanding the assumptions on which these forecasts are based and feeling confident of the factors driving market growth are particularly important.

• *Analyze the capabilities required to win market share in the most attractive markets.* Executives must talk to potential customers and evaluate the behavior of competitors to identify the specific capabilities needed to succeed in the markets.

• *Assess how well the company performs these capabilities relative to incumbents.* Executives must assess objectively how well their companies can perform these critical capabilities. If the company does not stack up well compared to competitors, there is a danger that the company will invest resources and fail to gain sufficient market share to offset the investment.

• *Invest in those markets where the company would enjoy a competitive advantage.* Executives must rank potential opportunity areas based on their profit potential and their company's likely competitive position in these markets. Executives should invest in the most attractive markets in which the company can expect to attain leadership.

A successful diversification into pharmacy retailing illustrates Wal-Mart's ability to grow organically. According to *Drug Store News*, Wal-Mart's twenty-five hundred stores with pharmacies generated $6 billion in prescription sales in 2000, making Wal-Mart the fifth-largest pharmacy business in the United States (after CVS, Walgreen, Eckerd, and Rite Aid). Former Wal-Mart CEO David Glass attributed its pharmacy retailing success to Wal-Mart's dedication to frugal experimentation. In a shareholder report, Glass noted that Wal-Mart has been able to locate a store or club next to the competition and beat the competitor every time. In Glass's view achieving this victory resulted from Wal-Mart's emphasis on growing organically with an eye toward continually improving its market position and operations.[1]

At the core of Wal-Mart's ability to gain share in new markets is the discipline it applies prior to committing resources. Wal-Mart enters markets where it knows it has the capabilities—such as purchasing in huge quantities, matching supply with demand for specific items in specific stores, and making a profit selling at lower prices—to offer customers a better deal than competitors. If Wal-Mart's capabilities compare favorably with those of incumbents, it attacks the market. If Wal-Mart lacks such competitive advantages, it avoids the market.

Wal-Mart's inherent strengths are the foundation of its success in the retail drug market—a hallmark of successful organic growth. These capabilities include marketing know-how, customer loyalty, operational ability, supply-chain expertise, and merchandising execution. Walgreen chairman and CEO L. Daniel Jorndt said that Walgreen perceives Wal-Mart to be the best retailer in America and that one of the five retailing keys to survival is having a strategy to deal with Wal-Mart. Vendor Dale Nepsa, vice president for Hyland's, a division of Standard Homeopathic, is impressed with Wal-Mart's drive to find and develop new products with sales potential. Nepsa called on Wal-Mart when Sam Walton had nineteen stores and still did the buying himself. Even after Walton delegated the buying function, he still attended trade shows to see what products were available. Then each purchasing executive in Wal-Mart would pick one item and try to make it the best item in the store that year. Nepsa praised Wal-Mart for its honesty, its ambition to be the best, its desire for the best price every day, and its timely payment of invoices. Wal-Mart partners with vendors representing 150 supplier companies to exploit local demand patterns, cut costs out of the supply chain, and maintain Wal-Mart's strategy of everyday low prices.[2]

Wal-Mart's first test of pharmacy retailing was a failure. According to *Mass Market Retailers,* in the early 1980s, Sam Walton was quoted as saying that deep discount drug store Phar-Mor was the only chain he feared. That reaction prompted Walton to start his own discount drug store. In 1983 Wal-Mart opened its first Dot Discount Drugs outlet in Des Moines, Iowa. Although it opened other units, by 1990 the experiment had ended.[3] According to *Drug Store News,* Wal-Mart sold Dot Discount Drugs to a group of local managers and investors in

Kansas City for a bit less than the amount it had invested in the stores. Wal-Mart had learned that a full-scale discount store with a pharmacy inside was a far more reliable producer than the deep discount drug store proved to be.[4]

Not only was Wal-Mart's initial experiment relatively inexpensive, but it also convinced Wal-Mart's executives that prescription departments served customers seeking convenience and value. As a result, pharmacies quickly became part of Wal-Mart's core discount stores.

Over the years Wal-Mart has invested in technology that pays for itself by cutting costs and enhancing sales in its pharmacy retailing operations. According to *Drug Store News,* Wal-Mart has upgraded pharmacy workstations and separate cash registers that enable customers to find what they need and pay for it more quickly. Furthermore, Wal-Mart has introduced automation depending on a store's volume of pharmacy sales. In low-volume pharmacies, Wal-Mart installed simpler computerized work modules; in high-volume locations it introduced conveyors and pill-counting and dispensing machines called Baker cells that can count six hundred tablets per minute. These investments also enable Wal-Mart to increase sales by cutting the time that customers spend getting in and out of the pharmacy department with their drugs. Wal-Mart is also testing robotic dispensing in some locations.[5]

Wal-Mart invests in technology that creates value for customers and pays for itself in lower costs or higher revenues. In this sense Wal-Mart's approach to technology epitomizes frugal experimentation. The technology does not cost Wal-Mart much over the long run because the improvements that the technology enables in its operations generate value that customers are willing to pay for or eliminate wasted operational steps, saving costs that the chain can invest in further improvements.

Wal-Mart's success in pharmacy retailing builds on its corporate strengths. According to Jim Martin, senior vice president of pharmacy, Wal-Mart applies the same customer service principles to its pharmacy departments as it does to the other parts of its business. This means direct contact between patients and pharmacists, efforts to monitor patients' drug therapy and outcomes, and in-store health screening services. Wal-Mart's screening service covers bone density, osteoporosis, cholesterol, and diabetes. According to Martin, Operation Detect Diabetes, offered in partnership with the American Diabetes Association, screened for diabetes in fifteen hundred Wal-Mart stores. The logic underlying the development of these new services—to use customers as a source of profitable innovation—exemplifies the power of frugal experimentation.

Wal-Mart is also negotiating tougher deals with third-party payers as it gains pharmacy market share. In 1999 it terminated its relationships with three major pharmacy benefit plans—Cigna Healthcare, Rx Price, and Health Source Rx—because they would not agree to Wal-Mart's tougher terms. At the same time, Wal-Mart is working with payers to cut the cost of prescription drugs through pharmacist interventions that help prevent incomplete orders, incorrect dosages and frequency, poor drug choices, and duplicate prescriptions. The company is also cutting drug costs through programs such as substituting less expensive generic drugs.[6]

Wal-Mart built its pharmacy retailing business from the inside. Its process illustrates several key principles. First, Wal-Mart has a clear understanding of its true strengths. Second, it recognized that pharmacy retailing was a big market that could add value to customers already visiting its stores and that it could bring in new customers who might buy other products. Third, Wal-Mart accurately assessed that it would be able to use its capabilities to compete effectively in the pharmacy retailing business. Fourth, its initial foray into the business was a small experiment from which Wal-Mart learned important lessons without losing too much money. Finally, Wal-Mart invested in its pharmacy retailing operations to cut costs and gain market share.

Peer companies often grow by investing in areas they don't understand. They are so frustrated with their core markets that they delude themselves into thinking that they will do better in a field that appears exciting even though they do not understand what is required to compete there. This mind-set can lead peer companies to spend significant resources attacking a new, exciting business opportunity whose magnitude is generally small now but is forecast to grow very rapidly. Because few significant competitors are in the market, management convinces itself that the company can win if it invests heavily up front. Ultimately, the market ends up being far smaller than anticipated; revenues are disappointing; and the company quietly closes down the venture.

Penney's failed Telaction experiment illustrates the dangers of investing significantly to enter a market in which a company is not equipped to compete. According to the *Chicago Sun-Times,* Penney's pulled the plug in April 1989 on Telaction, a twelve-month experiment in interactive home shopping that cost $106 million to develop and resulted in 164 lost jobs. Telaction featured products from Sears and Marshall Field's that were being test-marketed on cable TV systems in Illinois; however, both retailers ceased their participation in early 1989.[7]

Telaction, launched in February 1988, was intended to get consumers to buy clothing, housewares, and groceries by calling toll-free numbers after viewing the items on their TVs. The cable stations broadcast pictures of goods from various retailers on the screen, and the customer would use a push-button telephone to order the merchandise from Telaction. It quickly became clear that Telaction was a flop. In January 1989 Penney's hired investment bank Kidder, Peabody to find partners to finance Telaction, which never left the test phase. Robert B. Gill, Penney's vice chairman, acknowledged that partners were not willing to invest.

The venture was not a total failure; however, Penney's decided that it was not willing to incur its high up-front costs. In fact, Penney's claimed that 13 percent of the customers who watched Telaction ordered from it. Penney's failure with Telaction suggests that a company must specialize interactive home shopping along a few product lines and make it simple for viewers to use. For example, Home Shopping Network, which also depends on customers to place orders by telephone, has worked because it emphasizes value and selling action that makes people want to watch.[8]

Penney's experience with Telaction reveals a common set of behavioral symptoms associated with a "do the opposite" strategy. First, Penney's saw the success of Home Shopping Network as something that would be easy to replicate, so it slapped together a venture quickly. Second, Penney did not conduct an in-depth analysis of the capabilities needed to succeed at home shopping, and it did not determine whether it possessed these capabilities. Third, Penney invested over $100 million in Telaction, believing that its investment could preempt competition. Fourth, it was very quick to pull the plug when Telaction did not become profitable immediately, suggesting management's very limited commitment to Telaction.

The Wal-Mart and Penney cases reveal general principles about growing organically. First, for a company to grow organically, management must apply a disciplined process to screen out new markets that sound exciting but may not be profitable. Wal-Mart recognized that drug retailing tapped into many of its strengths, whereas Penney's judgment was tainted by the apparent excitement and novelty of interactive TV. Because Wal-Mart understood the magnitude of the drug retailing market and its potential sources of competitive advantage, it persisted with the development of the opportunity. By contrast, Penney lost interest in interactive TV after it lost money initially because it lacked an analytical foundation from which to justify continued investment.

Second, growing organically demands an unusual amount of objectivity about a company's true capabilities. Some executives find it challenging to dampen their natural optimism when evaluating the capabilities required to compete effectively in a new market. Such executives may find learning that their company lacks the capabilities needed to be successful in a potentially lucrative new market particularly difficult. In order to make an objective assessment, executives should gather data through an analysis of potential competitors' capabilities and customer needs.

Third, companies should approach organic growth in a sequence of experiments. They should be wary of investing heavily to build a huge presence quickly. Instead, executives should initially prototype their strategy in the new market to work out the kinks. Once the prototype is working well in one location, for example, the company should test how customers in a different location might receive it. As executives begin to appreciate how the new strategy can succeed nationwide, then the scale of the investments should grow—keeping consistent with the notion that investment should follow perceived demand.

Manage Development Risk

To manage development risk, executives must do three things. First, they must identify and thoughtfully assess potential risks. Second, they should monitor ongoing projects rigorously. Third, they should cut their losses as quickly as possible if a project becomes unattractive. Although this third prescription is often particularly difficult to follow, executives should follow it regardless of the magnitude of the sunk costs or the seniority of the project sponsor.

To manage development risk, executives must identify the major sources of risk in a development project. These include the risk that the market for the product is not big enough to offset the costs of bringing the product to market (market risk) or the risk that the product will not gain enough market share because it doesn't offer enough value relative to competitive alternatives (competitive risk). Executives should require development project leaders to analyze these risks and convince them they can be overcome. Executives should then decide which projects deserve more resources and which should be killed in order to free up resources for the more promising projects.

Managing development risk provides significant economic benefits. By funneling resources from failing projects to winning ones, companies can cut the cost of failure while shortening the time to bring a successful product to market. The biggest risk of pruning with rigor is that a company may cut a potentially promising project, thus eliminating a new product that could add to corporate revenues.

Executives seeking to manage development risk may consider the following tactics:

• *Form a cross-functional team to assess development risk.* Such a team might include participants from finance, marketing, sales, manufacturing, and R&D. The team would function most effectively if trained in techniques of development risk management.

• *Scrutinize development projects to pinpoint those with the greatest market and competitive risks.* The team would evaluate the specific assumptions underlying the forecasts of the market's size and profit potential as well as the analysis on which the assessment of the company's competitive position was based. The team would offer pessimistic and optimistic versions of these assumptions and calculate the possible upside and downside risks.

• *Identify potential initiatives to reduce these projects' risks.* Using the foregoing analysis, the team could develop possible techniques to limit the likelihood of these pessimistic scenarios and undertake the risk-reduction steps with the lowest cost and the highest chance of cutting project risk.

• *Cut projects whose risks the company cannot reduce cost-effectively and fund those that it can.* If these initiatives cannot sufficiently reduce risks in a specific project, the team should recommend it be canceled so that its resources could be shifted to projects with higher risk-adjusted returns.

• *Formalize the risk management process for future projects.* The team should formalize the process it uses to allocate resources to projects in order to apply it in the future.

Microsoft excels at managing development risk. It manages market risk by scanning the industry for successful new products that it currently does not sell. In this sense Microsoft outsources its innovation to other companies. According to the *Washington Post,* Microsoft did not invent the software industry, it copied it. Around 1980 an IBM engineer working to develop a personal computer (PC) published the specifications for its internal components, allowing other hardware makers to build compatible machines. This engineer's decision enabled the emergence of what came to be known as an IBM PC clone. Although IBM no longer makes PCs, companies from North America and Asia began creating PC components; clone makers assembled those components inside their own boxes, putting their names on the cases. A competitive marketplace emerged for components such as disk drives and power supplies. Machine prices dropped. Sales grew. The PC was everywhere.[9]

Microsoft was one of the companies that contracted to write an operating system for the IBM PC. Microsoft's operating system did not work very well. It spent $50,000 to license the software that became known as MS-DOS from another company, Seattle Computer Products, then reworked and patched it together. Microsoft's MS-DOS system sold along with the IBM-compatible PCs. Through bundling agreements with clone makers such as Compaq and Dell, Microsoft ensured that MS-DOS was installed on every machine that the manufacturer delivered.

Microsoft manages competitive risk by working closely with its customers to develop rapidly improving versions of an innovation that others originally developed. Microsoft's next PC operating system was Windows, whose graphical interface was copied from work at Xerox Palo Alto Research Center and later used by Apple. Windows, in its first two versions, also did not work well.[10] Its most recent version, Windows XP, is far more stable but still not perfect. Microsoft later developed software for word processing (Word), spreadsheets (Excel), and slide presentations (PowerPoint) based on innovations from WordPerfect, Lotus Development, and an acquired software company, respectively. Its Web browser software, Internet Explorer, was a reaction to Netscape's browser, and its Xbox gaming platform was a reaction to Nintendo's and Sony's.

Microsoft's financial results suggest that its approach to managing development risk works. In 2002, it was the world's largest software company, with $28 billion in sales, $8 billion in profit, and $39 billion in cash. Its chairman, Bill Gates, has been the world's wealthiest individual for over a decade.

The company's approach to managing development risk suggests several general principles. First, Microsoft usually reduces market risk before it makes a major commitment of resources. This means that it invests heavily when it perceives that another company in the industry is achieving significant growth as a result of a product that Microsoft does not currently sell. For Microsoft, a new competitor's revenue and stock price growth suggests that the market risk of attacking that competitor's market will be limited. By attacking markets that others have already pioneered, Microsoft reduces its development costs relative to competitors because it pours less money into failed initiatives, yielding a higher hit rate on those in which it does invest.

Second, Microsoft often invests over several years to develop improved versions of the targeted competitor's product. Its initial version is often not very competitive. However, Microsoft generally has greater financial resources and sharper programmers than its competitors. Thus, by working closely with customers, the company often finds a way to work out the bugs with its initial versions and ultimately develop a competitive product. Its approach to managing market and competitive risk enables it to achieve outstanding financial performance.

Peer companies manage development risks less effectively. They may invest too much money before ascertaining whether a market exists. Sometimes peer companies overestimate the competitiveness of the product under development, discovering only after spending significant resources that they can't recoup their investment. In some cases peer companies are slow to diversify away from a core market whose growth has slowed down. As a result, they find themselves unable to make a profitable entry into other more rapidly growing markets for which they lack the capabilities to mount an effective competitive assault.

Computer Associates (CA) failed to understand market risk in its core business and thus kept investing in it. According to *Computer Business Review*, CA's strategy of acquiring struggling mainframe software companies has led it into a strategic dead end. CA founder Charles Wang acquired more than seventy systems management, database, and applications software companies over his twenty-four-year tenure as CEO.[11]

CA's biggest weakness is that it generates most of its revenues from the upgrade and maintenance of mainframe products used for tasks such as sorting and backing up of data and the scheduling of batch jobs. Although the mainframe software market is large, it is growing at a relatively slow rate of 4 percent per year. This slow growth is not sufficient to justify lofty share price valuations. To accelerate CA's growth, Wang decided he wanted to get CA into the faster-growing computer services market. So in early 1998, his company bid

$9.8 billion in cash to acquire Computer Sciences Corporation (CSC), a leading provider of computer services.

Although CSC thwarted Wang's takeover attempt, Wang maintained his desire to diversify. In fact, Wang set a goal of generating $1 billion in services revenues by the close of its financial year in March 1999, hoping he could achieve the goal by acquiring several smaller computer services outfits. By 1998, after witnessing IBM's success with computer services and the slow growth of his core business, Wang had changed his mind about computer services.[12]

By August 2002 CA was still in a growth funk. Wang had replaced himself as CEO in August 2000 with a handpicked successor, Sanjay Kumar. Kumar had joined CA when it bought his company, UCCEL, in August 1987. According to Microsoft MoneyCentral, CA's revenues of $3 billion had actually shrunk at a 7 percent annual rate between 1997 and 2002. Furthermore, the company had a net loss of $825 million and its stock price had declined 75 percent in the previous twelve months to a nine-year low. CA's balance sheet presented a mixed picture: $1 billion in cash and equivalents but $3.3 billion in long-term debt. And Wang's goal of $1 billion in consulting revenue seemed far from CA's grasp when in the quarter ending June 30, 2002, CA's professional services revenue decreased 22 percent from $83 million in 2001 to $65 million.[13]

CA's inability to diversify out of its core market of mainframe software highlights some general principles of companies that fail to manage development risk. First, CA failed to manage market risk by delaying its decision to diversify away from the mainframe software market. CA's ability to survive in this moribund market reflected its strength at acquiring failing companies and cutting their costs. However, these companies became vulnerable to takeover partly because of mismanagement and partly because of the inherently limited profit potential of the market. In other words CA was slow to recognize that although it could grow in the short term by buying up losers, these acquisitions just made CA a big loser in the longer run. In fact, CA had transformed itself into the biggest player in an unattractive industry.

Second, once CA decided to diversify into computer services, it failed to manage competitive risk. The company was not aware that in order to be more attractive than competitive alternatives in the computer services industry, it would have to have top-notch consultants. CA did not realize that its strategy of reducing headcount during acquisitions would make retaining the best consultants very difficult, which gave CSC its competitive edge. Wang perceived that his strategy of acquiring and cutting, which had worked with mainframe software companies, would probably apply equally well to CSC's consultants. He did not recognize that such an attitude toward consultants would cause CSC's best assets to walk out the door as soon as they received their takeover cash. One reason CSC resisted CA's advances was that it perceived that acquisition by CA would weaken its competitive position. Wang, lacking a clear grasp of the requirements for competitive advantage in computer services, failed to manage the competitive risk of his push into that market.

Partner Internally

Partnering internally is hard to do and valuable to companies that can do it. It means encouraging different departments within a company to work together to develop a new product or a better process. Partnering internally is difficult to do well because it requires people to put significant energy into a process that has a chance of benefiting their company in the longer run more than it benefits their department in the short term. The process depends on fostering the values and incentives illustrated in Chapter Three.

Partnering internally taps into the creativity of people in different departments whose ideas could lead to new products and better processes. It can also reduce the cost of a failed idea. An idea that might seem great to an engineer might be so difficult to manufacture or distribute that it should be killed. Alternatively, manufacturing or logistics staffers might be able to suggest changes to the idea that could make it more profitable for the company. Partnering internally can increase the odds of a profitable new idea and can cut the costs of failed new product or new process ideas.

By contrast, firms that choose not to partner internally have a much more difficult time growing profitably. Such firms tend to promote ideas sponsored by the most powerful departments. Generally, such ideas are very expensive to implement or often fail to generate the revenues or profits needed to offset the investment in their development. In such cases problems with these ideas are identified only after the company has invested significant resources in their development. If a firm chooses to continue to pursue the new idea, the rework (or duplication of work) leads to costly delays that may further diminish the potential returns.

Executives seeking to reap the benefits of partnering internally may use the following tactics:

• *Identify key functions to participate in internal partnering for product and process innovation.* Innovation within a company typically crosses functional boundaries. Therefore, executives aspiring to achieve product and process innovations must be prepared to lead cross-functional teams that will identify opportunities for innovation and make the right opportunities a reality.

• *Develop a process that captures the input of these functions from brainstorming to implementation.* To capture the genius within the company, executives must design and manage a process that unlocks the creativity that can emerge from the interaction of the functions involved in the product or process innovation.

• *Communicate the purpose and responsibilities of the internal partnering process and implement it.* A key success factor for internal partnering is executives' willingness to commit the time needed to make innovation real. Given the skepticism that often accompanies efforts to encourage teams from different functions to cooperate, only executive commitment to the process can overcome the resistance needed to achieve tangible results.

• *Create financial and qualitative incentives for profitable product and process innovation and desirable teaming behavior.* In addition to executive commitment, executives should offer financial incentives—in the form of team bonuses—as well as peer reward ceremonies that enable employees to have the satisfaction of being publicly recognized by their peers for behavior that executives are seeking to encourage companywide.

Smucker's Appleseed Project illustrates the benefits of partnering internally. According to *Optimize,* the company is the market leader in the peanut butter and jelly categories since its 2001 purchase of Jif from Procter & Gamble. Through its Appleseed Project, Smucker is seeking new ideas by challenging cross-functional teams of employees to develop innovative ideas for products or improvements in corporate culture. These teams consisted of employees from all different levels of Smucker's organization, selected customers, and outside consultants. Teams met for nine months, after which the company presented the best ideas to internal venture capitalists for corporate funding.[14]

So far, at least one significant success has emerged from the Apple-seed Project. According to Richard Smucker, the company's president and co-CEO, Uncrustables, prepackaged peanut-butter-and-jelly sandwiches on crustless bread, have generated significant revenues (although the company will not disclose how significant). Even though Uncrustables cannibalized existing sales, the new product increased the company's overall profitability. After one team suggested such a product, Smucker acquired a small existing brand. Uncrustables emerged from Smucker's market research that suggested that the average family decides what to eat for dinner at 4 P.M. and that people like handheld products they can take in their car. Uncrustables addressed both these research insights: because the sandwiches were popular with children, they were a soft sell for parents trying to feed their children dinner; and because Uncrustables lacked crusts, they were less messy to eat in the car and required little additional effort for parents.[15]

The Appleseed Project has led to other new ideas. According to the *Plain Dealer,* in 1999 Smucker opened its first retail store on Strawberry Lane three miles south of its Orville, Ohio, headquarters. The 3,100-square-foot Simply Smucker's store offers 350 Smucker products and gifts from fruit salsa to strawberry banana preserves. The Appleseed Project also reinforced the notion that all manufacturers are fighting for supermarket shelf space and that therefore Smucker must market more directly to the consumer. In response Smucker launched an Internet site and a new catalog.

These ideas worked well because they took into account the specific requirements of the various functions needed to bring them from conception to the consumer. The successful introduction of, say, strawberry banana preserves resulted from teaming among Smucker's different functions. Consumers, whose opinions were tapped by marketing staff and consultants, identified the preserves as a desirable gift item. Smucker's fruit buyers and growers offered insights into the costs of making the product, while its retailing staff helped identify the best way to present and market the product in the store. Without the cooperation of these different functions, the product might not have been as effective.

Smucker's decision to focus its growth strategy on its employees and core products resulted from a failed experiment that cost the company $84 million. In 1994 Smucker bought frozen-pie maker Mrs. Smith's for $84 million from Kellogg. Smucker learned that the business was more seasonal than it had expected. Furthermore, Smucker failed in its efforts to market a new line of low-fat frozen pies that Mrs. Smith's had developed just before Kellogg sold it to Smucker. Smucker discontinued this line and struggled with the entire Mrs. Smith's division for two years before unloading it for $80 million.

The biggest lesson of the Mrs. Smith's experiment was that Smucker's growth would emerge from partnering internally. Now Smucker executives stick with their core products. They look to their employees and customers to identify growth opportunities such as providing the fruit base used in Dannon yogurt or the fruit filling in Kellogg's Pop-Tarts. According to Richard Smucker, consumers eat in new ways, and Smucker has an opportunity to provide them with fruit in new forms—whether in jams, juices, Pop-Tarts, or Dannon yogurt.[16]

Smucker's approach to internal partnering reveals some general lessons. First, internal partnering works best in a culture that values human relationships, between management and employees and between employees in different departments. Second, internal partnering yields the best results when an outside partner—the customer—contributes to the new ideas. Whether through market research, focus groups, or participation in brainstorming sessions to devise new products, bringing the customer into the loop, as Smucker did in developing Uncrustables, makes a big difference in the quality of the new products. The best new product ideas seem to come not from listening to customer complaints about existing products but from understanding the fundamental changes in customer's lives and envisioning new products that can help customers adapt to these changes. Third, internal partnering means that growing through acquisition will succeed only rarely because an acquired company must fit within the acquirer's culture and capabilities, a test that is extremely difficult to pass. Finally, although internal partnering yields the best results, it has flaws. For example, it can be slow, can disappoint those whose ideas do not receive funding, and still generates some failed experiments. Nevertheless, internal partnering is the most cost-effective approach to growth because it minimizes expensive false starts while maximizing the potential for successful new products and better processes.

Some peer companies pursue an approach in which the CEO comes up with a big thought and spends huge amounts of money on the idea. In most cases this approach results in an expensive failure that the company readily pretends did not happen. Admitting that the

CEO was responsible for wasting resources on a failed growth idea would mean acknowledging that the CEO was human and would be a career-limiting move for anyone seeking the CEO's favor. The weakness in the approach is that ideas are not sufficiently tested against the realities of the marketplace before they receive investment. As a result, the company may spend millions on the idea and only later discover that the market is too small; the product does not deliver enough value to gain market share; or the inherent profitability of the market is limited.

This syndrome seems to have infiltrated credit card issuer Capital One when it decided to enter the cell phone market. According to the *Richmond Times-Dispatch,* Capital One's wireless telecommunications venture, America One, lost $57 million in the second quarter of 1999 on gross revenue of $67 million. Richard Fairbank, Capital One's CEO, decided to enter the cell phone business after making what he thought was a brilliant proclamation: "A cellular phone is just a credit card with an antenna!"[17] Fairbank saw wireless as a service that people buy and then pay a monthly bill. In his view the capabilities that enabled Capital One to excel in the credit card business could yield big market share gains in wireless as well.

Fairbank started America One by reselling Sprint PCS's air time and using direct marketing to sell phones. He admits that Capital One made mistakes. For example, the cell phone market proved to be much more competitive than Capital One had anticipated. Fairbank found that some competitors actually pay potential customers to take their cell phones. Capital One responded by cutting advertising with the expectation that it would be ready to jump back in when the wireless market recovered.[18] Within a year, Fairbank's boast turned into a quiet whimper as Capital One closed down America One. According to *CardFAX,* a Capital One spokesperson (not Fairbank) noted that the rates of return on the America One venture were lower than other Capital One investments. America One discontinued operations as a wireless reseller in October 2000, when it sold seventy-two thousand customer accounts to Sprint and sought buyers for other accounts.[19] In total Capital One lost an estimated $250 million on Fairbank's America One brainchild.

Capital One's experience reveals some general principles of a top-down approach to growth initiatives. First, the top-down approach depends on an organization with a CEO cult in which employees succeed on the basis of their degree of obeisance to the CEO. Second, the top-down approach thrives in an environment that neither encourages nor rewards thoughtful analysis of a new idea from employees and customers. Third, the top-down approach thrives when the board tends not to challenge the CEO's requests for capital. Finally, the top-down approach tends to affix blame for an expensive failure somewhere besides its true source—the CEO.

Partner Externally

Although the skills needed to succeed are similar, the economic benefits of partnering externally may exceed those of partnering internally. Partnering externally creates new business opportunities by working with organizations outside the firm such as suppliers, competitors, and customers. Because partnering externally can create new markets or expand existing ones, it has the potential to generate new profits for the firm that can exceed those emerging from a new product or better process. In order to achieve these benefits, executives must have the vision to conceive of new ways of working with outside organizations. In order to make such visions real, executives must persuade partners that adopting the visions will give them higher revenues, lower costs, or both.

Partnering externally, if done well, can generate economic benefits for the initiating firm and other participants. Frequently, information technology can enable suppliers, competitors, and customers to lower their joint costs. Specifically, technology-enabled initiatives can lower administrative costs such as placing orders, sending invoices, or issuing payments. Such initiatives can also lower business risks such as producing inventory in amounts that exceed demand or developing new products that customers don't want to buy. Other systemwide initiatives can increase revenues by introducing new products that are less costly to make and distribute and that many customers are willing to buy.

Nevertheless, executives should not underestimate the commitment of resources required to make external partnership succeed. During the late 1990s, it was popular to issue press releases touting partnerships among high-tech companies. Often the companies involved did not follow up such press releases with sufficient organizational commitment to generate meaningful results. In general, partnerships succeed when they satisfy mutual needs. Should such partnership opportunities emerge, executives may seek to assign a person or even a department to ensure that these opportunities pay off.

Executives seeking to reap the rewards of partnering externally make use the following tactics:

• *Participate in industry consortia for their own industry as well as those of suppliers and customers.* Particularly in technology-intensive industries, companies can achieve significant benefits by setting and gaining industrywide agreement on specific standards for communicating with suppliers and customers. These standards can help the initiator to build a strong market position.

• *Lead systemwide strategy initiatives that conceive and analyze ways to create profit growth for all participants.* Once such initiatives become apparent, their management can be quite challenging because partners might feel concerned that they are ceding competitive advantages in the process. Therefore, it is essential to identify initiatives that will create a "bigger pie" for all participants. To make such initiatives effective, executives must assign individuals who are exceptionally good at managing complex political situations.

• *Invest time and capital to implement these initiatives so that they deliver the promised benefits for their partners and their firms.* The key requirement for achieving meaningful results is to devote the people and the financial resources needed to carry the idea from conception to implementation.

Merck-Medco, the managed care subsidiary of pharmaceuticals company Merck, partnered externally to cut the cost of prescription drugs. Rob Epstein, Merck-Medco's chief medical officer, noted that the company partners with physicians, pharmacists, payers, and patients. According to *Chain Drug Review,* Merck-Medco's innovations reduced the rate of increase in drug spending per member from 16.4 percent in 1999 to 14 percent in 2000. It achieved this improvement by implementing clinical programs and technologies to cut prescription costs while enhancing patient care.[20]

Epstein acknowledged that new medicines and an aging population will inevitably drive up drug spending. However, he believes that Merck-Medco clients have capped these increases without sacrificing quality of care. For example, the company holds down costs by filling members' prescriptions for brand-name drugs with generic drugs. In one case, within one month of introducing a generic alternative, Merck-Medco replaced 90 percent of the patented subscriptions with generics. This saved plan sponsors and members $2 million per month.[21]

The Merck-Medco case suggests some general principles for partnering externally. First, partnering externally works effectively if it creates a bigger opportunity for all participants. Until it becomes clear that all parties are likely to be better off, participants may be somewhat guarded about revealing too much about their capabilities. Second, partnering externally is a distinct skill that executives must learn and practice. Executives would be better off taking a targeted executive education program on partnering, or spending several years earlier in their career trying to find and manage smaller partnerships, rather than learning how to manage significant corporate partnerships for the first time through on-the-job training, when significant revenues may be at stake. Third, successful partnerships begin with the press release, but their true measure is the tangible results they generate. During periods of economic expansion, too many external partnerships end with the press release. Finally, external partnerships represent a significant management challenge. In order for such partnerships to continue to deliver results, all participants must articulate their expectations clearly. Furthermore, companies must follow processes to monitor participants' achievement of these expectations and to take corrective action promptly if performance slips.

3M

Diversified manufacturer 3M taught itself how to experiment frugally during its earliest years. Despite its success, it became somewhat moribund in the late 1990s and decided to bring in an executive who had lost out in a struggle for the CEO slot at General Electric. 3M's survival for more than one hundred years flows from its ability to experiment frugally.

3M as a Living Company—Secret of Longevity

3M started out in 1902 making sandpaper. Today it makes fifty thousand products including Scotch tape, Post-it Notes, Scotchgard fabric protectors, respirators, optical films, insulation, drugs, and fuel cells. Its 2001 revenues totaled $16 billion.[22]

Much of 3M's culture comes from its former president and chairman of the board, William L. McKnight. McKnight believed that as 3M grew, delegating responsibility and encouraging men and women to exercise initiative became increasingly necessary. He acknowledged that achieving this would require considerable tolerance because the people to whom 3M delegated authority and responsibility would want to do their jobs in their own way. McKnight anticipated that these people would make mistakes.

However, he thought that if a person was essentially right, the mistakes he or she made would not be as serious in the long run as the mistakes management would make if it tried to tell 3M people exactly how to do their jobs. In McKnight's view management that is destructively critical when employees make mistakes kills initiative. He saw that having many people with initiative was essential if 3M was to continue to grow.

3M's survival is largely a result of its ability to retain this spirit of innovation despite its size and history. A story from 1916 helps illustrate the value that 3M places on disciplined financial management, listening to customers, and developing solutions to their problems.

At 10 A.M. on August 11, 1916, 3M executives were gathered to hear 3M's president, Edgar B. Ober. Ober announced that 3M had achieved a goal that its managers had been waiting for (and doubting they would ever achieve). He proclaimed that 3M was out of debt and its future looked bright. Not only had 3M's business more than doubled since 1914, but for the first time in its history, it had enough left after expenses to pay a dividend.

The credit for this turnaround, a struggle since the company's founding in 1902, was due in large part to a product that was an extension of 3M's original interests in abrasives. In 1914 the company launched a new abrasive cloth made with aluminum oxide, which it branded Three-M-ite. Three-M-ite did a better job of cutting metal than did natural mineral. The automotive and machine tool industries were Three-M-ite's biggest buyers until America's entry into World War I, when large quantities of sandpaper were needed to build automobiles and other vehicles used in the war effort.

The 3M product would be even more successful when, quite by accident, plant superintendent Orson Hull drew the sheet of abrasive cloth over the sharp corner of an iron bar and broke down the adhesive backing in a way that made the sheet more flexible. Now production workers could get at otherwise inaccessible places on car parts they were sanding, abrading curved metal surfaces with greater efficiency.

The key to 3M's longevity has been its ability to repeat this pattern of frugal experimentation to solve customer problems that represent significant market opportunities. Three-M-ite's repurposing is a small example of a broadly repeated pattern at 3M: engineers work with customers seeking solutions to their problems by applying 3M technology. Without spending too much money, 3M engineers find a promising lead through trial and error and refine the lead until it works effectively for the customer. Once the initial customer's problem is solved, 3M finds many other customers willing to pay for the newly discovered solution to a common problem.

3M's Rule of 15 Percent for Personal Research

A belief in encouraging experimentation and discovery has fostered the innovative products and technologies for which 3M is known. The company has many programs that encourage employees, including the 15 percent rule, which allows them to spend part of their work time exploring experiments.

In addition, technical employees can apply for 3M Genesis Grants, which provide corporate money for innovative projects that are not funded through standard channels.

Shigeyoshi Ishii's new adhesive is one of many examples of products that emerge from 3M's culture of innovation. Ishii is a senior chemist in the electronic and electronic handling and production products division of Sumitomo 3M. Ishii's one dream when he joined the company in 1987 was to develop a new product that would have a major sales impact. That desire has always guided his work.

Six years later, his opportunity arose. Semiconductor-package manufacturers told Ishii that they were searching for a low-cost adhesive that could reliably bond organic substrates to inorganic materials such as metal and silicon. Using the 15 percent of work time that 3M allots for self-directed projects, Ishii began developing an adhesive with superior flexibility, heat resistance, and out-gassing characteristics along with high-performance bonding. He overcame many challenges including the need for specialized laboratory facilities. He had to coordinate his research needs with the equipment availability at a vendor and a public technology center. It was difficult for him, but he got the work done.

Ishii also credited the support of his 3M colleagues throughout the years of research. He drew on the advice and assistance of a number of 3M specialists. No one turned him down; they all made time for his project. He had all the encouragement he needed to pursue his innovation. His unique semiconductor package adhesives, which manufacturers use to bond carbon-based substrates such as light-emitting diodes with inorganic materials such as silicon and metal, have had the market impact he dreamed of when he joined 3M. They also helped Ishii receive the 2000 3M Innovator Award.

According to Ishii, innovators need to take a hands-on approach to research. He allowed that past experiments offer important information. However, he does not believe that a researcher should rely on other people's data when that data is critical to determining the validity of the researcher's new idea. He believes that the first step in true innovation is to plan the researcher's experiments and confirm the researcher's outlook. Following this, Ishii believes, the researcher is in the strongest position to convince colleagues to support his or her work.

At the core of 3M's 15 percent rule is an important insight into creative people: they thrive on a blend of time spent musing on a problem by themselves along with the need for help and recognition from colleagues whom they respect. 3M's ability to drive innovation over one hundred years reflects its ability to attract such people and create an environment in which they can thrive.

3M Conglomerate of Competences

Over its history 3M's ability to profit from happy accidents has led it into a broad range of industries. As a result, 3M enjoys market leadership in many of the segments in which it competes. Its current organization structure enables 3M to focus its new product development for specific markets while sharing corporate resources in a fashion that enhances the company's efficiency without sacrificing the delivery of services to the operating units. 3M applies these capabilities to markets in sixty countries, and it earns half its revenues outside the United States.

3M Invited an Outsider to Be CEO

The arrival of 3M's current CEO, Jim McNerney, from General Electric must have come as quite a shock to 3M employees. As McNerney often repeats, there is only one of him and seventy-five thousand 3M employees, so he must tread carefully in his efforts to change the culture. Undoubtedly, McNerney was brought in to improve 3M's performance when it was clear that 3M had not developed internally a leader who would be capable of delivering the results that its

shareholders expected. For example, for the five years preceding Mc-
Nerney's tenure, 3M's stock price had risen 35 percent, while the Standard & Poor 500 had increased 60 percent.

From General Electric, McNerney has brought the ability to manage corporatewide initiatives that help invigorate employees and
improve corporate performance. Under McNerney's direction 3M
launched five initiatives in 2001 that contributed to 3M's bottom line:

- 3M's indirect-cost control initiative, which saved over $500 mil-
  lion compared with 2000 (3M expected another $150 million of
  savings from this initiative in 2002.)

- 3M's sourcing initiative, which saved over $100 million in 2001,
  with another $150 million expected in 2002

- eProductivity, with which 3M believed it could generate $50 mil-
  lion of benefits in 2002

- 3M acceleration, which reallocated R&D resources to larger,
  more global projects

- Six Sigma, which focuses on higher growth, lower costs, and
  greater cash flow and from which 3M expected over $200 mil-
  lion of operating income benefits in 2002[23]

3M's Lessons on Frugal Experimentation

3M spent much of its first fourteen years struggling for survival. However, frugal experimentation spurred the profitable growth that
enabled the company to survive for over one hundred years. Five general lessons emerge from 3M's experience. First, its management recognized that growth comes from the ability to exploit opportunities
that happen by accident. By giving its employees the chance to turn
such accidents into products, 3M created a self-propelling growth
engine. Second, the company experienced so much success through
these happy accidents that it created formal processes such as the 15
percent rule to institutionalize the process of profiting from them.
Third, 3M's growth pattern is like that of a spider plant, which sends
several offshoots away from the base in search of fertile ground in
which to plant roots. Although not all the offshoots will survive,
enough will find a profitable home so that the overall plant expands.
Put another way, 3M's growth was a result of its ability to diversify into
new markets that take advantage of its inherent strengths. Fourth, 3M

is careful not to get carried away with any single idea by limiting the resources that it can allocate to the ideas and by requiring champions of new ideas to persuade their colleagues based on intensive research. Finally, 3M has created an environment in which creative people have a chance to be rewarded for their successes through peer recognition.

MANAGEMENT LEVERS

The 3M example illustrates the power of experimenting frugally. As we've seen throughout this chapter, different companies have different ways of putting this principle into effect. Experimenting frugally leads to profitable growth, whereas the alternative can lead companies down very expensive dead ends. Executives seeking to turn their organizations into frugal experimenters should take the following steps:

- *Let people develop ideas.* To experiment frugally, companies need to give their people a chance to develop their ideas for new products and better processes. An environment that encourages creativity depends on management's values. If executives operate in a top-down fashion, they will have difficulty empowering their people. However, if executives are open to the benefits of frugal experimentation, then they can look to 3M's 15 percent rule and Smucker's Appleseed Project as models for how to empower people systematically to generate profitable growth.
- *Work with customers.* To experiment frugally, companies should invest in ideas that create value for customers. The best way to do this is to work with customers early in the product development process to get their feedback on ideas before spending too much money. Many of 3M's best new product ideas emerged from such collaboration.
- *Kill losing product ideas, not their developers.* Another key element to frugal experimentation is the ability to take resources away from losing ideas before spending too much money. For executives an important process challenge is to kill losing ideas without destroying the spirit of innovation that moves the entire organization to develop its ideas. To the extent possible, executives should give the developers of failed ideas a chance to use their talents on other projects. Sometimes ideas that failed initially can be the source of great new businesses. Wal-Mart's pharmacy retailing success is a case in point.
- *Celebrate successes.* Creative people enjoy being recognized for their success. Executives can celebrate success in a way that motivates

their entire workforce. Yet the cost of these celebrations is small in comparison to the creativity that they unleash. 3M's Carleton Society is an annual awards ceremony within the company that recognizes the contributions of a handful of employees. Its motivational power is a model for executives looking for ways to celebrate new product success.

VALUE QUOTIENT

Tactical-level analysis can help executives pinpoint opportunities for improvement. If you perceive that your organization can improve in the way it applies the principle "Experiment frugally," such analysis can help identify how best to improve the way your organization performs targeted activities.

Exhibit 4.1 can help you calculate your company's Value Quotient through two levels of analysis. The first level of analysis is binary, meaning that you can use the worksheet as a checklist to determine whether or not your company performs the specific tactics on the list. If your company does not perform any of the tactics within a specific activity, then it should consider initiating such tactics. The second level of analysis is analog, meaning that the worksheet can help pinpoint opportunities to improve how well your company performs a specific tactic that it has already been performing. To raise your company's score on a particular tactic, you may wish to initiate an in-depth process to change the way your organization performs that tactic along the lines developed in Chapter Nine.

To conduct the binary and analog levels of analysis, your company should gather data through interviews with employees. Ideally, your company should use objective third parties to identify an appropriate sample of interviewees, develop interview guides, conduct the interviews, and analyze the results. The outcome of collecting and analyzing the data will be specific scores for each tactic. Although assigning these scores requires judgment, they should be calibrated by comparing the scores with the Value Leaders and other best-of-breed competitors.

Scores for each tactic range from excellent (five) to poor (one). If an organization does not perform the tactic at all, it receives a score of zero. To calculate the activity scores, the analyst can average the scores for the tactics supporting that activity and round the average to the nearest whole number. To illustrate how a score might be

Experiment Frugally: Activity and Tactics	Score

Grow organically

☐ Identify rapidly growing markets that could benefit from the company's strengths. _____

☐ Evaluate the size, growth rate, and profit potential of these markets. _____

☐ Analyze the capabilities required to win market share in the most attractive markets. _____

☐ Assess how well the company performs these capabilities relative to incumbents. _____

☐ Invest in those markets where the company would enjoy a competitive advantage. _____

Manage development risk

☐ Form a cross-functional team to assess development risk. _____

☐ Scrutinize development projects to pinpoint those with the greatest market and competitive risks. _____

☐ Identify potential initiatives to reduce these projects' risks. _____

☐ Cut projects whose risks cannot be reduced cost-effectively and fund those that can. _____

☐ Formalize the risk-management process for future projects. _____

Partner internally

☐ Identify key functions to participate in internal partnering for product and process innovation. _____

☐ Develop a process that captures the input of these functions from brainstorming to implementation. _____

☐ Communicate the purpose and responsibilities of the internal partnering process and implement it. _____

☐ Create financial and qualitative incentives for profitable product and process innovation and desirable teaming behavior. _____

Partner externally

☐ Participate in industry consortia for the industry as well as those of suppliers and customers. _____

☐ Lead systemwide strategy initiatives that conceive and analyze ways to create profit growth for all participants. _____

☐ Invest time and capital to implement these initiatives so they deliver the promised benefits for their partners and their firms. _____

Total _____

Exhibit 4.1. Value Quotient Worksheet: Experiment Frugally.

Key: 5 = excellent; 4 = very good; 3 = good; 2 = fair; 1 = poor; 0 = not applicable.

assigned for a specific tactic, consider the tactic "Evaluate the size, growth rate, and profit potential of these markets." If your company has not identified such markets, it could not evaluate them and therefore would be scored zero. On the other hand, if your company has recently completed a detailed analysis of the size, growth rate, and profit potential of such markets, it would receive a score of five.

CONCLUSION

Frugal experimentation creates value for partners and employees and profitable growth for shareholders. To practice frugal experimentation, executives can follow the four activities described in this chapter. The examples of 3M, Wal-Mart, Merck-Medco, Smucker, and Microsoft give executives models for how these activities can deliver frugal experimentation's benefits.

CHAPTER FIVE

Trust Is Vital

(Fulfill Your Commitments)

F ulfilling your commitments means saying what you intend to do and doing what you said. Executives make explicit and implicit commitments to employees, customers, suppliers, shareholders, and communities. Honest executives meet these commitments. Doing the right thing is not enough. Executives must also communicate their intent to do the right thing. Honest executives communicate their intent because the communication teaches others about the value the executive places on honesty. Furthermore, the communication makes the recipient expect results. When these are delivered, trust is built.

By definition, fulfilling your commitments is far easier said than done. Companies that walk the talk believe that the purpose of a business is to establish and foster long-term relationships. The interest in long-term relationships—whether with employees, customers, investors, or suppliers—causes companies that fulfill their commitments to communicate what they intend to do and then do it. These companies realize that long-term relationships depend on trust and that trust emerges from being honest.

Executives can measure the strength of these bonds by tracking the level of turnover in employees, suppliers, customers, and even shareholders. If companies keep turnover low, they are doing a good job of selecting the right people and giving them a reason to maintain their relationship with the company. The lower turnover in these relationships makes these companies more productive than those with higher turnover. Once a company's executives are convinced of the business value of fulfilling their commitments, the details of implementing this principle are not so difficult to master. If a company's executives do not see the principle's business value, the company's board may need to decide whether to replace its executives with those who do. And once a company's executives are persuaded of the principle's value, the rest of the organization tends to follow suit.

LINK WITH VALUE LEADERSHIP

Fulfilling your commitments creates the trust on which society depends in order to function. Employees start working at a new company because they trust that the company will pay them periodically for their effort. Customers purchase a product because they believe that the price they pay for the product will be offset by its promised benefits. Suppliers deliver goods because they trust the company to pay their bills. Shareholders buy stock in a company because they trust its executives will increase the value of their investment. And communities offer a favorable environment because they trust the company will pay its taxes, employ its citizens, and help keep the land on which it operates clean and safe.

ECONOMIC BENEFITS

Fulfilling your commitments enhances an organization's efficiency by sustaining trust between the firm and its stakeholders. A firm that communicates and delivers on its intent to treat employees fairly will attract talented employees, motivate them to work for the good of the company, and minimize the likelihood and costs of employee lawsuits. A firm that communicates and delivers on its intent to deliver good value to customers will sell more products to those customers and incur smaller product liability claims. And a firm that communicates and delivers on its commitment to communicate honestly with investors and treat their money with care will attract more loyal shareholders and incur lower costs for shareholder lawsuits. Fulfilling your commitments is the right, and often the most cost-effective, thing to do.

Fulfilling your commitments is important throughout an economic cycle. During times of economic expansion, executives may feel pressure to stretch the limits of honesty. For example, sustaining a rising stock price may depend on exceeding quarterly earnings estimates by a penny. The cost of missing this target could be a plunge in stock price leading to a significant drop in executives' net worth. Under such conditions executives may be faced with the choice of slipping over the boundaries of generally accepted accounting principles (GAAP) to meet the earnings target. Although being dishonest may enable the executive to hit the earnings target in the short run, pressure in the longer term to meet ever higher targets inevitably leads to behavior that causes the house of cards to collapse. The result is that a visible subset of all dishonest executives goes to jail and their companies go bankrupt.

During times of economic contraction, fulfilling your commitments is equally important but often more consistent with the cultural zeitgeist. During economic contractions the general public looks for scapegoats to bear society's guilt for the excesses during the prior period of economic expansion. Typically, the scapegoats are among those individuals who most visibly profited from the economic expansion and violated laws and ethical standards in the process. In order to avoid being tossed out of office by angry voters, politicians seek to appear to be part of the solution by scrutinizing and jailing the scapegoats and passing new laws to prevent the future recurrence of the excesses. In such an environment of recrimination and punishment, most executives become more vigilant to assure that they are not swept up by the popular rage. In short, being honest means going with the grain during periods of economic contraction. It is during the subsequent period of economic expansion that it becomes increasingly more challenging for profit-driven executives to be honest in the face of bad news that could cut their net worth.

CASES

This chapter illustrates the benefits of fulfilling your commitments. It details the care that Southwest Airlines took to pick CEO James Parker, an honest leader with a penchant for getting results, to succeed legendary cofounder Herb Kelleher. It contrasts Parker's honesty with the rise of Canadian milkman Bernie Ebbers to CEO of WorldCom. Ebbers used a $7 billion accounting shell game and a string of increasingly bigger acquisitions to keep WorldCom's stock price rising, until the whole house of cards blew away. The chapter continues with an argument for the use of cash instead of accrual accounting and presents evidence suggesting that companies that report honestly do better in the stock market than those that exaggerate their results. It contrasts Microsoft's revenue reserve accounting travails with the accounting investigations of Computer Associates, which allegedly manipulated its financial statements so that its top three executives could receive a $1 billion options package. The chapter illustrates how Johnson & Johnson (J&J) used its credo to enhance the way it serves its employees, customers, and communities. It also examines CEO Steve Ballmer's efforts to infuse Microsoft's people and products with integrity.

ACTIVITY ANALYSIS

Fulfilling your commitments depends on performing three activities:

- **Hire and promote honest people.** An essential starting point for being honest is to hire and promote people who behave honestly. People whose internal compasses direct them toward honest behavior are more likely to behave honestly in their jobs. If the company promotes honest people, those inside the company will be more inclined to behave honestly; and potential employees with honest natures will be attracted to the company.

- **Account honestly.** Companies that value honesty will also report their financial results honestly. Honest accounting means staying within accounting guidelines instead of stretching them to make results look better than they really are. It also means exposing and communicating bad news early rather than burying and obfuscating it.

- **Treat employees, customers, and communities fairly.** Being honest also means providing fair treatment to employees, customers, and communities. Fair treatment means that executives have a responsibility to communicate high standards. Communicating these standards will lead employees, customers, and communities to expect fair treatment. The real test is how well and how consistently companies' daily actions fulfill these stakeholders' expectations.

Hire and Promote Honest People

Executives who aspire to build an honest company can make their jobs much easier by hiring and promoting honest people. If its procedures assume that every employee is dishonest, a company is likely to be far less productive because the processes put in place to prevent dishonesty will add costs and time to its activities that customers generally are not willing to pay for. Therefore, it makes economic sense to take great care during the hiring process to screen out dishonest people. Firms need cost-effective processes for identifying dishonest people before they are hired, such as checking numerous previous employer references, criminal records, credit ratings, landlords, and financial records.

Executives seeking to hire and promote honesty may consider the following tactics:

• *Conduct behavioral interviews with potential employees to test their integrity.* In a behavioral interview, an executive might ask a question that would test the potential employee's honesty. If the interviewer detected a tendency to exaggerate or misrepresent, the executive could immediately screen the potential candidate out from further evaluation.

• *Review all interviewers' impressions of the candidate.* Following the interview process, all the interviewers should caucus to compare notes on a candidate. If one of the interviewers noticed a tendency to dishonesty, other interviewers might echo the trait; the observations could therefore help to screen out a candidate early in the process or sensitize subsequent interviewers to the potential issue.

• *Check references, résumé details, and other sources carefully before extending an offer.* During periods of economic expansion, in which making offers quickly might be perceived as essential to hiring the employees most in demand, some companies might tend to be less cautious about checking these details; in times of economic sluggishness, when there is less of a sense of urgency about closing a deal quickly, more companies might be more meticulous. Companies that fulfill their commitments are consistently meticulous about checking these details, regardless of employment market conditions.

• *Monitor employee integrity as a criterion for promotions.* Executives should monitor employee integrity as a condition for promotions and further employment. Although egregious violations of integrity would be obvious grounds for dismissal, more subtle forms of not fulfilling commitments might be grounds for delaying a promotion. For example, if an employee made a commitment to deliver certain results, such as meeting a sales target, and failed to do so, such an outcome might represent one of three things: a factor outside of the employee's control; an opportunity to improve the employee's skill, which the company could address through training; or an unsolvable problem that would warrant the employee's dismissal from the company.

Just as hiring honest people makes for a better work environment, promoting honest people has benefits that spread to all a firm's stakeholders. According to the *Dallas Morning News,* Southwest Airlines' promoting James Parker, known for his humility, honesty, and effectiveness, to succeed legendary cofounder Herb Kelleher had very positive repercussions. On June 19, 2001, Parker became CEO, running Southwest in a triumvirate with chairman Herb Kelleher and president and chief operating officer Colleen Barrett.[1]

The modest Parker noted on his ascension that he would not waste "a nanosecond" trying to replace the outgoing Kelleher's engaging personality. Parker had a reputation for combining honesty, fairness, toughness, and a willingness to fight to protect Southwest. In giving Parker his CEO title, Kelleher noted that Parker was an altruistic person and a leader who focused on helping employees. He cited Parker's tendency to benefit other people at his own expense, his empathy, and his great wit. Finally, Kelleher pointed out that Parker felt a sense of personal completeness that freed him of the need to imitate others.[2]

Those close to Parker found his honesty to be deeply ingrained. As a child, Parker was a solid performer with a bright mind. Born in San Antonio, Texas, he spent much of his childhood in Fort Worth. In sixth grade at South Hills Elementary School, he won a citywide speaking contest sponsored by the Optimist Club. Parker said his first career goal was to become a journalist; however, he realized that doing his best writing took him too long, thereby making it impossible for him to function effectively as a reporter.

Parker attended the University of Texas, earning a bachelor's degree and a law degree. Betsy Julian, a Dallas lawyer who was one year behind Parker at the University of Texas, met him through the Young Democrats chapter, where he was president. Julian described Parker as an honest, straight-arrow person that people could trust. Julian emphasized that people could trust Parker's word and depend on him to act well and decently.[3]

Parker became assistant attorney general of Texas in 1978 when he met Herb Kelleher, whose law firm served Southwest. In February 1986 Parker followed Kelleher—who had become Southwest's chairman, CEO, and president—as the airline's general counsel. Danny

Bruce, aviation director at Dallas for nineteen years until retiring in 1999, said Parker could be nice or tough, depending on the situation. Bruce was confident that Parker would look after Southwest. He described Parker as straightforward, honest, and strong.[4]

Southwest's decisions to hire Parker and promote him to the CEO slot suggest general principles about hiring and promoting honest people. First, Southwest's cofounder, Herb Kelleher, took a personal interest in hiring Parker after working with him. Kelleher knew Parker for twenty-three years before choosing him to replace Kelleher as Southwest CEO. Kelleher recognized that his choice of successor would be one of the most fundamental decisions on which others would judge his tenure. Kelleher based his decision on more than two decades of working with Parker.

Furthermore, those who knew Parker both before and during his Southwest tenure noted honesty as one of his most predominant personality traits. Parker's honesty works for him because it induces people to trust him.

Second, Kelleher's choice of Parker, and the fact that he highlighted his criteria for choosing Parker, sends a strong message to aspiring managers within Southwest that Parker's personality traits of honesty, fairness, and respect for others are worthy of reward. As a result, Southwest's most ambitious people will be even more motivated to develop a reputation like Parker's. And this will benefit Southwest stakeholders such as employees, customers, and shareholders.

Finally, Kelleher's reference to Parker as a strong leader and a complete individual suggest that other beneficial personality traits often accompany honesty. By choosing such a CEO to replace him, Kelleher inadvertently sent a message to others: often the best CEO is one whose personality will function naturally in the role of the leader rather than one who must fit his or her personality into the job by force. Although Southwest's revenues and profits declined in the year following Parker's appointment as CEO, it was the only airline to hire new employees following the events of September 11, 2001. Parker's leadership skills helped enable Southwest to grow and fare well relative to its peers during a very difficult period.

Whereas Southwest offers a compelling example of the benefits of hiring and promoting honest people, the story of WorldCom paints a very different picture. According to the *New York Times,* WorldCom's former CEO, Bernie Ebbers, was a huckster who succeeded in hoodwinking scores of bankers and investors even though Ebbers lacked basic management skills or understanding of the telecommunications business. Ebbers's "qualifications" as WorldCom CEO were his tenure as a high school coach, a hotel operator, and a Canadian milkman.[5]

WorldCom's bankruptcy was the result of Ebbers's inability to manage a string of acquisitions coupled with $7 trillion of fake profits that he used to pump up WorldCom stock to fuel the acquisition machine. After sixty-five acquisitions, WorldCom's operations remained disconnected. Some customers would find their phone service shut off and would wait for days to get it back on. Customers received multiple bills even after they had switched to another service provider. Furthermore, insiders and analysts agreed that Ebbers was outmatched in the competitive telecommunications industry. For example, Susan Kalla, an analyst at Friedman, Billings & Ramsey, noted that although Ebbers was charming, he lacked a working knowledge of his business.[6]

Ebbers got his foot in the door of the telecommunications industry by using cash from a chain of Mississippi hotels to bail out a failing telecom start-up. In 1983 a group of Mississippi businessmen formed a telephone company, LDDS Communications. LDDS was soon losing money and became dependent on cash from Ebbers, then the owner of thirteen budget hotels and an investor in LDDS. When Ebbers announced he would no longer fund LDDS, its directors appointed him CEO. Ebbers accepted because he had invested so much money in LDDS that he felt he needed to control how it was managed in order to recover his investment.

Although Ebbers had no telecom industry experience, he began buying up other telecom companies. By 1988 his company had accounts in four states. Ebbers paid little attention to the details of operations but when 1996 deregulation enabled competition in the local telecom market, he used LDDS's stock price to pay $12 billion for MFS Communications, a local telecom provider that itself had just acquired UUnet Technologies, an Internet service provider.

Thus began a cycle of using fake accounting to overstate earnings after a WorldCom acquisition. The overstated earnings fueled investors' enthusiasm for WorldCom stock, which gave Ebbers the currency to make another acquisition, beginning the cycle anew. WorldCom's accounting fraud depended on subtracting billions of dollars from its profits through a write-down of the value of certain assets it acquired. WorldCom's big charges against postacquisition earnings were intended to generate bigger losses in the current quarter following smaller ones in future quarters, thereby enhancing expected profits. Specifically, WorldCom took large charges for R&D that it could convert to a reserve fund that WorldCom could use if it needed a boost in earnings.

The value of this reserve fund depended on WorldCom's ability to acquire ever bigger companies. In 1997 Ebbers fed the ever expanding maw of WorldCom's acquisition machine by winning a bidding war for MCI with a $30 billion offer. Insiders believed that WorldCom had wildly overpaid for MCI. So Ebbers's fake accounting factory sprang into action to offset the purchase premium. Specifically, WorldCom reduced MCI's book value (the value of the equity: assets minus liabilities) by $3.4 billion, simultaneously increasing goodwill by the same amount. If the company had not written down the $3.4 billion, WorldCom would have charged it off against earnings in four years. By shifting the expenses to goodwill, WorldCom amortized them over decades, artificially pumping up profits for the MCI acquisition. The Center for Financial Research and Analysis estimates that WorldCom's accounting trickery boosted 2000 earnings per share (EPS) by 14 cents a share to its reported $1.40 from what the center calculates should have been $1.26.

Ebbers's acquisition factory began to implode in June 2000, when the Justice Department shot down WorldCom's $145 billion bid for Sprint. With Ebbers cut off from acquisitions as a source of growth, WorldCom's inability to manage operations was unmasked. For example, in August 2000 Marc Perkel's Springfield, Missouri–based software company stopped working, thanks to WorldCom's misguided decision to turn off his company's phone lines. When Perkel called customer service, he was told that he was not listed as a customer. After several frustrating attempts to resuscitate his phone service, one of the WorldCom employees pointed out that her operations only covered former MCI customers, not WorldCom accounts.

Perkel, whose account was eventually found on the MCI side, inadvertently experienced a serious operational weakness: WorldCom could acquire, but not integrate and manage, those companies. As a result, dozens of conflicting computer systems remained; local network systems were repetitive and failed to work together properly; and billing systems were not coordinated. Perkel eventually moved to San Francisco and canceled his WorldCom phone service. However, WorldCom continued to bill him for over a year, adding charges each month, for phone lines to an office that no longer existed.[7]

The WorldCom saga reveals the dangers of a dishonest CEO. His ability to occupy the CEO slot at WorldCom in the first place reveals a mismatch between Ebbers's background and knowledge and the position's requirements. Ebbers's ability to survive in the position as long as he did was the result of a rare confluence of events. Industry deregulation, both the 1984 breakup of phone monopoly AT&T and the 1996 Telecom Act, lowered the barriers to entry into the industry. Furthermore, the booming stock market and hungry lenders created the currency for serial acquisitions that pumped up WorldCom's stock price and masked Ebbers's lack of operational ability. After World-Com's bankruptcy, it became public knowledge that Ebbers kept his money machine rolling through accounting trickery that painted a false picture of his acquisition strategy's profitability. In the short run, a company can mask the mismatch between the skills of the CEO and the requirements of the job. In the long run, however, this mismatch emerges to the light of harsh scrutiny that often creates huge costs, particularly for shareholders and customers.

The comparison of Southwest Airlines and WorldCom reveals general principles about hiring and promoting honest people. First, honesty (or lack thereof) starts at the top. In too many companies, results are the only thing that matters, and the way those results are achieved is irrelevant. If the CEO holds this view, then everyone else in the organization will act accordingly, regardless of the words in the company's value statement. Conversely, if the CEO gets results honestly, the organization will emulate that behavior. Second, the company must institutionalize through formal processes the hiring and promoting of honest people. Companies must be disciplined in order to keep dishonest people from receiving employment offers. One dishonest individual can wreak great damage on a company's reputation. For companies with strong core values, such damage can be extremely costly. Third, companies should take integrity into account when promoting employees. Promotions communicate to other employees what behaviors the company values. As a result, executives should recognize that other employees are likely to emulate the behavior of those who get promoted.

Account Honestly

Honest accounting reflects accurately the underlying economic reality of a business. It reports revenues, costs, and profits accurately, letting investors know when business operations are good and when they are suffering. WorldCom, America's biggest bankruptcy, achieved much of its size with the help of $7 trillion in dishonest accounting. World-Com was simply the latest in a string of accounting scandals that came to light beginning in late 2001 based on accrual accounting.

Under accrual accounting a company counts income when the sale occurs and counts expenses when the company receives goods or services rather than when a check arrives or leaves a bank account. Simply put, accrual accounting allows companies to count revenues before they receive cash and to defer expenses even though cash has gone out the door. For example, by capitalizing its expenses, WorldCom was able to keep expenses off its income statement and therefore falsely report profits.

The concept of accrual accounting is at the core of very complex accounting policies that give accountants leeway to essentially falsify numbers to satisfy investors and lenders. Here are some other examples:

Energy traders use mark-to-market accounting for long-term energy contracts; this method allow traders to forecast the value of long-term contracts and inflate their revenues well in excess of the cash they actually receive from those contracts during the period of revenue reporting. Furthermore, energy traders counted as revenues the dollar value of the energy they were trading rather than the amount of cash they received as a result of the trades, a much smaller figure. Traders received bonuses based on the bigger numbers, so they had every incentive to overstate how much they made.

Telecommunications companies engaged in capacity swaps in which they recognized revenues for trading unused transmission capacity between telecom providers even though no cash had actually changed hands. Global Crossing, Qwest, and WorldCom all allegedly conducted such cash-free transactions to boost reported revenue.

Companies that have made huge acquisitions, such as AOL Time Warner and WorldCom, must write off the value of the goodwill and intangible assets they receive when they paid more than book value for a company. In April 2002 AOL took a $54 billion write-off, although its amount was based on complex value estimates that the company did not disclose. In January 2003 AOL continued this pattern by taking a $45 billion write-off.[8]

Accrual accounting leaves plenty of room for such gaps to emerge between economic reality and what companies report in filings to the U.S. Securities and Exchange Commission (SEC). And exposing accounting scandals such as WorldCom or Enron does not happen through regular financial reporting; it happens when disgruntled former insiders leak documents or new CEOs conduct special investigations. Given the complexity of accrual-accounting procedures and the incentives to abuse them, investors have very little reason to trust reported numbers.

A potential solution is to abandon accrual accounting and go to cash-basis accounting. Under a cash basis accounting system, which publicly traded firms generally do not use, a company reports as revenues the amount of cash in its bank account during the period when it received that cash. Similarly, the company counts expenses during the period when cash left the company's bank account.

Although gaming such a system is not beyond the means of a determined executive, cash-basis accounting would leave fewer avenues for deceiving investors and lenders and would go a long way toward restoring trust in our capital markets. The biggest disadvantage of using cash-basis accounting is the costs that companies would incur to adopt it. In order to put the change into effect, the SEC would need to mandate the change. The benefits of the change—far more transparent financial results, less manipulation of accounting rules by lobbyists, and ultimately greater confidence in public company financial reporting—would outweigh its cost.

Even within the framework of a potentially flawed accrual-accounting system, companies that report their earnings honestly perform better in the stock market than those who misrepresent their earnings. According to *Investment News,* the closer companies' reported pro forma EPS are to their GAAP-compliant primary EPS, the better their stock prices perform. Douglas Cote, portfolio manager at Aeltus Investment Management in Hartford, Connecticut, identified companies with honestly reported earnings and compared their stock market performance to those of companies with questionable earnings.[9]

To do so, Cote developed "honest EPS," which subtracts primary EPS from reported earnings per share. Companies file primary EPS with the SEC using GAAP. By contrast, EPS reported in press releases are often pro forma, calculated without necessarily following GAAP. Nevertheless, Wall Street analysts often use the pro forma numbers to develop consensus estimates of how much money a company will earn. Cote's idea was that a company that inflates its reported EPS relative to its primary EPS might be perceived as misleading investors and therefore experience weaker stock market performance.

Cote tested his hypothesis rigorously. He analyzed eight years of Russell 1000 Growth stock results. He calculated each stock's honest EPS, ranked them from best to worst, and divided the ranking into five subgroups (or quintiles). He then calculated each quintile's subsequent one-month return every month for a year. He found that the stocks with the best honest-EPS rankings outperformed those with the worst rankings by a compound annual return of 11 percent. Over the eight-year period through 2001, stocks with the most honest EPS returned 14.92 percent compounded annually, while those with the least honest EPS returned only 3.95 percent. During the first quarter of 2002, the stocks with the most honest EPS outperformed the worst by 14.6 percent. The biggest margin between the most honest and the least honest stocks was 33.14 percent in 2000.

The companies that performed best and worst in Cote's analysis are revealing. In general, the best-performing companies tend to be leaders in their markets that grow organically, whereas the worst performers are high-tech companies seeking market leadership through acquisitions. The list of the best included Fannie Mae, Freddie Mac, Comcast, Electronic Data Systems, and MBNA. The average difference between primary EPS and reported EPS for those companies over eight years was only 99 cents. Among the worst were Qwest, JDS Uniphase, Broadcom, Agere Systems, and VeriSign. The average difference between primary and reported EPS was -$26.33; in other words, the reported EPS of the worst companies overstated their primary EPS by $26.33 over the eight years.[10]

Cote's analysis, although not establishing an immutable rule, certainly suggests that honesty in reporting has economic benefits in addition to ethical ones. It is possible that the superior stock market performance of honest reporters reflects a shift in investor sentiment from favoring high-tech acquirers during the late 1990s to unsullied organic growers during the chastened early 2000s. As we noted earlier, when society seeks to purge the excesses of a boom period, honesty becomes fashionable. In future boom periods, a big challenge for executives will be continuing to produce honest financial reports when less honest reporters garner the highest stock market valuations as they did during the late 1990s. Nonetheless, Cote's analysis does reinforce the notion that honesty pays.

The complexity of accounting rules we discussed earlier reveal the frustrations facing managers seeking to report honestly and the challenges facing investors seeking to distinguish companies on the basis of their accounting honesty. Value Leaders tend toward conservatism in their accounting, whereas some peer companies may go over the line to make their financial results look better than their economic fundamentals would suggest.

Executives seeking to account honestly should employ the following tactics:

• *Appoint a CFO with a reputation for integrity and conservative accounting policies.* Given the critical importance of the CFO's integrity, companies must be particularly cautious in assuring themselves of the CFO's past performance. Such caution might take the form of checking credit reports and criminal records, verifying résumé details, and interviewing dozens of references from throughout the candidates' careers.

• *When in doubt, interpret accounting policies conservatively.* Companies must have the courage to report bad news and to maintain conservative accounting policies, particularly when more aggressive competitors are adopting less conservative policies and reporting supposedly better numbers as a result.

• *Be consistent in financial communications with analysts, employees, and investors.* Companies must be consistent in communicating financial results and forecasts to all consumers of the information. They must recognize that gaps between current and previous statements can cause investors to lose confidence in management, which can endanger the company's share price and the careers of its executives.

• *Reward financial staff for conservative accounting practices.* Companies should measure and reward conservative accounting practices as part of the performance evaluation and compensation process for financial staff.

Microsoft's accounting woes in the late 1990s reveal that the line between honest and dishonest reporting can be a bit fuzzy. According to the *Asian Wall Street Journal,* in February 2002 the SEC launched an investigation into whether Microsoft understated its earnings through the use of revenue reserves. Rick Sherlund, who follows Microsoft for Goldman Sachs, reacted to this investigation by noting that Microsoft was actually being conservative in its revenue recognition, the opposite of the aggressive revenue recognition policy that tends to raise red flags for stock analysts. The SEC remained concerned that Microsoft was using its revenue reserves to smooth out earnings, a practice that could be construed as misleading to investors.[11]

It remained unclear which revenue reserves the SEC referred to in its complaint. In fact, two possible sources of such reserves appeared to result from complying with GAAP. For example, Microsoft estimated revenues that it expected to generate in the last month of a quarter and then reconciled the actual revenues with the estimated ones in the subsequent quarter. In addition, it maintained a deferred revenue account that estimated the value of long-term software contracts, taking down the value of these accounts to reflect the portion of the contracts earned in each period. Microsoft's practice, known as revenue smoothing, is common, and the company worked with the SEC to make sure it complied with SEC regulations.[12] Microsoft ultimately settled with the SEC. According to *Reuters News,* in 2002 Microsoft stopped its revenue-smoothing practice, in exchange for which the SEC dropped its investigation.[13]

Microsoft's experience with revenue smoothing helps reveal the sometimes subtle issues associated with honest accounting. First, Microsoft's accounting practices appeared for the most part consistent with GAAP and SEC regulations. Nevertheless, the company settlement with the SEC suggests that perhaps Microsoft, although following reporting practices within the guidelines, may have been pushing the edge of these guidelines' intent. This suggests that in general firms are better off reserving their creativity for their products rather than for accounting. Second, Microsoft's cash balances appear to have continued to grow, which suggests that its business strategy is working and that therefore the overall trend in Microsoft's financial reports is consistent with the underlying economic reality. Ultimately, executives seeking to report honestly must make sure that their financial reports consistently present their business's underlying economic reality, erring on the side of conservative interpretations of principles and regulations. As we will see at the end of this chapter, Steve Ballmer is revamping Microsoft's organization to enhance its reputation for honesty.

Computer Associates (CA) offers a far less subtle example of breaking the rules of revenue reporting to enrich management. According to the *Wall Street Journal,* in May 2002 the SEC was investigating whether CA had artificially inflated its revenues in order to make an executive compensation package more valuable. Specifically, investigators were looking into whether CA executives manipulated revenue from software-license contracts to increase the company's stock price by meeting goals in a $1 billion compensation package for senior executives. The beneficiaries of the stock grant that the company awarded in June 1998 included CA chairman Charles Wang, CEO Sanjay Kumar, and executive vice president Russell Artzt.[14]

Investigators alleged that CA artificially inflated revenues to meet goals that would trigger enormous stock grants to its top executives. According to the *Wall Street Journal,* the Justice Department and the SEC were investigating whether CA inflated revenue by $500 million in its 1998 and 1999 fiscal years to enrich its senior managers. In May 1998, because CA shares hit a $55.13 trigger price and stayed there for a time, Wang, Kumar, and Artzt received a special incentive stock award then worth $1 billion.

The Justice Department and SEC were investigating why CA overstated its revenue for the period preceding and following the stock grants. They focused on CA's May 2000 accounting move to reduce by $1.76 billion, or about 10 percent, the revenue it had previously reported for the three years that ended in March 2000. The downward revision, made when the company filed its Form 10-K annual report with the SEC, included hundreds of millions of dollars that CA retroactively cut from its revenue in the fourteen months before the May 1998 stock award to its top three executives, including $513 million for the year ended March 1998 and part of the $587 million cut from 1999.

CA's earnings did not change in the wake of the "reclassification" because the lost revenue was offset by a commensurate reduction in expenses. In a footnote to CA's 2000 annual report, the company attributed the revision to a change in the way CA accounted for software leases. In announcing the original 1998 results in May 1998, Kumar bragged about "record" revenue and earnings that he attributed to "strong worldwide demand for CA software."[15] In fiscal 1999 the downward adjustment totaled $587 million, also about 11.2 percent, and the $663 million taken off in 2000 amounted to a 9.8 percent reduction.

Kumar's original announcement had the desired effect on CA's stock. In July 1998 CA stock climbed above $60 a share. But later that month, Kumar warned that the Asian economic turmoil and Y2K fears led the company to expect that its revenues and earnings growth would slow. On July 22, 1998, CA dropped from $57 a share to $39.50.[16]

CA's manipulation of financial statements to benefit its top three executives' compensation package clearly punished CA investors. For example, in the twelve months ending August 2002, CA's stock lost 73 percent of its value. Furthermore, CA's dishonest reporting reveals some general principles. First, the company believed that it could manipulate its financial statements and use this manipulation to enrich its top executives. Not only did CA believe that it could violate the law so brazenly, but its top executives believed that they would not be caught. This arrogance underscores the absence of serious corporate governance at CA. Top executives could never expect to get away with such a fraud unless they believed that they could manipulate their board and their auditors to disregard their illegal behavior.

Second, CA's actions reveal a high-handed attitude toward employees and shareholders. Essentially, CA's top three executives' actions reveal an implicit belief that employees and shareholders are pawns in the executives' game of self-enrichment. The executives clearly did not concern themselves with the impact that their accounting and compensation trickery would have on the livelihoods of employees or shareholders.

Although CA's dishonest reporting has some unique elements, it reveals a general trend toward weak corporate governance that seems to thrive particularly during periods of economic expansion. Although the high priests of corporate ethics bray loudly during the subsequent periods of economic contraction, the challenge facing executives is how to account honestly during all phases of the economic cycle.

Treat Employees, Customers, and Communities Fairly

Although most companies seek to project the image of a good employer, the test of that image is the way a company treats its employees, customers, and communities. Fair treatment of these stakeholders closes the loop between a company's stated intentions and its actions. As we noted earlier in this chapter, honesty entails meeting commitments so that both the statement of the commitment to treat stakeholders fairly and the way the firm treats stakeholders are consistent.

Executives seeking to treat customers, employees, and communities fairly may consider the following tactics:

• *Define standards of fair treatment.* To develop such standards, executives must interview customers, employees, and key community members to learn how they expect to be treated in their interactions with the company. Executives should use these interviews as a basis for establishing specific measures that can enable the company's stakeholders to quantify the fairness of their treatment.

• *Communicate the standards to customers, employees, and communities.* Executives must engage customers, employees, and communities in a dialogue that results in common agreement on the specific standards that they should expect in their interaction with the company. Depending on the nature of the relationship, companies should formalize these standards of conduct in contracts with stakeholders.

• *Link manager and employee evaluations and compensation to conformance with the standards.* In setting performance objectives, reviewing performance, and determining pay and bonuses, executives should incorporate these performance standards. Only by linking standards of fair conduct to performance measurement and compensation of managers and employees can companies be confident that the interests of their employees will align with the principle of fair treatment.

• *Survey customers, employees, and communities to gauge their perception of how well the company follows the standards.* In order to encourage fair treatment of a company's customers, employees, and communities, executives must invest in a system that measures how well a company behaves relative to the specific standards we alluded to earlier. This system should be based on periodic feedback from customers, employees, and communities collected and analyzed by objective third parties.

Johnson & Johnson (J&J) has made an effort to renew the beliefs of its founder by encouraging managers and employees to internalize its credo, a one-page summary of the company's responsibilities to be fair, honest, trustworthy, and respectful in dealings with its customers, employees, and communities. According to *Executive Excellence,* the outcome of this process has been a value system that encourages management to treat stakeholders with respect. Former CEO Ralph S. Larsen renewed Robert Wood Johnson's more than sixty-year-old credo by blending its principles into the mainstream of management. Larsen lifted the credo beyond a statement of responsible decision making and turned it into a management tool.[17]

The revitalization of J&J's credo began under Larsen's predecessor, James Burke. According to the *California Management Review,* soon after assuming the CEO slot, Burke assembled twenty-eight senior managers to challenge the credo. He asked them to talk about whether they could really live by the document. In Burke's view pretending to believe in the credo if J&J was not willing to live by its principles made no sense. Burke recalled that people "stayed up all night screaming at each other." When they were done, they had updated the credo. They then took it to all J&J operations, released a revised credo in 1979, and committed the organization to it.[18]

As we noted in Chapter One, J&J's response to the 1982 Tylenol crisis infused the credo with meaning and earned global admiration. In the fall of 1982, McNeil Consumer Products, a J&J subsidiary, faced a crisis when seven people on Chicago's West Side died mysteriously. Authorities determined that each of the people that died had ingested an Extra-Strength Tylenol capsule laced with cyanide. J&J responded by taking immediate responsibility for the problem, withdrawing all thirty-one million bottles of Extra-Strength Tylenol capsules from the market at a cost of $150 million. J&J had done a great job of infusing its credo, specifically its emphasis on treating customers and communities with respect, into its employees. As a result, J&J managers began pulling Tylenol off the pharmacy shelves before J&J's CEO, who was in an airplane at the time the news broke, even knew about the problem. Six weeks later J&J reintroduced the product with new triple-seal tamper-resistant packaging. As a result, J&J earned itself a global reputation as an exemplary corporate citizen.

In 1983 J&J's credo was tested again when Zomax, a drug for intense pain, was linked to twelve deaths caused by allergic reaction. Although fifteen million patients were using Zomax without side effects, the twelve deaths again challenged J&J to live up to its credo. Despite Zomax's benefits, J&J withdrew it from the market.

The Zomax incident made J&J management believe that it needed to embed the credo more deeply into J&J's management processes, because the world was watching. As a result, then-CEO James Burke launched a 1985 program to make the document relevant to all employees. Burke asked J&J's seventy-seven thousand employees to evaluate how well management was performing relative to consumers, employees, communities, and stockholders. To encourage frankness the company kept all responses confidential. Managers received the feedback, discussed deficiencies, and took corrective action. Ultimately, even skeptical employees gained a new respect for how the credo could make J&J better.

When Ralph Larsen became chairman, he made his own mark on the use of the credo as a management tool. Larsen extended the use of the credo beyond a means of reporting how well managers performed in the past. He used the credo to increase employee involvement, enhance productivity, communicate company values and objectives, get input into strategic plans, and identify and close gaps between J&J's principles and its daily actions. Larsen's concept of standards of leadership changed managers' daily behavior. Specifically, Larsen encouraged managers to support the credo's values, communicate about the credo purposefully and consistently, and reward behavior that was consistent with credo principles.

Larsen also encouraged managers to base hiring and promotion decisions on the credo. For example, when managers discuss promotion opportunities with employees, they discuss credo values first and then business results. The activities associated with credo values include the following:

- Behaving with honesty and integrity
- Treating others with dignity and respect
- Applying credo values
- Using results of customer and employee satisfaction surveys to improve the business
- Balancing the interests of all constituents
- Managing for the long term

In addition to rewarding those who follow the credo, Larsen had to deal with violations of credo policy and clearly outlined the consequences of such infractions.[19]

J&J's revitalization of its credo provides general principles for fair treatment of employees, customers, and communities. First, Burke's intellectual honesty in testing his managers' belief in J&J's credo is noteworthy. For a company to paper over its unethical behavior with an inspiring statement of beliefs is far easier than is operating an organization that lives every day according to those beliefs. If a firm has trouble living up to a statement of beliefs, then employees, customers, and communities should be skeptical of any other claims that the company makes. Simply put, fair treatment of employees, customers, and communities begins with a genuine commitment to living a company's beliefs.

Second, J&J recognized that each new generation of managers and employees must reinvent its beliefs, drawing on tradition as well as personal experience. Burke renewed the credo in advance of the Tylenol scare, tested it during the Zomax incident, and subsequently embedded it into J&J's management performance evaluations. Larsen went even further by using the credo for hiring and promotion decisions. J&J's willingness to adapt the credo to changing generations of managers and new challenges reflects the company's commitment to live by its stated beliefs rather than hypocritically saluting a piece of paper on the wall while violating its intent in daily actions.

Third, J&J responded meaningfully to the way its actions raised global expectations of its behavior. The company's response to the Tylenol scare put J&J in the global spotlight as a company that was committed to treating employees, customers, and communities fairly. Its willingness to embrace its role as a global value leader led to changes in its operations that improved its performance. And this improved performance kept the pressure on J&J both externally and internally.

Finally, J&J linked the credo to its incentive systems. By measuring people based on how well they followed the credo, J&J communicated the importance of the credo throughout its organization. By rewarding those who followed the credo and punishing those who did not, the company infused the credo with meaning. The ultimate test of a company's ability to treat its employees, customers, and communities fairly comes in its daily actions.

TRANSFORMING MICROSOFT

Microsoft, which grew to become one of the world's most successful companies, has never been thought of as a paragon of honesty. As we noted earlier in this chapter, Microsoft appears to have come close to crossing the line of GAAP in accounting for revenues in order to produce more consistent quarterly earnings improvements. This accounting issue was not among the most egregious; nevertheless, it exemplifies a Microsoft culture that pursued competitive advantage in ways that often challenge the spirit, if not always the letter, of the law.

After cofounder Bill Gates handed over the CEO title in 2000, his successor, Steve Ballmer, assumed the challenge of infusing Microsoft with integrity in its dealings with employees, customers, and industry peers. Ballmer perceived that Microsoft needed to do a better job of communicating and meeting its commitments. Specifically, it needed to deliver high-quality, secure products to its customers; be a trustworthy business partner; conduct honest communication between executives and managers and across functions within the company; and do a better job of explaining its business performance and prospects to investors. According to *Business Week*, Ballmer's efforts focused on fashioning Microsoft into a long-lasting company that could be more successful in its second twenty-five years than it was in its first by imbuing Microsoft with integrity and making sure it had a more positive impact on customers and partners.[20]

In June 2002 Ballmer communicated his plan for meeting this goal in an all-company memo entitled "Realizing Potential." Ballmer's memo detailed a new mission statement—"To enable people and businesses throughout the world to realize their full potential"—and described the path to achieve the mission. It outlined management processes to improve cross-functional coordination, tighten account-ability, and speed up decision making. For example, Ballmer instituted ways to gets sales and product development functions to work together. He empowered line executives to run their businesses with less supervision. And he demanded that his engineers, sales force, and managers improve the quality of Microsoft's products and services.

Ballmer's new management processes are designed to get Microsoft people to do their jobs better. For example, employees now grade their supervisors; a new accounting system lets managers evaluate spend-ing decisions; and top executives meet each quarter off-site for brain-storming meetings. Each new process is intended to flow into the next to accelerate decisions and later measure their outcomes.

Furthermore, Ballmer introduced new corporate values, whose adoption became part of each employee's annual performance evalu-ation. Specifically, he required employees to attest personally to their agreement with the values at the beginning of the evaluation period. Ballmer also intended to pay employees, in part, on the basis of how well they acted in accordance with these values. He wanted Microsoft's core values of honesty, integrity, and respect to make the company a valued corporate citizen in the minds of customers and partners. Although Ballmer tried to transform Microsoft into a good corporate citizen, competitors such as Sun Microsystems and SAP remained skeptical of the sincerity of Microsoft's transformation. Furthermore, Microsoft had yet to resolve fully its antitrust battles, although Ballmer did settle the revenue accounting matter and has settled many cases that temporary workers, competitors, and customers have brought.

In the two years before his "Realizing Potential" memo, Ballmer struggled in his efforts to manage Microsoft. He first tried to reorga-nize the company by customer group. His intent was to link product development groups more tightly with users. However, Ballmer's first reorganization failed. Decisions about products like Windows were spread across too many of the new divisions. Ballmer eventually found a way to make the CEO job his own. Several eye-opening management experiences—such as reorganization experiments, meetings with executives at other companies, and reading of management books—led Ballmer to solve problems systematically.

The result of Ballmer's quest was a set of management processes—some adapted from other companies—that he believed would work at Microsoft. These eight processes include the following:

• *Measuring executive performance with the organizational health index (OHI).* Based on a concept from Procter & Gamble, the index surveyed employees who rated their bosses' leadership skills.

• *Developing management.* Ballmer studied General Electric to develop a new system for identifying and promoting promising managers.

• *Using Executive P&L to divide the company.* Executive P&L, a management performance measurement tool, divided Microsoft into seven businesses and gave each unit's leader the numbers needed to measure the unit's performance. Previously, managers would know the costs of developing a product but not the cost of selling it. With Executive P&L, they could see all the product's costs, giving them the information they needed to allocate resources without reviewing their decision with Ballmer. Senior vice president Doug Burgum liked Executive P&L. In June 2002, for example, he presented Ballmer his financial plan for his corporate-applications group. Although Ballmer questioned a large R&D increase, he ultimately told Burgum that Burgum had the responsibility to decide how to spend the money. Burgum, who had previously been CEO of Great Plains Software, said that the review felt like a good board meeting.

• *Using Rhythm of the Business as a planning calendar.* Rhythm of the Business was a planning calendar that Microsoft initiated in late May with seven days of business-plan reviews. In October 2001 Microsoft's twelve senior vice presidents met for two weeks to analyze their organizational structure and development needs. In November leaders of its seven business units brainstormed for a week to identify new opportunities. In January, after the results of Microsoft's annual customer satisfaction survey arrived, these seven executives met for four days to analyze the results.

• *Instituting management sync weeks.* Management sync weeks occurred quarterly and coordinated themes and strategies among executive staff and board members. Their intent was to coordinate Microsoft's key decision-making groups.

• *Encouraging a collaborative work style.* Ballmer wanted managers who collaborated well and finished projects on time. He gave power to executives who fit his requirements, such as Office applications executive Jeff Raikes, CFO John Connors, and sales chief Orlando Ayala. Ballmer dismissed those who did not fit, such as former president Richard Belluzzo, who often did not know his business's financial performance as well as Ballmer did.

• *Coordinating across the industry.* Ballmer visited Silicon Valley six times a year and developed a friendship with former Oracle president Ray Lane, a partner at the leading venture capital (VC) firm Kleiner Perkins. Ballmer initiated the Microsoft VC Summit in 2000, which became an annual opportunity for venture capitalists to learn about Microsoft's plans.

• *Building credibility with customers.* Microsoft needed to build credibility with customers. In the summer of 2002, it surprised corporate customers with a licensing plan to receive automatic software upgrades. Jim Prevo, chief information officer at Green Mountain Coffee in Waterbury, Vermont, did not like the plan because it locked Prevo into a series of software upgrades that he was not certain would be useful for Green Mountain Coffee. Pressure from customers led Microsoft to postpone the deadline for upgrading licenses twice and loosen the rules. Despite the changes, analyst surveys suggested that many customers did not like the revised plan.[21]

It remains to be seen whether Ballmer's transformation of Microsoft will be effective. From the time he took over as CEO in January 2000 to August 2002, the company's financial performance was mixed: its revenues grew 22 percent, from $23 billion to $28 billion; its EPS declined from $1.71 to $1.41; and it lost 57 percent of its stock market value, a whopping $342 billion. On a positive note, Microsoft's net profit margins remained a strong 27.6 percent, and its cash balance grew from $30 billion to $39 billion. Over the longer run, the outcome of Ballmer's "Realizing Potential" initiative will appear in qualitative indicators such as customer satisfaction, industry leadership, management "bench strength," and product development effectiveness, as well as traditional financial measures.

MANAGEMENT LEVERS

Ballmer's efforts to transform Microsoft highlight the significant challenges facing executives who want to infuse their organizations with integrity. As we have noted throughout this chapter, being honest means communicating commitments to stakeholders and meeting these commitments through action. Adhering to this principle demands comprehensive and systematic change. Steve Ballmer, in an effort to make his mark, undertook this change process at Microsoft.

His efforts suggest the following management levers for being honest:

• *Take the initiative.* In general, it takes a change in executive leadership to spur a reexamination of a company's integrity. However, the best time to launch such an initiative is before an external shock demands such a reexamination. As we saw, James Burke launched a reconsideration of J&J's credo in advance of the Tylenol scare, thereby better preparing J&J intellectually for the subsequent challenge.

• *Challenge and refine values.* As we noted earlier, each generation of management should feel compelled to challenge the values and beliefs it inherited from the previous generation. Such a challenge may incorporate much of what came before; however, management must be willing to act according to whatever set of values ultimately emerges. By challenging the values received from previous generations, the current generation incorporates what made sense, rejects the rest, and adds what is needed to create a complete set of values in which the current generation believes. If management is hypocritical about its own values, neither communicating those values to stakeholders nor mobilizing the organization to operate according to the values will be possible.

• *Align executives with new values.* As we saw in the cases of Microsoft and J&J, when a company adopts new values, it is crucial that all executives subscribe to these values in their words and actions. The CEO should show the door to those who will not or cannot behave in accordance with these values. Although such harsh action is difficult, it is a necessary part of aligning the organization with the new values. It builds a unified executive team and sends a signal to the company's stakeholders that the company will live by its new values.

• *Create management processes to implement values.* The most time-consuming aspect of being honest is creating the management processes to assure that employees conform to the principle in their daily actions. As we saw in the case of Microsoft, these processes extend to the behavior of the organization vis-à-vis all stakeholders. The company must create management processes to ensure excellence in financial reporting, product development, customer service, and industry relations, as well as in interactions between executives, managers, and individual contributors. As Ballmer's example indicates, creating such processes often emerges from a deep understanding of the company, a review of best practices, and a process of trial and error.

• *Measure outcomes.* What gets measured gets done. In transforming an organization, executives must measure progress regularly and comprehensively. The measures ought to be both qualitative and quantitative. The qualitative factors should relate clearly to the management processes and might include the ability to follow corporate values, results of customer satisfaction surveys, employee evaluations of management and peers, progress in management development and succession, quality of financial reporting, and industry perception of the company and its leaders. The quantitative factors should be conservative financial results, not pro forma ones.

• *Provide incentives accordingly.* Executives need to dole out rewards and punishments in accordance with how well individuals perform relative to these measures. Companies should measure and pay individuals according to their performance in factors over which they have some measure of control. Ultimately, executives' credibility will be measured—internally and externally—on the basis of how well they live up to their commitments.

VALUE QUOTIENT

Tactical-level analysis can help executives pinpoint opportunities for improvement. If you perceive that your organization can improve in the way it applies the principle "Fulfill your commitments," such analysis can help identify how best to improve the way your organization performs targeted activities.

Exhibit 5.1 can help you calculate your company's Value Quotient through two levels of analysis. The first level of analysis is binary, meaning that you can use the worksheet as a checklist to determine whether or not your company performs the specific tactics on the list. If your company does not perform any of the tactics within a specific activity, then it should consider initiating such tactics. The second level of analysis is analog, meaning that the worksheet can help pinpoint opportunities to improve how well your company performs a specific tactic that it has already been performing. To raise your company's score on a particular tactic, you may wish to initiate an in-depth process to change the way your organization performs the tactic along the lines developed in Chapter Nine.

Fulfill Your Commitments: Activity and Tactics	Score

Hire and promote honesty

☐ Conduct behavioral interviews with potential employees to test their integrity. _____

☐ Review all interviewers' impressions of the candidate. _____

☐ Check references, résumé details, and other sources carefully before extending offer. _____

☐ Monitor employee integrity as a criterion for promotions. _____

Account honestly

☐ Appoint a CFO with a reputation for integrity and conservative accounting policies. _____

☐ When in doubt, interpret accounting policies conservatively. _____

☐ Be consistent in financial communications with analysts, employees, and investors. _____

☐ Reward financial staff for conservative accounting practices. _____

Treat customers, employees, and communities fairly

☐ Define standards of fair treatment. _____

☐ Communicate the standards to customers, employees, and communities. _____

☐ Link manager and employee evaluations and compensation to conformity with the standards. _____

☐ Survey customers, employees, and communities to gauge their perception of how well the company follows the standards. _____

Total _____

Exhibit 5.1.   Value Quotient Worksheet: Fulfill Your Commitments.
Key: 5 = excellent; 4 = very good; 3 = good; 2 = fair; 1 = poor; 0 = not applicable.

To conduct the binary and analog levels of analysis, your company should gather data through interviews with employees, customers, suppliers, analysts, and shareholders. Ideally, your company should use objective third parties to identify an appropriate sample of interviewees, develop interview guides, conduct the interviews, and analyze the results. The outcomes of collecting and analyzing the data will be specific scores for each tactic. Although assigning these scores requires judgment, they should be calibrated by comparing the scores with the Value Leaders and other best-of-breed competitors.

Scores for each tactic range from excellent (five) to poor (one). If an organization does not perform the tactic at all, it receives a score of zero. To calculate the activity scores, the analyst can average the scores for the tactics supporting that activity and round the average to the nearest whole number. To illustrate how a score might be assigned for a specific tactic, consider the tactic "Conduct behavioral interviews with potential employees to test their integrity." If your company does not conduct such interviews, it receives a score of zero. On the other hand, if your company has extensive experience conducting such interviews, regularly weeds out ethically challenged potential candidates as a result, and has not encountered problems related to the integrity of its people, it would receive a score of five.

CONCLUSION

To fulfill their commitments, executives must create expectations that they will be good corporate citizens and then shape their organizations to fulfill these expectations through daily actions. Achieving these lofty prescriptions requires massive effort, yet the payoff exceeds that investment. Fulfilling your commitments during periods of economic expansion and contraction generates society's trust and confidence. These rare and valuable assets help a company to work more efficiently with its customers and partners, draw and motivate the best people, and generate financial results that attract a base of loyal and richly rewarded shareholders.

CHAPTER SIX

Success Can Breed Failure
(Fight Complacency)

F ighting complacency is a management process for weeding out arrogance. Success contains the seeds of its demise. When a company achieves market leadership, it often develops habits that prevent it from sustaining that leadership. Success comes from offering customers better value than do its competitors. In some companies this success leads to a culture of entitlement that rewards those who are skilled at winning internal battles for pay, promotion, and perks while punishing those who pay more attention to external matters. As a result, the formerly successful company loses market share to more adaptive upstarts who themselves can fall prey to complacency.

LINK WITH VALUE LEADERSHIP

Fighting complacency supports Value Leadership. A company that has been successful for a period of time faces the creeping danger that its executives will become too comfortable in their success. This comfort can make them less focused on improving the company. As a result, the company's employees, customers, and communities can begin to feel that the company takes them for granted. This feeling makes them more open to better offers from competitors. If a company does not put in place mechanisms for fighting complacency, it will drift away from following Value Leadership. If a company fights complacency, however, it will deepen the loyalty it has built with employees, customers, and communities.

ECONOMIC BENEFITS

As a result, these executives' companies sustain faster growth than their peers. For example, the eight Value Leaders grew 35 percent faster than their peers. Specifically, their five-year sales growth rate averaged 16.5 percent compared to the 12.2 percent rate of their industries. The ultimate source of Value Leaders' superior performance is that their executives view their success as temporary and vulnerable rather than as an entitlement.

CASES

This chapter illustrates how companies fight complacency. It describes the prescience of Wal-Mart's founder, Sam Walton, who learned from the failure of his first employer, J. C. Penney, to hire a strong successor; finding the right successor represented the most significant challenge to preserving Wal-Mart after Walton's departure. The chapter further demonstrates how Wal-Mart encourages a healthy paranoia that puts endless pressure on managers and employees for sustained results, focusing on the few areas that need improvement rather than the many that are doing well. It further describes how Goldman Sachs launched a successful attack on the staid British investment banking market and rewarded the leading proponent of this success. The chapter concludes with a case study of how Johnson & Johnson (J&J) revitalized its once moribund research laboratories and spurred further growth in its noninvasive surgery business.

ACTIVITY ANALYSIS

To fight complacency executives must perform three activities:

- **Plan CEO succession.** To keep a start-up vital after its founder has left, executives must select carefully those who will succeed them. In so doing they must select a CEO who can balance overseeing formal management processes with seeking out new business opportunities that keep the company growing.

• **Sustain a healthy paranoia.** As a company becomes larger, it must add more sales each quarter just to sustain historical growth rates. In order to achieve this goal, executives must instill a healthy sense of paranoia and insecurity through formal processes such as systematic performance measurement and frequent corporate meetings that apply pressure to improve products and processes.

• **Attack new markets.** Another danger facing successful companies is that they grow to dominate markets whose needs are mostly saturated. As a result, these companies can meet their growth targets only by attacking big markets in which they do not have a significant presence.

Plan CEO Succession

Planning CEO succession can determine the future of a company, particularly during the transition from a founding CEO to the first "professional" CEO. If the initial transition does not go well, a successful firm can swiftly manage its way to mediocrity within a few years of the founding CEO's departure. If the transition is done properly, the company can continue the growth trajectory that the founding CEO established, with nary a hiccup. An effective transition from postfounding CEO to next-generation CEO is similarly crucial in determining whether a successful firm can sustain its market leadership. Furthermore, an average performing company can significantly enhance its position by making the appropriate transition to a new CEO.

The key difference between firms that manage these transitions successfully and their peers is the will to focus executive attention on how the choice of successor will influence the long-term future of the company. Whereas peer companies may be less systematic in their process of selecting successors, Value Leaders pick successor CEOs who have the skills that the board believes will be needed to lead the company into the future. In short, fighting complacency depends on empowering a new CEO who can sustain the best of the old while driving the right new management principles.

Executives seeking to plan CEO succession can use the following tactics:

• *Plan for succession at least five years before the current CEO's planned retirement date.* Such a plan might include ranking five to ten internal candidates by their qualifications for the CEO job as well as specific developmental plans, including job rotations and training, to enhance their ability to perform well in the CEO job.

• *Draw from a pool of high-potential executive candidates and expose them to new jobs to test how well they adapt to unfamiliar situations.* The company must continue to pull in new candidates to replace those who leave the company or cannot meet the tests as they rise up the ranks. After sending candidates on to each new job, management should rerank them so that each candidate knows where he or she stands.

• *Expose CEO candidates to the entire company's operation and introduce them to the board of directors.* The job rotation plan should give the most promising candidates an opportunity to understand and manage all of the company's important business operations. The top candidates should also have a chance to meet board members, who can begin to develop their own assessments of the various candidates.

• *Leave the incumbent CEO in a clearly defined advisory capacity for the incoming CEO.* Once a new CEO has taken over, the previous CEO must leave any executive capacity. A new CEO cannot develop and perform effectively if the previous CEO is overseeing the successor's work. Nevertheless, if the retired CEO is willing to act as an advisor, he or she can provide valuable guidance.

Sam Walton, founder of Wal-Mart, is among those who acted on a deep recognition of the importance of picking the right successor as a means of keeping Wal-Mart from becoming complacent. According to the *Chicago Sun-Times,* Walton exploited the complacency that accompanied the tenures of the postfounder generations of CEOs at J. C. Penney and Kmart. When Walton opened his first store, for example, Kmart was the dominant discount retailer; yet within twenty-five years, Kmart had fallen far behind Wal-Mart. Kmart lost ground to Wal-Mart not only because of competition from Wal-Mart but because of its own complacency and incompetence. Like Wal-Mart's, Kmart's initial success was due to a talented entrepreneur, Harry Cunningham, who shaped Kmart and operated it effectively until his retirement.[1]

The seeds of Kmart's demise were planted after Cunningham's departure: Kmart chose traditional corporate managers to succeed him. These traditional managers were comfortable managing budgets; however, they lacked the entrepreneurial feel for how to adapt to changing market conditions that spurred Cunningham's drive in building

Kmart. For example, many of his successors could not grasp the changes in the marketplace and in technology that by the late 1960s made it possible for managers to track and refill inventory quickly.

Although Kmart and Wal-Mart got started with clear though different strategies, Wal-Mart stayed in touch with its customers and adapted to their changing needs, whereas Kmart became complacent and suffered accordingly. Kmart served the suburbs and the maintenance needs of the automobile that had spurred them, but Wal-Mart targeted the small towns that national corporations declined to serve. Although both discount retailers had ample resources, Wal-Mart kept its costs low and remained alert to its customers' needs and tastes. In fact, Walton himself polished the handle on Wal-Mart's big front door or made sure someone else did. By contrast, Kmart concentrated on opening new stores and failed to maintain existing stores, which became shabby. Furthermore, Kmart became complacent about its merchandise assortment.

A would-be Kmart savior, Joe Antonini, admitted that he felt depressed visiting an old Kmart. Wal-Mart, seeing the opportunity of weak competition in the suburbs, moved itself into the suburbs that Kmart formerly dominated. Antonini's Kmart remained inefficient and vulnerable; for example, Kmart required managers at each of its 673 stores to fill out order books by hand and mail daily invoices to headquarters. In 1987, when Antonini took over Kmart, it held 35 percent of the discount retail market, while Wal-Mart held 20 percent.[2]

Antonini had ambitious plans to compete with Wal-Mart. According to the *Financial Times,* he tried to revive Kmart through three initiatives: first, he spent $3 billion to overhaul twenty-four hundred discount stores by widening aisles and adding gardening and pharmacy centers. He also strove to create fifteen combination stores of 140,000 to 160,000 square feet—twice the size of a traditional Kmart—which featured discount retailing and groceries. Second, he built specialty stores such as the Pace warehouse clubs and OfficeMax office equipment, furniture, and computer stores. Third, he sought overseas expansion, purchasing twelve retail outlets in Czechoslovakia in 1992.[3]

Antonini's initiatives failed. In 1994, when Antonini left, Kmart held 23 percent of the discount retail market, while Wal-Mart controlled 42 percent.

Walton also learned much about what to do and what to avoid from his first employer, J. C. Penney, whose unconventional ideas about retailing Walton used and refined. Like Kmart, however, J. C. Penney was unable to maintain the creative spark that led to its initial success. J. C. Penney found itself struggling through various makeovers in a vain attempt to find a profitable formula to generate consistent profit growth.[4] The most important lesson Walton learned from J. C. Penney and Kmart was that managing the transition from an entrepreneurial founder to the next generation of management could determine the long-term viability of the firm.

Wal-Mart's success did not interrupt Walton's interest in new business ideas. He continued to experiment with new retailing concepts, fighting complacency himself and assuring that his successors would continue his focus on self-renewal. According to *Chain Drug Review,* Wal-Mart's success and Walton's growing celebrity did not make Walton complacent. Instead, he continued testing new formats such as the membership warehouse club and the hypermarket. For example, in 1983 the first Sam's Club opened; and in 1987 Wal-Mart introduced its first Wal-Mart Hypermart USA in Garland, Texas, a 220,000-square-foot store that presaged Wal-Mart's rapidly growing Supercenter format, which combines a supermarket with general merchandise. Walton foresaw the importance of the Supercenter format after opening the first such store in Washington, Missouri, in 1990. Walton, who died of bone cancer in 1992, did not live long enough to see the Supercenter's emergence as Wal-Mart's primary source of growth in the second half of the 1990s.[5]

However, Walton did have the prescience to choose David Glass as his successor in 1988. Following Glass's appointment, Wal-Mart experienced twelve years of rapid growth. It expanded internationally in 1993 when it opened stores in Mexico, followed in 1994 by its entry into Canada. During Glass's tenure as CEO, the firm extended its presence to Argentina, Brazil, Germany, and Korea. In 1997 Wal-Mart topped $100 billion in sales and had established itself as the industry leader in the use of information technology (IT) to improve supply chain efficiency.

In 2000 Glass retired, passing the CEO baton to Lee Scott. Scott, who had impressed his bosses with his leadership of Wal-Mart's logistics group, subsequently headed up its merchandising. During his tenure Scott saw Wal-Mart exceed $200 billion in sales in fiscal year 2002, a mere five years after Wal-Mart sales hit $100 billion. With the Neighborhood Market format ready for introduction and additional global markets awaiting Wal-Mart's entry, Walton's effective job of CEO succession appeared ready to leave Wal-Mart in a position to exceed $300 billion in sales.[6]

Planning CEO succession is the most important weapon in a company's fight against complacency. The foregoing discussion of Wal-Mart and its peers reveals some general principles. First, the transition from the founding CEO to the second generation is often the most crucial. In making this transition, the founding CEO must resist the temptation to appoint a successor who will make the founder look good by preserving the founder's legacy. Instead, the founding CEO must attempt to foresee the challenges that the business will face in the future and hire and groom candidates who will be best able to meet these challenges. For example, Sam Walton found in David Glass a successor who shared Walton's obsession with low costs and customer service while adding skill in the application of IT and effective operation in international markets.

Second, once a company botches the passing of the CEO baton, getting the company back on a path of self-renewal is very difficult. As we saw in the cases of Kmart and J. C. Penney, the original founders were gifted entrepreneurs who spent so much time on corporate expansion that they neglected CEO succession. The result of this neglect was that the subsequent generations of CEOs were financial managers who lacked a feeling for the industry. Thus, when customer needs changed, new technologies emerged, or upstart competitors introduced new formats, the financial managers failed to recognize and respond to the changes until financial performance began to suffer. At this point the managers tended to respond in the only way they knew—by cutting costs. Ultimately, Kmart and J. C. Penney sought out CEOs with a reputation for effective turnarounds. Kmart's turnaround ended in bankruptcy, and J. C. Penney's remains a work in progress. In both cases the original founders' neglect of CEO succession led to decades of mediocre corporate performance.

Finally, CEO succession must be an important part of an incumbent CEO's job. For most CEOs, concerns about meeting financial targets take center stage. Furthermore, CEOs enjoy their jobs and find planning for the day that those jobs will end uncomfortable. Nevertheless, CEOs, like all corporate employees, are valuable to companies only to the extent that they perform services that benefit the corporation. If they neglect succession, they are placing their personal interests ahead of their employees' interests. To fulfill their obligations, CEOs must envision the company's future and develop talent that can lead the company effectively. For example, CEOs must assess which markets might generate the most attractive growth opportunities ten years hence and understand the capabilities needed to compete effectively in these markets. At the same time, CEOs need to develop a deep cadre of future leaders by offering them career opportunities to develop these same capabilities. The ultimate judgment of a CEO's effectiveness is whether that CEO selects a successor who keeps the company on a growth track along the lines of global leaders like Wal-Mart or on a path to bankruptcy like Kmart.

Sustain a Healthy Paranoia

Picking the right CEO is a crucial starting point for fighting complacency; however, the CEO must keep the pressure on employees and competitors by sustaining a healthy paranoia. Such paranoia keeps companies alert and shortens their reaction time as customer needs change, new technologies emerge, or upstart competitors introduce new ways of competing. Although maintaining a healthy paranoia may come naturally to an aspiring market leader, pushing forward a company that has already achieved great success is not easy. A successful company must have a unique corporate mind-set to overcome its tendency to rest on its laurels. Such a corporation believes that a certain amount of paranoia is healthy if it drives already successful companies to reach even higher to maintain the lead over current and potential competitors. In fact, this healthy paranoia can alter the very structure of an industry, raising mobility barriers for competitors seeking to take an incumbent's customers. Healthy paranoia is binary: either the CEO embodies it or not. If not, there is no way to train a CEO to develop it, and thus a company and its employees are at risk of falling prey to the growth-sapping features of corporate complacency.

Executives seeking to convert this healthy paranoia into action may use the following tactics:

• *Pick performance measures that force employees to monitor and respond to competitors—both the expected and unexpected ones.* Such performance measures might include changes in market share for the company and its competitors, emergence of new technologies that might offer customers a better value proposition, or changes in customer's level of satisfaction with the company's products.

• *Communicate these measures to employees and incorporate them in their performance objectives.* Through all-company meetings and frequent e-mail and other communications, executives should announce and reinforce these measures and the reasons for applying them. Executives should incorporate these measures into employee performance objectives. Executives should hold periodic business performance review and planning meetings, asking questions of managers and employees to reinforce the urgency of these matters.

• *Compare actual results from these measures to targets.* Executives should also reinforce the importance of these measures by developing and using systems that compare actual results to targets. Executives should probe for in-depth understanding of variances between actual and planned results and take appropriate action to remedy negative trends.

• *Allocate incentives accordingly.* Executives should reinforce the importance of fighting complacency by rewarding employees who perform well on the measures designed to sustain the company's competitive advantages.

Among the measures that seem to sustain the performance imperative are customer satisfaction, growth and profit goals, and productivity targets. These indicators can motivate an organization when it applies them openly, fairly, and consistently to an entire employee population. In short, the way executives apply such performance management systems determines their effectiveness.

To apply such systems successfully, management must focus attention on opportunities for improvement. For example, if customers are very satisfied with a company in nineteen specific areas but dissatisfied with one aspect of the company, Value Leaders will focus management attention on the one aspect that needs improvement rather than crowing about the nineteen areas that are going well. This focus on opportunities for improvement sends important messages to employees. First, it lets people know which problems have the greatest urgency. Second, it communicates management's sense of urgency and dissatisfaction with the status quo. Finally, it helps employees understand that corporate success is not an end point to be celebrated but a process of reaching for ever higher levels of performance.

Wal-Mart offers insights into the process for making such performance management systems work. According to *Fortune,* Wal-Mart's management is driven by a unique blend of confidence and a fear of falling behind. At Wal-Mart's biannual conventions, these traits reveal themselves. Rather than holding such conventions in cool spots in the summer and warm ones in the winter, Wal-Mart saves money by holding its January conference in a snowy locale like Kansas City, Kansas, and its August convention in steamy Dallas, Texas.[7]

The January 2000 meeting in Kansas City mixed confidence with fear. For example, one part of the Kansas City coliseum celebrated Wal-Mart heroes along with a sign proclaiming "We Are Wal-Mart. We Are Winners. Winners Win." At the same convention center, Wal-Mart executives discussed the company's failings in food marketing. And the concern about Wal-Mart's opportunities for improvement extend to corporate headquarters, where a weekly Friday morning meeting of two hundred managers harps on imperfections that Wal-Mart must fix in the next week to avoid a sales disaster.

The Friday morning meetings focus on details that range from out-of-stock merchandise to analysis of competitors' strategies. A meeting held in 1999 included a discussion by current CEO Lee Scott of out-of-stock Kathie Lee "trousers socks" at a store that Scott had recently visited, a reminder by former CEO David Glass to put out Halloween candy early so that customers would eat it and need to come back for more, and a forty-minute analysis of pharmacy competitor Walgreen.[8]

These examples reveal the tremendous emphasis that Wal-Mart executives place on customers and competitors. Specifically, Wal-Mart executives communicate a persistent message that managers need to eliminate customer dissatisfaction while remaining mindful of how competitors seek to exploit any such dissatisfaction to take market share from Wal-Mart. The company keeps the pressure on its managers to stay ahead, making it impossible for complacency to find a foothold.

Wal-Mart's efforts to fight complacency extend from its retailing operations to its information technology (IT) department. According to *Chain Store Age,* Wal-Mart's chief information officer (CIO), Kevin Turner, believes that a certain level of paranoia among Wal-Mart's IT professionals produces positive results. Turner's April 2000 speech to a retail systems conference in Chicago focused most heavily on the personal development of Wal-Mart's IT professionals. Turner articulated his belief that retail IT professionals are among the smartest group of people in retailing. He observed that if CIOs could harness the retail IT genius of their staffs, IT skills could become a significant source of competitive advantage, making it possible for retail CIOs to become CEOs. Turner suggested that IT employees, rather than unquestioningly performing the work assigned them, should use their intellects to challenge the business logic of application development decisions and infrastructure projects. Turner said that Wal-Mart tries to foster some paranoia and insecurity as a way to spur its IT professionals to higher levels of performance. Because of the company's size, Turner believed that employees could begin to feel insulated from competition and new technologies. Therefore, he found that encouraging a bit of paranoia spurred them to take on greater responsibility and led to improved performance.[9]

Turner noted that the absence of this mind-set may have allowed new competitors to take market share from traditional retailers. In fact, Amazon recruited many of Wal-Mart's IT employees. By 2000 Turner was worried about the competitive threat from Amazon, which had 17 million customers, 73 percent of whom were repeat purchasers. He also noted with a mixture of admiration and fear that Amazon shipped 99 percent of its orders on time through December 23, 1999—significantly better than Wal-Mart's performance during that period. And Turner observed that Amazon was learning more about product fulfillment and merchandising, making it a potentially formidable competitor to Wal-Mart.

His concerns about upstart competitors extended to eBay as well. As Turner observed, competitors such as eBay start off with none of the constraints facing a manager of an established company. Specifically, their lack of customers, legacy systems (older computer technology that must be either replaced or bridged when a company installs the latest technology), infrastructure, and budget problems actually give these new competitors an advantage over big companies like Wal-Mart. He noted that his retired father enjoys using eBay to collect fishing lures. Online auctioneer eBay is getting the attention (and often the business) of people who have been Wal-Mart customers. Turner advised traditional retailers to think like eBay, tapping great ideas that may appeal to a different retail market.[10]

Turner's observations about the motivating power of paranoia and insecurity clearly reflect how Wal-Mart's values pervade all its business functions. Although the threat from Internet retailers does not seem to have cut into Wal-Mart's growth very significantly, the fear that these retailers induced in Wal-Mart's organization reflects the company's ability to keep its people from resting on their laurels despite becoming the world's largest company.

Wal-Mart's ability to keep the pressure on its people even extends to its offerings in high fashion, a segment that most "sophisticated" people would conclude was beyond Wal-Mart's ability to serve. *New York Times* fashion reporter Cathy Horyn sheepishly admitted that she buys clothes at Wal-Mart. Due to its perceived lack of sophistication, she was embarrassed to admit her Wal-Mart purchases. Yet she noted that Wal-Mart sells more clothes than any store in the world—about $25 billion worth. Horyn's Wal-Mart purchases started small: sandals in 1997 and a $13 fleece top in 2001. By 2002, however, her Wal-Mart clothing buying spree took off. Horyn applauded Wal-Mart's failure to advertise its clothing, but she was disappointed with its failure to supply customers with knowledgeable sales assistance or mirrors to see how clothes might look.[11]

Wal-Mart's $25 billion clothing retailing business flowed from its investments in developing the capabilities needed to compete effectively there. In the late 1990s, many of Wal-Mart's suppliers moved into Bentonville, Arkansas, where Wal-Mart is headquartered, to respond more effectively to the company's requirements. Furthermore, Wal-Mart executives visit Europe to track the latest trends. For example, Celia Clancy, a senior vice president for women and children's apparel, and Claire Watts, a senior vice president for product development, travel to Europe regularly to visit stores and Première Vision, the fabric fair in Paris.

As a result, Wal-Mart offered popular merchandise for fall 2002, such as low-rise pants, denim dresses with lace-up necklines, and patchwork. Since 1997 Wal-Mart has increased its fashionable clothing selection at the lowest prices, paying particular attention to clothing fit. Before selling a garment, Wal-Mart sends it to Bentonville, where technicians fit it to be more in line with U.S. sizes. Wal-Mart's merchandising skills were rewarded with an August 2002 *Consumer Reports* article that named the company's Faded Glory jeans the best-fitting denim brand on the market. Referring to fashion columnist Horyn's comment about jumbled merchandise and a lack of mirrors, Wal-Mart senior vice president Clancy acknowledged that Wal-Mart's clothing presentation represented an "opportunity." Her comment is Wal-Martese for "We know we have a problem here, and we are working to solve it."[12] Clancy's comment demonstrates how deeply Wal-Mart's culture of self-improvement permeates the thinking of its executives and employees.

Wal-Mart's ability to keep competing reveals general principles. First, the company does not view its relative size as a reason to slack off. Many companies equate size with success and view success as a reason to kick back and enjoy its spoils. Wal-Mart's ability to maintain a healthy paranoia despite its success is the principal reason that it can keep competing. If a company does not maintain this sense of insecurity, it is ultimately doomed to forfeit its market leadership to hungrier competitors.

Second, Wal-Mart fuels its healthy paranoia with information about its markets. Specifically, Wal-Mart executives monitor customers and competitors to identify opportunities to improve its business. It monitors customer satisfaction and creates a sense of urgency about taking action to remedy sources of customer dissatisfaction. Wal-Mart also analyzes its toughest competitors to understand the sources of their success and to hone strategies to blunt competitive incursions.

Finally, Wal-Mart institutionalizes its healthy paranoia. Its biannual celebrations both boost employee morale and excoriate employees to improve. Its Friday morning managers' meetings transmit a sense of urgency about addressing customer concerns and developing strategies to cope with tough competition. These formal processes drive Wal-Mart employees to get off their laurels and solve problems that keep the ever restless Wal-Mart from standing still long enough to become vulnerable to competitors.

Attack New Markets

One of the great challenges facing successful companies is the saturation of their core markets. When a big company has satisfied most of the demand among the customer group it originally set out to serve, its very success constrains its ability to grow in that market. Some companies respond to this challenge by sticking with their core customers and products—a recipe for stagnation. Others attempt to acquire their way into what appear to be new fast-growing markets, only to discover that they overpaid and lack the skills needed to compete effectively. Both of these approaches reflect intellectual sluggishness born of complacency.

Executives seeking to attack new markets may choose the following tactics:

• *Set financial goals and mission statements to drive people toward the goals.* Executives take command of their company's destiny by setting ambitious goals for growth and by defining a mission that inspires current employees and attracts new ones. The drive to achieve should be ambitious yet achievable.

• *Brainstorm, analyze, and rank ideas for markets and products to realize the goals.* Executives should encourage the company to generate many creative ideas for achieving these goals. Once the creativity has produced a long list of ideas, however, executives must analyze the ideas in order to enable management to spend the most time on the ones with the greatest profit potential.

• *Identify and assess the company's capabilities to win in the high-priority markets.* Although a new market may have the potential for high profit, executives must evaluate how much of this profit potential their company can capture. To complete such an analysis, they must understand the capabilities required to build a successful position in that market. Furthermore, executives must assess how well their company can perform these capabilities relative to companies already competing in that market. If the company appears poised to do a better job than incumbents, then the company should enter the market.

• *Develop a plan of attack and implement it with vigor.* To enter the new market, executives should develop a plan of attack and implement the plan vigorously. Such a plan might specify target customers; the specific customer needs on which the company will focus; the products and services the company believes will offer customers superior value; as well as the functional policies required to design, build, sell, distribute, and support these products. Executives must also allocate the people and capital needed to turn the plan into actions that get results.

Goldman Sachs's invasion of the European investment banking market represents just such a successful attack. Because Goldman was founded in New York and had derived most of its business from the United States, such an attack was not without challenges. According to the *Sunday Telegraph,* Goldman's thirst for beating its competitors helps explain its successful entry into the European investment banking market.[13]

Goldman launched its entry into Europe's investment banking market in 1986 by opening an office in London, leveraging its core capabilities to achieve success in a new arena. Goldman's entry was abetted by its status as a partnership of 146 rich partners; a 1991 *Fortune* survey of Wall Street's wealthy found that 40 percent were Goldman partners. Furthermore, Goldman's 1991 profits were thought to total $600 million, yielding a relatively high 30 percent return on equity. Goldman's wealth offered a strong foundation of capital to finance a successful European investment-banking business. And its partnership structure assured that its hiring and investment decisions would be thoroughly vetted.

Beyond its wealthy partners, Goldman's principles also contributed to its successful entry into Europe. For example, Goldman's staff was indoctrinated in Goldman's fourteen principles at company gatherings. These principles include always putting clients first and maintaining the highest ethical standards in Goldman employees' professional and private lives.

Goldman launched its entry into Europe after setting itself the goal of becoming a global bank. Prior to 1986, its European presence was limited to serving American clients in Europe and some European companies in the United States. By 1991 its new London offices employed one thousand people. Speakers at the new office's June 1991 opening were former British Premier Margaret Thatcher and Goldman Sachs International's chairman, Eugene Fife, who boasted that Goldman's European operation accounted for a quarter of the firm's total profits.

Goldman earned these profits through trading, a traditional Goldman strength. Specifically, its London-based trading operation dealt in bonds, oil, precious metals, coffee and agricultural commodities, foreign exchange, swaps, options, and derivatives.

Moreover, Goldman built its organization by hiring people and training them to operate in its culture. It spent heavily on training its salesmen, traders, and researchers, whom Goldman assumed had picked up un-Goldman-like work habits from previous employers. The organization encouraged its new London hires to work as a team, cutting those with big egos down to size.

But Goldman's most aggressive London department was corporate finance. This department was led by former Oxford tennis star John Thornton and his European chief, Donald Opatrny. Goldman's London corporate finance unit gained significant market share during the takeover wars of the late 1980s by developing a reputation as a defender of companies facing hostile bids, declining to act on behalf of aggressors. By pursuing its defense-only strategy, Goldman differentiated itself from competitors such as Deutsche Bank or Warburg. The source of this differentiation was that CEOs trusted Goldman and thus shared information—realizing that, unlike its competitors, Goldman would not take information from a company and then represent a company making a hostile bid for it. The driving force behind Goldman's success was paranoia: Goldman required itself to be *excellent* at all its business activities, believing that if a client saw Goldman as *equal* to its competitors, then Goldman would be out of business.

By 1991 Goldman's leadership in corporate finance was undisputed. It had done sixty-four privatization transactions around the world, helping primarily with British and U.S. transactions. It took over the privatization of British Telecom from scandal-ridden Salomon Brothers. Goldman also developed a strong reputation for multicountry offerings such as the underwriting of Swedish utility

Norsk Hydro's rights issue in eight countries; led an international equity deal for Volkswagen; and conducted the first debt issue that was not led by the Swiss, with warrants for Ciba-Geigy.

Goldman's five-year rise to prominence in London earned the respect of its competitors. Sir David Scholey of SG Warburg, then Britain's leading homegrown investment bank, considered Goldman different from Warburg, harder and determined to be the best.[14]

But earning Scholey's respect was certainly not the greatest reward for Goldman's success in Europe. In a culture where stars are cut down to size, someone still needs to emerge as a leader. John Thornton, whose leadership of Goldman's London corporate finance unit helped propel its growth, appeared poised by 2002 to take over as CEO of the entire company. According to the *Financial Times,* Thornton's reputation for aggressive pursuit of new business helped propel him to the top of Goldman Sachs. By April 2002 Thornton, then Goldman's president and co–chief operating officer, moved back to the United States after fifteen years in Britain. Thornton was believed poised to become co-CEO along with John Thain, succeeding Hank Paulson as CEO by 2004.[15] Ultimately, Thornton was unable to climb all the way to the top of the Goldman pyramid. According to the *Observer,* in March 2003 he announced his departure from Goldman to take a position as a professor at Beijing's Tsinghua University. Some speculated that he ran out of patience when it became clear that CEO Hank Paulson had no imminent plans to make his job available.[16]

During Thornton's tenure in London, he developed a fearsomely aggressive reputation for himself and Goldman Sachs. Apocryphal stories of Thornton's aggressiveness abound: he once telephoned a staffer six times on his wedding day to argue about a deal that was falling apart, and he told a CEO that he would slit the throats of his team and drink their blood if they did not win the deal they were sent to close. Although such aggressiveness might appear counter to Goldman's emphasis on subverting the individual's ego to the interests of the team, Thornton's aggressiveness was necessary to gain market share in the stodgy British banking industry, and he seamlessly welded his interests to advancing Goldman's interests.

Thornton's first opportunity to take advantage of his competitors' complacency came during British Tyre and Rubber's hostile bid for Thomas Tilling in 1983. The target's traditional investment bankers did not call their client for three days, whereas Thornton spent seventy-two hours at Tilling's office before his British counterpart arrived. After Thornton transferred to London in 1987, he appeared at the office of a leading British company's CEO without an appointment. He just sat and waited until he got one, and that CEO awarded Thornton the deal he sought. Following his 1999 promotion to Goldman's presidency, Thornton spent less time in London—instead spending his time roving throughout Goldman Sachs—troubleshooting and searching out top talent.[17]

Goldman Sachs's successful expansion into Europe reveals general lessons for attacking new markets. First, Goldman recognized that Europe was a large market in which the company could compete effectively. Goldman decided that it wanted to become a global investment bank and that building a strong position in Europe was central to achieving its goal. Furthermore, it realized that its capabilities would be a source of competitive advantage in Europe. Specifically, it saw that its wealthy partnership structure, business principles, sense of urgency about outperforming competitors, and operational skills in trading and corporate finance gave Goldman an advantage over incumbents.

Second, Goldman was able to translate this vision into reality. It got the results it wanted by hiring local staff and inculcating them with Goldman's culture and way of operating. It also applied these resources in a unique way that differentiated it from competitors, for example, aggressively pursuing new business or following corporate finance's "defense-only" strategy regarding takeover advice. The way Goldman applied its resources in London enabled it grow to one thousand employees in a mere five years while generating a quarter of the firm's global profits. Not only was Goldman able to conceive of the right strategy, but it was able to execute the right strategy very effectively.

Finally, Goldman rewarded the individual whom it deemed responsible for its successful European strategy. By promoting Thornton to president and putting him in a position to take over the firm as co-CEO, Goldman was sending a strong signal to others in the firm regarding what succeeding at Goldman would require. With his aggressive pursuit of Goldman's growth, Thornton enriched his partners and left them confident that he could lead the company into a wealthier future. Despite Thornton's departure, the ascendancy of such a strong new business generator let others at Goldman know that complacency could never lead to advancement.

REVIVING JOHNSON & JOHNSON'S R&D

Companies that have allowed themselves to become complacent are not necessarily fated for a future of mediocrity. Although dislodging a company from complacency is difficult—often requiring a series of jarring wake-up calls—companies can revitalize themselves if they are willing to take the right steps.

These steps apply the three activities we discussed earlier in a pressured turnaround effort that often cuts costs, revives revenues, and instills a spirit of self-renewal. The first step is often to put in place new executives who have proven their abilities in the past and are ambitious for career growth. Such executives will be able to look at a business problem with a fresh perspective and take action aggressively and persistently in order to deliver the results that will propel them up the career ladder. The second step is for these ambitious new executives to take a fresh look at the company, examining its flaws as an upstart competitor would do, looking for vulnerabilities. Such vulnerabilities might include slow decision making, lack of responsiveness to changing customer needs, ignoring market-share losses to new competitors, or failure to use technology to increase productivity. The final step is to develop and implement a plan to fix these flaws and get results. This final step often takes most of the time and effort on the part of the entire organization, and thus executives must communicate their plans broadly and frequently to keep people performing and reaching to achieve broad goals.

Johnson & Johnson (J&J) brought its once moribund research labs back to life in the late 1990s and in so doing unleashed a stream of new drugs. According to *Forbes,* this turnaround was spurred by some serious setbacks that drove J&J to change the way it managed its R&D labs. In 1998 CEO Ralph Larsen realized that J&J's growth was slowing down. Although its consumer business in baby powder and Band-Aids was doing fairly well, J&J's medical-device division was losing its share of the coronary stent market. And its $9 billion pharmaceutical business faced serious challenges.[18]

J&J's pharmaceutical business lacked sufficient new drugs, and some of its existing products were struggling. For example, five potential drugs failed in late stages of development: regulators nixed treatments for multiple sclerosis and premature labor, and stroke and diabetes drugs failed in large-scale trials. Furthermore, J&J lost a battle over rights to a new version of Procrit, its anemia drug. Sales growth slowed to 5 percent in 1998, and profits fell 9 percent as J&J took a restructuring charge. CEO Larsen recognized that J&J's real problem was that it had become complacent and had lost touch with changes in the pharmaceutical industry.

J&J's drug lab, for example, was fetid with mediocrity in the mid-1990s. Its labs in Raritan, New Jersey, and Springhouse, Pennsylvania, had produced only one drug for testing in 1995 and 1996 combined, compared to an industry average of six. J&J scientists became so dependent on licensing compounds from other peers that they had lost the will and the ability to develop their own.

J&J's drug researchers acted as though changes in regulatory requirements were irrelevant. For example, in the 1990s regulators took a much harsher view of drug side effects; however, J&J developed drugs with a 1980s mind-set in which only effectiveness mattered. Ergoset, a diabetes drug that J&J had licensed from Ergo Sciences, was rejected by the Food and Drug Administration in 1998. In 2000 J&J was forced to withdraw its heartburn drug, Propulsid, losing $1 billion in sales, after users suffered irregular heartbeats.

By December 2001 J&J had successfully revitalized itself. Its stent business was regaining market share by leading the industry in developing drug-coated devices that could cut the risk of arteries reclogging. More significantly, J&J's drug business, which provided roughly half of the company's total revenue and 62 percent of its operating profit, looked poised to introduce promising new drugs.

J&J's pharmaceutical research lab had increased almost sixfold the number of promising new drugs in five years. By the end of 2001, it had thirty-five in early trials, including treatments for diabetes and arthritis, compared to six in 1996. By 2002 J&J hoped for fifty new drug candidates. To improve its results in the interim, Larsen paid $5 billion to acquire biotech firm Centocor in 1999 and $11 billion for Alza, which is developing new forms of drug delivery, in March 2001.

The turnaround at J&J can be attributed to several Larsen initiatives. He divided J&J's medical devices and drugs into two separate divisions and named a promising executive, William Weldon, to manage the drug business. Larsen cut layers of bureaucracy from J&J's drug research laboratories and increased its budget 50 percent in three years to $3.5 billion. Larsen also assigned Per Peterson to be the first executive to manage all J&J drug labs and appointed him to the company's thirteen-member executive committee, the first scientist ever to join this committee.

Peterson was eager to revive J&J's R&D labs. The company had recruited Peterson from Scripps Research Institute in La Jolla, California, in 1994 to run its basic research. Peterson was promoted to run J&J's drug R&D in 2000 and charged to enhance its productivity.

Peterson first cut management, removing three of the six layers between scientists and the research chief. He chopped twenty-four departments and their executives, each focusing on a different disease group, replacing the hierarchy with small teams of twelve biologists and chemists who report to lab heads. Instead of studying only one disease, each team could focus on any drug targets or diseases within a category. Peterson's organizational changes helped revitalize the labs by freeing researchers to work on topics that interested them rather than assigning them to a narrow area of research. By unleashing researcher creativity and self-motivation, Peterson was able to generate far higher levels of productivity.

Peterson also shook up J&J's Janssen Pharmaceutica unit in Belgium, laying off 40 percent of its researchers in June 2001 while recruiting outside replacements. William Murray, a chemist at J&J's Raritan lab, noted that Peterson challenged researchers, giving them a broad idea of what he wanted and letting the researchers develop solutions.

Peterson's initiatives spurred a bevy of promising drugs. At J&J's new lab in La Jolla, California, scientists developed a compound in human trials that could cut jet lag and memory loss. The compound blocks a newly discovered receptor known as H3, the third in a family of cell-surface proteins that receive messages from the hormone histamine. H3 was discovered by a former Scripps colleague of Peterson. On the East Coast, other J&J researchers developed an arthritis drug to block an enzyme that releases toxic immune proteins in arthritic joints. A second J&J team developed a diabetes drug that cuts blood sugar and cholesterol levels. A third group mapped proteins to develop new drugs for the digestive system. All three were in early human trials as of December 2001.

J&J also changed the way it funds drugs under development to increase its odds of market success. In 1999 William Weldon, who became J&J's CEO in 2002, set up a committee to evaluate a compound's readiness for early human testing. In 2000 he formed a second group, which decided whether a compound was likely to outperform competitors sufficiently to warrant investment of several hundred million dollars in large-scale clinical trials. Peterson participated on both committees and had veto power. In 2000 he voted down two drugs that J&J had licensed after deciding they were only as good as existing drugs. He also vetoed an internally developed drug for migraine headaches when results showed it offered no advantages over Glaxo's Imitrex. According to Peterson, J&J would have invested in both prior to 1998.

Although whether J&J's promising drugs will translate into profit growth remains to be seen, J&J's turnaround seems to have revitalized its drug development efforts.[19]

MANAGEMENT LEVERS

The J&J turnaround story suggests that a well-established company can fight complacency. Many large companies need an external shock to the system to get them to realize that they need to shake up their organizations. Once the realization occurs, most executives recognize that taking the steps needed to spur performance improvement is well within their power. At J&J, better results flowed from cutting management layers, hiring new staff, and providing a work environment in which researchers felt challenged to innovate.

Executives seeking to achieve results along the lines of J&J may seek to pull the following management levers:

• *Bring in some new executives.* Complacent companies are often run by complacent managers. As we saw in the case of J&J, the new executives do not necessarily need to come from outside the company. In fact, companies with a process for developing highly talented executives inside the company may be better off, because these new executives can get results faster. An outside executive would likely need to spend valuable time building credibility inside the company before taking meaningful actions. This chapter's section "Plan CEO Succession" provides a framework for developing such executive talent.

• *Look at the company from the outside in.* Thanks to an emerging new generation of management, J&J was able to empower a pair of executives who could look at the company as it appeared to customers, competitors, and regulators. Taking a fresh and objective look at a company as it appears to outsiders is an essential first step to fighting complacency. J&J's fresh look revealed an organization that was out of touch with changes in its markets, was top-heavy with bureaucracy that made bad decisions, and did not put enough emphasis on research productivity. Without this outside perspective, J&J could not have begun its battle with complacency. This chapter's section "Sustain a Healthy Paranoia" offers ideas on how to look at the company from outside in.

• *Cut costs that do not add value.* J&J's review from the outside in revealed a significant opportunity to cut out layers of bureaucracy that slowed down decision making and yielded bad decisions about allocating resources. It also identified individuals whose attitudes and abilities did not fit with J&J's new emphasis on research productivity. By cutting these costs, J&J eliminated barriers to improvement while boosting its profits. This management lever is a natural outcome of sustaining a healthy paranoia.

• *Enhance competitiveness.* Although cutting away barriers is a useful first step, fighting complacency also depends on affirmative actions, such as those designed to enhance the company's competitiveness. J&J's emphasis on evaluating drugs in process based on their competitiveness clearly enhances their profit potential. The company also took steps to unleash researcher creativity while focusing their attention on areas with compelling promise. J&J's turnaround efforts reveal that just a shift in management focus from internal to external factors can go a long way toward fighting complacency. This management lever is also part of sustaining a healthy paranoia.

VALUE QUOTIENT

Tactical-level analysis can help executives pinpoint opportunities for improvement. If you perceive that your organization can improve in the way it applies the principle "Fight complacency," such analysis can help identify how best to improve the way your organization performs targeted activities.

Exhibit 6.1 can help you calculate your company's Value Quotient through two levels of analysis. The first level of analysis is binary, meaning that you can use the worksheet as a checklist to determine whether or not your company performs the specific tactics on the list. If your company does not perform any of the tactics within a specific activity, then it should consider initiating such tactics. The second level of analysis is analog, meaning that the worksheet can help pinpoint opportunities to improve how well your company performs a specific tactic that it has already been performing. To raise your company's score on a particular tactic, you may wish to initiate an in-depth process to change the way your organization performs the tactic along the lines developed in Chapter Nine.

To conduct the binary and analog levels of analysis, your company should gather data through interviews with employees, customers, suppliers, analysts, and shareholders. Ideally, your company should use objective third parties to identify an appropriate sample of interviewees, develop interview guides, conduct the interviews, and analyze the results. The outcomes of collecting and analyzing the data will

Fight Complacency: Activity and Tactics	Score

Plan CEO succession

☐ Plan for succession at least five years before the CEO's planned retirement date.   _____

☐ Draw from a pool of high-potential executive candidates and expose them to new jobs to test how well they adapt to unfamiliar situations.   _____

☐ Expose CEO candidates to entire company's operation and introduce them to the board of directors.   _____

☐ Leave the incumbent CEO in a clearly defined advisory capacity for the incoming CEO.   _____

Sustain a healthy paranoia

☐ Pick performance measures that force employees to monitor and respond to competitors, both the expected and unexpected ones.   _____

☐ Communicate these measures to employees and incorporate them in their performance objectives.   _____

☐ Compare actual results on these measures to targets.   _____

☐ Allocate incentives accordingly.   _____

Attack new markets

☐ Set financial goals and mission statements to drive people toward the goals.   _____

☐ Brainstorm, analyze, and rank ideas for markets or products to realize the goals.   _____

☐ Identify and assess company's capabilities to win in the high-priority markets.   _____

☐ Develop a plan of attack and execute it with vigor.   _____

Total   _____

Exhibit 6.1.   Value Quotient Worksheet: Fight Complacency.
Key: 5 = excellent; 4 = very good; 3 = good; 2 = fair; 1 = poor; 0 = not applicable.

be specific scores for each tactic. Although assigning these scores requires judgment, they should be calibrated by comparing the scores with the Value Leaders and other best-of-breed competitors.

Scores for each tactic range from excellent (five) to poor (one). If an organization does not perform the tactic at all, it receives a score of zero. To calculate the activity scores, the analyst can average the scores for the tactics supporting that activity and round the average to the nearest whole number. To illustrate how a score might be assigned for a specific tactic, consider the tactic "Plan for succession at least five years before the CEO's planned retirement date." If your company has no succession plan, it would receive a score of zero. On the other hand, if your company has recently completed a succession plan that includes, say, five experienced internal candidates for the CEO position ranked by their degree of readiness as well as five candidates for each of their jobs, similarly analyzed, then it would receive a score of five.

CONCLUSION

Fighting complacency is essential for a company's long-term vitality. Although mediocre companies can survive, they eventually become zombies. They lose their best people, and the most desirable customers defect to companies with more interest in offering better value. Fighting complacency starts with the right CEO. But that CEO must keep the pressure on employees to resist the siren song of success and reach for ever higher levels of performance relative to customer needs and competitor strategies. The good news for executives is that the tools for fighting complacency are not so difficult to employ once management is determined to use them.

CHAPTER SEVEN

Profit Is Vital

(Win Through Multiple Means)

T he principle "Win through multiple means" is an approach to strategy that enables a company to sustain market leadership. Winning through multiple means enables executives to develop sound strategies based on research into the three foundation stones of strategy: customers, capabilities, and competitors. Winning through multiple means flows from three activities: understanding the customer, building diverse capabilities, and sustaining competitive superiority. In order to sustain market leadership, companies that win through multiple means must maintain a continuous flow of accurate information about changes in these three foundation stones. As long as a winning company remains alert to these changes and adapts effectively to them, it is likely to sustain its market leadership.

LINK WITH VALUE LEADERSHIP

Winning through multiple means creates value for many of a company's stakeholders. First, it creates value for customers over a long period of time because the company keeps improving the quality of its products or services in order to stay ahead of competitors. This commitment to superior value in turn provides a compelling reason for customers to make repeat purchases which can increase the profitability of each customer relationship insofar as the customer loyalty cuts the cost of customer churn. Second, winning through multiple means creates value for employees because winning inspires employees to exert themselves to solve customer problems. Winning motivates employees to keep winning. Third, winning through multiple means creates value for suppliers because a market-leading firm generally increases the volume of its purchases. For most suppliers, the marginal benefits exceed the costs. Benefits include the ability to predict demand, to plan capacity increments, and to attract more customers because the supplier works with a market leader. Costs may include customers demanding lower unit prices and collocation of facilities. Finally, a market leaders' shareholders benefit from the higher profits generated from the use of their capital.

ECONOMIC BENEFITS

Winning through multiple means leads to superior results. For example, the eight Value Leaders who win through multiple means earned average five year net margins over twice their industry averages and grew sales 35 percent faster over the same 1997 to 2002 period. Specifically, the eight Value Leaders earned average five year net margins of 16.7 percent compared to 8.0 percent for their respective industries. And the Value Leaders' five year sales growth was 16.5 percent as compared to 12.2 percent for their industries. While Value Leaders' superior growth and profitability are due to several factors, winning through multiple means is clearly an important one.

CASES

The chapter brings the principle of winning through multiple means to life by presenting case studies and extracting lessons from them. It details how Goldman Sachs dominates the market for emerging-market debt by outperforming competitors in the way it meets seven specific requirements of customers in that market. The chapter also relates how Goldman decided it wanted to increase its share of the junk bond market and proceeded to assemble the capabilities needed to do so, spurred by the hiring of a leading market maker from competitor Bear Stearns. Chapter Eight contrasts Goldman's success with

Merrill Lynch's steady loss of leadership in initial public offerings (IPOs) due to its failure to sufficiently cultivate relationships with institutional investors. It continues with a discussion of how MBNA has been able to sustain its strong credit card market position through diverse capabilities that enable the company to expand profitably into new markets while limiting its risks from competitive attack in its existing markets. The chapter continues with an examination of Southwest Airlines, whose ability to hire and manage team-oriented and capable individuals enables it to develop new ideas that keep Southwest ahead of competitors seeking to replicate its strategy. The chapter concludes with a case study of J. C. Penney's ongoing efforts to turn itself around with the techniques we will now explore.

ACTIVITY ANALYSIS

Winning through multiple means enables executives to develop sound strategies based on research into the three foundation stones of strategy: customers, capabilities, and competitors. Winning through multiple means flows from three activities:

- **Understand the customer.** Executives must initiate strategy development by understanding the specific criteria that customers use to choose among various competitors' products.
- **Build diverse capabilities.** Executives should next assemble the capabilities to outperform competitors in many different functions and in diverse product or market segments.
- **Sustain competitive superiority.** Executives must stay ahead of scrambling competitors by analyzing their strategies and coming up with new ways to keep ahead of them in the struggle to win business from customers.

Understand the Customer

Executives aspiring to lead their industries must understand their customers at a fine level of granularity. This means that executives must gather information about their customers from many different perspectives and with increasing frequency. Specifically, aspiring market leaders must understand the overall size and growth rate and key trends of their markets as well as detailed differences in buying behavior among small segments of target customers. Executives must understand these differences to retain their existing customers and win over potential customers. Furthermore, aspiring market leaders must recognize that a slice-in-time market research report is only a useful starting point. Only by maintaining a near-constant flow of feedback from customers—through tracking purchases, analyzing customer service, and collecting feedback—can executives maintain the level of vigilance needed to stay ahead of competitors.

Competitive battles are won and lost on the basis of how well companies meet the specific purchase criteria of their customers. Such criteria vary by product and by customer group. For example, a middle-income purchaser of a car with two elementary school students would have different purchase criteria than an affluent teenager purchasing her first car. The family car purchaser might be concerned primarily with the car's safety record, seating space per passenger, price, and cost of maintenance, whereas the teenager might care most about the car's appeal to her school friends, its color, and how quickly its windows moved up and down.

To understand the customer, executives may use the following tactics:

• *Assemble representative customers within the relevant market segments.* It is often useful to assemble groups of early adopters within a market segment because they tend to be interested in trying new products and because they enjoy being seen as experts by their more numerous fellow customers in the mass market.

• *Ask the customers to list and rank the criteria they use to consider purchases among competing products.* By conducting individual interviews with customers in the target market segments, executives should seek an understanding of the specific criteria the customers use to select among competing products within the category. Executives should ask the customers to describe the criteria in ways that are easy to measure and to offer their ranking of the relative importance of the criteria in making the purchase.

• *Ask them to articulate how well the company's products satisfy the customer purchase criteria relative to competitors'.* Executives should then ask customers to articulate how well the various companies' products perform relative to these purchase criteria. Such an analysis can expose opportunities for a new entrant to take market share.

Goldman Sachs has applied these tactics in several situations in which it was seeking to establish dominance in a new market. When Goldman sets its sites on a new market, it conducts careful analysis, not wanting to risk its hard-earned reputation and capital on a new market unless Goldman feels that it will be better off. The company researches the needs of customers in the new market and seeks out vulnerabilities both in its own capabilities and those of its competitors. It then figures out whether it can close the gaps in its own capabilities, potentially by hiring from outside, in order to assemble an industry-beating set of capabilities.

Goldman's dominance in the market for trading emerging-market debt illustrates the usefulness of this analysis. According to the *Banker,* Goldman Sachs outperforms its peers in satisfying the most critical customer purchase criteria of emerging-market debt managers. The publication polled debt managers from twenty-six countries, asking them to score emerging-market debt traders Goldman Sachs, JP Morgan, Salomon Smith Barney, Deutsche Bank, BNP Paribas, Credit Suisse First Boston, and Morgan Stanley. Senior debt managers rated banks on a four-point scale from excellent (four) to poor (one) on seven criteria:

- Ability to provide new and innovative ways of funding
- Speed and efficiency of execution
- Depth of distribution
- Support for bonds in the aftermarket
- Skill in working in difficult market conditions
- Straightforwardness and ability to deal with the customer
- Skill at arranging meetings and presentations with investors

Goldman was the winner overall. However, as Table 7.1 illustrates, it did not come out as the best in all categories.[1]

For example, in what most issuers consider one of the key categories, the ability to provide new and innovative ways of funding, Goldman was ranked second, with a score of 3.75, behind Deutsche Bank and Salomon Smith Barney, which tied for first with 3.8 each. In the area of skill in working in difficult market conditions, Goldman placed seventh with 2.75 points, while Salomon was first with 3.4. Deutsche won in the category of depth of distribution with a score of 3.4, compared with 3.25 for Goldman.

Goldman attributes its leadership to its ability to innovate. John McIntire, Goldman's managing director and cohead of Latin America, noted that in 1996 the company introduced an innovative

Criteria	Goldman Rank	Goldman Score	Leader	Leader Score
Overall score	First	3.27	-	-
Meeting and presentation skills	First	3.60	-	-
Execution speed and efficiency	Fourth	3.20	JP Morgan	3.40
New and innovative funding	Second	3.75	Deutsche Bank	3.80
Skill in difficult markets	Seventh	2.75	Salomon Smith Barney	3.40
Depth of distribution	Second	3.25	Deutsche Bank	3.40
Straightforward or easy to deal with	Second	3.30	BNP Paribas	3.40
Support for bids after market	Third	3.10	Credit Suisse First Boston	3.50

Table 7.1.   Customer Ranking of Emerging-Market Debt Trading: Goldman Sachs.

Source: "Goldman Sachs Dominates in Emerging Markets," *Banker,* Aug. 1, 2001, p. 49.

debt-trading scheme called the Brady exchange. McIntire said Goldman was positioning itself to compete for the next phase of financing emerging markets, which he believes will resemble the current market for developed-market debt. Specifically, he expects emerging markets to seek more active management of interest rates and currencies. McIntire also believes that Goldman will be able to sustain its lead into the future due to its foreign exchange, derivatives, and commodities operations. Finally, he attributes Goldman's leadership to senior relationships in emerging markets, macroeconomic research, integrated capital markets, syndication, and distribution.[2]

Given Goldman's internal emphasis on winning, this slice-in-time report card for Goldman's position in emerging-market debt offers mixed lessons. The analysis itself is the starting point for executives aspiring to market leadership. It reveals the purchase criteria that customers use to select among competing suppliers. But the analysis leaves open several important issues. First, the seven criteria are not explicitly ranked. For the criteria to be of most use, customers should rank the purchase criteria and allocate one hundred points among them, placing the most points on the most important criterion. Such ranking would explain why Goldman was top-ranked overall despite its failure to win on all the criteria. Second, given Goldman's desire to remain in the lead, this analysis reveals significant opportunities for improvement. The ranking of the decision criteria might help Goldman to focus its improvement efforts on criteria most likely to help it sustain its leadership position.

The ability to use insights into customer purchase processes to enhance market position is a crucial element of winning through multiple means. Executives must have the intellectual humility to recognize that the customer's perception of weakness in certain decision criteria represents opportunities for improvement. However, it is not always immediately obvious what action to take to improve the customer's perception. For example, Goldman was ranked seventh in its skill in difficult markets. What could Goldman do to improve its ranking in that area? Did it need to move more experienced people into the department? Did it need to adopt different policies to cope with difficult market conditions? Or did it need to widen its base of investors who could share the risk under such conditions?

Goldman has demonstrated its ability to improve its market position, thereby resolving such questions. Its hunger for a share of a lucrative new market drove it to take three strategic initiatives. First, Goldman talked to customers in the market that it aspired to dominate. In so doing, Goldman learned that potential customers perceived it as lacking the depth of commitment needed to serve their needs. In fact, customers saw Goldman as having such a blue-chip reputation that customers were concerned that serving them would somehow be at odds with the company's culture. Second, Goldman initiated a hiring program to attract a raft of professionals perceived as being able to bring a significant chunk of new business to the company due to customers' perceptions that these individuals had the skills needed to serve customer needs well. Third, Goldman created an organizational home for these new hires that would enable them to excel at serving customers while being embraced by the Goldman culture. And finally, it communicated its newly acquired capabilities and commitment to potential customers in order to start the process of winning them over.

For example, in the late 1990s, Goldman used this approach to improve its market position in junk bonds. According to the *Wall Street Journal,* Goldman's ambitions for market leadership in junk bonds were so strong that it decided to hire a junk-bond–market kingpin as a partner to spearhead its efforts. In 1999 Goldman prided itself on being the top-ranked underwriter of U.S. stock issues, first in merger and advisory deals, and the leader in initial public stock offerings. To its disappointment, Goldman's rank in the market for issuing high yield was fifth, behind smaller rival and market leader Donaldson, Lufkin & Jenrette (DLJ). Although Goldman had moved up from eighth in 1997, it had not been a significant participant even as the junk-bond market had doubled in size between 1996 and 1999.[3]

Goldman understood that potential customers did not consider it to be very committed to the market. To address this concern, Goldman decided to raise its profile in the industry by investing significantly in hiring a high-profile executive and sponsoring a conference on junk bonds for key issuers and investors. In September 1999 Goldman hired David Solomon, cohead of investment banking at Bear Stearns, to join Robert O'Shea at Goldman as cohead of global high-yield and bank business. To raise its profile among both issuers and investors, Goldman hosted eight hundred people at an October 1999 conference at the Venetian Resort Hotel in Las Vegas, Nevada. Grateful attendees listened to presentations from 130 high-yield issuers and were entertained by Cirque du Soleil and Jay Leno.

The conference did change potential customers' perceptions of Goldman's commitment to the junk-bond market. One portfolio manager who attended the three-day conference said that it was something he expected from DLJ, not Goldman. Marc Rowland, CFO of oil and gas producer Chesapeake Energy of Oklahoma City, had previously issued $730 million of junk bonds through Bear Stearns. Rowland remarked that prior to the conference, he never would have thought of approaching Goldman to handle junk bonds. The conference opened Rowland's mind to just such a possibility.

Goldman's hiring of Solomon, who generated millions of dollars in high-yield deals for Bear Stearns, was only the most visible of many hires it made to beef up its junk-bond–market position. Others include Roger Gordon, former head of high-yield research at DLJ; Mark Rose, telecommunications junk-bond analyst from Credit Suisse First Boston; and Dirk van Doren, a former high-yield and equity analyst at Bear Stearns specializing in energy companies. Harry Resis, high-yield portfolio manager at Scudder Kemper Investments, noted that Goldman's hiring of Solomon sent a strong signal to the junk-bond industry that Goldman was not only serious about aspiring to market leadership but that it was among a small number of firms that could actually achieve market leadership.

Goldman's deep pockets enabled it to offer a compensation package for Solomon, including stock options, estimated at several million dollars a year. Goldman anticipated that a larger share of the high-yield market would more than offset its investments in Solomon and his new colleagues, while Solomon looked forward to repeating the fun he had developing Bear Stearns's junk-bond business by building a premium brand in the junk-bond market at Goldman.

Goldman's initiatives to enhance its junk-bond market position hinged on its strength in certain geographic markets and its ability to coordinate the work of its junk-bond and mergers and acquisitions (M&A) departments. Solomon and O'Shea noted that junk-bond issuers wanted to deal with firms with global capabilities. In 1999 Goldman grabbed the largest share of new-issue underwriting in Europe's then-growing junk-bond market. From Goldman's European success, Solomon and O'Shea learned that its ability to win junk-bond underwriting assignments grew out of M&A roles. O'Shea saw this trend emerging in the United States as well. For example, in October 1999 Goldman advised the now-bankrupt telecommunications firm Global Crossing on its $1.65 billion proposed acquisition of the telecom unit of Britain's Racal Electronics. Later that month, that M&A advisory role helped Goldman win the competition to manage a $765 million bank loan to finance the transaction. Dan Cohrs, Global Crossing's CFO at the time, noted that until recently he would not have thought that Goldman was capable of participating in the financing of such transactions.[4]

Other junk-bond–market trends played into Goldman's strengths. Companies themselves, rather than leveraged buyout firms, have begun to issue junk bonds. Because Goldman traditionally had stronger relationships with companies than with these firms, this shift to issuing corporate junk bonds played into Goldman's traditional strengths. The company also benefited from an increase in the proportion of junk-bond transactions that took place across borders, playing into Goldman's strong presence in Europe and Asia.

Finally, Goldman responded to another critical junk-bond–market requirement—the willingness to seek business from smaller companies. Although Goldman had traditionally been known for its large, prestigious clients, it began seeking out junk-bond business from smaller clients in the $300 million to $500 million revenue range, for example, Argosy Gaming, which attended Goldman's junk-bond conference. Dale Black, Argosy's CFO, pointed out that Argosy would not have been among Goldman clientele prior to its focus on gaining share in the junk-bond market. Elaine Stokes, a high-yield trader at Loomis Sayles in Boston, said that Goldman had always attempted to make a market in junk bonds, even when other investment banks would not respond to her requests to trade in them. Scudder's Resis said that his evaluation of Goldman's commitment to the junk-bond business had improved substantially. Goldman's willingness to do what was needed to take junk-bond market share had impressed Resis.[5]

As a consequence of its 1999 strategic initiatives, Goldman increased the size of its junk-bond business significantly. According to *Thomson Financial,* Goldman was ranked third in the global high-yield underwriting market in 2000 and 2001, up from fifth place in 1999. Specifically, Goldman underwrote $10 billion in high-yield bonds from thirty-nine issued in 2001 and $6.6 billion from twenty-four issues in 2000.[6] Although Goldman's goal of leadership in the junk-bond market remained elusive, its increased volume of underwriting junk bonds most likely far exceeded the costs it incurred to generate that volume increase.

Goldman's progress in gaining junk-bond market share reveals the importance of understanding the customer. Goldman's ambition for greater market share enabled it to engage in several acts of intellectual humility. First, it recognized that potential junk-bond clients did not perceive that it was a significant player in the junk-bond market. In response to this recognition of weakness, Goldman hired from the outside an executive who had the stature in the junk-bond market that the company needed to jump-start its drive to increase its share of the market. In order to overcome the challenge that Solomon would face in being accepted within the company's culture, Goldman paired him with a Goldman executive, O'Shea. Second, Goldman recognized that it needed to take a dramatic step to communicate to potential customers its new commitment to junk bonds, so it sponsored the Las Vegas conference. Third, Goldman executed a strategy that built on insights into the emerging requirements of junk-bond clients. The company was well positioned, for example, to address the junk-bond market's need to wed M&A with junk-bond issuance and to conduct cross-border transactions. Ultimately, Goldman's market share gains in junk bonds reflect its willingness to identify and overcome its weaknesses in delivering the capabilities that its target customers demanded.

The failure to overcome such weaknesses leads to the opposite result: lost market share. Indifference to their changing needs leads customers to seek out suppliers who care about these needs and are willing to invest to meet them. In many cases a firm that has achieved some level of success begins to pay less attention to erosion in market share, particularly in a line of work that accounts for a relatively low proportion of its overall business.

In some cases Merrill Lynch occasionally suffered due to its failure to understand and adapt to changing customer needs. At times Merrill felt very comfortable discounting the significance of changes in the market. Its overall business was doing fairly well, so the weaker performance of one unit did not receive much management attention. Merrill's management did not focus on understanding the changing needs of its customers until it became very obvious that its inattention was allowing huge amounts of revenue to go to its more responsive competitors. Merrill's very success in selling stocks through brokers blinded it to changes in the market that did not immediately affect its brokers' commission levels.

The decline of Merrill Lynch's share of the initial public offering (IPO) underwriting market in the late 1990s reveals the dangers of losing touch with the changing needs of customers. According to the *Dow Jones Online News,* Merrill's loss of IPO market share resulted from its relatively weak capabilities in institutional trading, a critical requirement for developing the distribution skill needed to attract new IPO underwriting customers. Specifically, Merrill's share of the IPO market fell to 12.9 percent in 1997—second behind top-ranked Goldman Sachs—from 19.2 percent in 1993 when it was ranked number one in IPO underwriting.[7]

Part of Merrill's market share decline is attributable to the popularity of high-yielding real estate investment trusts and closed-end bond funds, which individual investors liked in 1993 because they had relatively high yields when interest rates had fallen sharply. By contrast, in 1996 and 1997, much IPO business was in technology, a historically weak area for Merrill. Although Merrill's 4.7 percent share of 1997 technology IPOs was higher than its 1993 share, Merrill fell far behind the market leader Goldman Sachs, which gained 12.4 percent of 1997's technology IPO market.

Merrill's market share erosion could be explained in part by its weakness in technology, but its deeper problem is that one of its self-defined strengths—its retail franchise—was a weakness in the IPO market. Through its tens of thousands of retail brokers, Merrill had a significant retail distribution capability. During the late 1990s, however, it became apparent that the key to gaining IPO market share was building strong relationships with institutional investors.

Between 1993 and 1997, for example, most major institutional firms increased their share of the IPO market while retail firms lost IPO share. Goldman's share popped to 15.4 percent in 1997 from 10.4 percent in 1993; Credit Suisse First Boston's share rose to 5.5 percent from 2.8 percent during the same period; and DLJ boosted its IPO market share to 4.9 percent from 3.8 percent. During the same period, retail firms saw their IPO market share shrink. Salomon Smith Barney's market share fell to 4.6 percent in 1997 from 9.5 percent in 1993; PaineWebber Group, which held an 8 percent share in 1993, had 1 percent in 1997; and Prudential Securities, which had a 2.9 percent share in 1993, only had 2.2 percent in 1997.[8]

Merrill was unable to respond effectively to this change in customer needs. Institutional investors helped increase demand for IPOs because the institutions made so much money "flipping" IPO shares on the first day of trading. Between 1995 and 2000, for example, the stock price of companies conducting IPOs would increase 100 percent or more on the first day. Institutional investors, who brought huge fees to the investment banks for trading stocks, were rewarded for this business by receiving shares of IPOs at the pre-IPO price. The institutions would then turn around and sell these shares on the day of the offering in the secondary market at prices that were double or higher than the prices that they had paid earlier in the day. Institutional demand for such easy money was virtually unlimited during this period. A company seeking to raise money in the IPO markets thus needed to do business with an investment bank that could bring such institutional investors to the table.

Its perceived strength among retail investors hurt Merrill in the IPO market of the late 1990s. Its strength among retail investors may have led it to focus on the "wrong" customer for the IPO market. To succeed in that market, Merrill needed to adapt to the changing needs of the small companies seeking to raise capital through IPOs. If it had focused on the needs of these companies rather than those of the retail investors, it might have invested more heavily in building an institutional capability. Clearly, the investment banks with such capabilities reaped a growing share of IPO underwriting during this lucrative period. Merrill's failure to meet the need of the right customers—as some of its competitors had done—cost it significant profit.

Understanding the customer is a crucial starting point for winning through multiple means. Goldman's ability to understand the subtle interplay between customer needs and its own capabilities contributed greatly to its ability to lead in emerging-market debt and to enhance its share of the high-yield bond market. Merrill's inattention to significant changes in who the real IPO market customer was caused it to lose its market leadership. These case studies suggest that executives aspiring to market leadership must remain vigilant in three areas. First, they must track changes in relative market position among competitors and understand the underlying reasons for the changes. Such changes may reveal shifts in the locus of buying power. Second, executives must conduct in-depth market research to pinpoint specific customer purchase criteria, ranking the criteria and learning how their firm stacks up in the eyes of customers. Finally, aspiring market leaders must overcome the natural tendency to ignore bad news emerging from such analysis and be willing to take substantive action to overcome weaknesses.

Build Diverse Capabilities

Although understanding the customer is a crucial first step for gaining market share, aspiring market leaders must choose carefully the capabilities that they use to battle for the customer. Such companies understand that challengers will analyze how they sustain market leadership so that the challengers can neutralize their competitive advantages. Over the long run, market leaders realize that they cannot keep competitors from finding out how they conduct business so successfully. As a result, the only way that they can hope to protect their market share is by making it difficult for competitors to replicate their capabilities.

One way to do this is by building diverse capabilities, outperforming competitors in many different functions and in diverse product or market segments. Building diverse capabilities means that, for example, an airline, such as Southwest Airlines, beats competitors through its choice of many activities including the airports where it locates its gates, the airplane models it flies, the level of its food service, its low ticket prices, its quick gate turnaround times, and its unique hiring practices.

If the company outperforms competitors in many different activities, then established or upstart competitors have far more difficulty replicating the strategy. Established competitors find it hard to copy diverse capability-based strategies because the established companies believe that the cost of copying the strategy will exceed the incremental profits. Upstart competitors who try to replicate the strategy may find that the diverse capability-based competitor has locked up some of the best competitive "real estate." For example, an upstart trying to compete with Southwest might find that the market leader has already locked up gates at the best airports for its strategy or that the ability to hire and develop the right people is far more difficult to achieve in practice than it appears on the surface.

Building diverse capabilities pertains not only to the skills required to compete but to the scope of competition. It means that the diverse skills enable a company to compete in several distinct market segments where these skills are valuable competitive weapons. The benefit of competing in diverse markets is that a loss of share in one such segment would not damage the entire business as long as the operations of the other segments were sufficiently independent of the damaged segment. Thus, building diverse capabilities requires a detailed understanding of how a company's capabilities can facilitate competition in different market segments and how to bolster the barriers protecting those segments from damage to any one segment.

Executives seeking the benefits of building diverse capabilities may consider the following tactics:

• *Understand incumbent strengths and weaknesses in meeting customer needs.* Executives can gain this understanding by referring to the customer evaluation of competitors discussed earlier. For competitors whose products rank most highly on the key customer purchase criteria, executives should analyze the key capabilities required to deliver this superior performance. Executives should also seek insight into how these companies perform these capabilities so well.

• *Assess how well the company performs the activities needed to outperform competitors in satisfying unmet customer needs.* Using the insight into competitor capabilities, a company's executives must conduct a strategic audit of its own capabilities to assess how well the company performs these activities relative to incumbents. This analysis can help executives determine their company's strengths and weaknesses relative to incumbents.

• *Close the capability gap by hiring, acquiring, or partnering.* Executives could then determine whether the company's weaknesses could be bolstered. If so, executives could initiate a search process that would begin by identifying the world's best performers—corporations and their key employees—of the desired capabilities. Executives could rank these performers based on their potential fit and their willingness to merge (if companies) or to switch employers (in the case of key employees). Depending on a cost-benefit analysis, executives could conclude this process by acquiring the company with the best position in the desired capability or hiring the key employees who could best close the capability gap.

• *Make the capabilities difficult for competitors to copy.* Executives must not merely match the capabilities of competitors in their target market. They must develop capabilities that customers will perceive as measurably superior and that competitors will find difficult to copy due to some barrier to entry such as a patent or some complex know-how.

MBNA used these four tactics in building its business. First, it defined the market in a way that would favor its strengths. By doing so, it did not need to worry about competitors quickly replicating its strategy and taking market share. Second, MBNA bolstered its initial advantages by investing in technology to generate new customers more efficiently and to retain the most profitable customers by offering them better customer service. Third, it chose to expand its business geographically into markets where potential customers would view MBNA's strengths as offering them superior value.

MBNA's pattern of profitable growth reflects this approach. *American Banker* attributes MBNA's profitable growth to its diverse capabilities, from which it draws competitive advantage in multiple market segments. Spun off from parent MNC Financial in 1991, MBNA had distributed its cards to members of twenty-eight hundred affinity groups such as the American Dental Association by 1993. By winning endorsements for its cards from professional associations, alumni organizations, recreational clubs, and smaller banks and thrifts, the company emerged as the United States' third-largest issuer of MasterCard and Visa cards.[9]

MBNA's competitors could not match its diverse capabilities in the affinity business. Whereas its competitors sent mail solicitations to an unscreened list of potential customers, MBNA marketed to the U.S.'s most creditworthy customers by targeting the 105 million members of its affinity partners. Chuck Cawley, MBNA's CEO, pointed out that the company targeted members of affiliate groups that have settled down in life and are likely to use credit cards responsibly. Its choice of target customers helped shield it from forces that hurt competitors, such as pressures on rates and fees, diminished consumer confidence, and new competitors from outside the banking industry. In 1992, for example, MBNA's income rose 14 percent, to $149 million, while its late payments and loan losses stayed well below industry averages.

In addition to MBNA's careful targeting of affiliate group customers, its success was also attributable to its ability to manage risks differently than traditional banks. According to former MBNA chairman Alfred

Lerner, the company grew by taking "zillions" of very small risks instead of a handful of very large risks as traditional banks do.[10] As a result, in 1992 MBNA's loan losses averaged 3.33 percent of total loans, well below the 5.7 percent that the five largest issuers of Visa cards experienced and better than the total issuer loss average of 4.9 percent.

Furthermore, MBNA succeeded in attracting customers whose ability to pay back credit card debt was superior to those of competitors' customers. For example, the average 1993 MBNA customer was a homeowner who earned $55,000 a year, had been steadily employed for fifteen years, and had paid bills on time for fourteen years. Furthermore, that customer generated higher-than-industry-average fees for the company. That customer's average account balance was $2,166, compared with $1,419 for the industry, and conducted thirty-eight transactions a year, versus thirty for the average bank card holder.

MBNA achieved these superior customer demographics as a consequence of two key sources of advantage: its upscale affinity partners and its credit culture. Its process for screening applications is an important element of its credit culture. Each MBNA application is screened both by a computer and a credit analyst. MBNA's employees are genuinely interested in ensuring that they attract the best customers for their company. In 1992 its credit card loans grew 15 percent. MBNA added 630 new organizations to its affinity group list and 1.5 million new cardholders to its customer base. In 1993 it sought agreements with another six hundred targeted groups. Although MBNA expected to expand overseas, considerable growth opportunities arose from thousands of U.S. graduates entering the medical, teaching, law, and dental professions who became eligible for membership in some of the one hundred university alumni clubs with which MBNA had partnerships.

Cawley, who closed MBNA's first affiliate marketing deal with his alma mater, Georgetown University, excelled at giving up less to the affinity group and getting more from the group than most competitors. Banks typically pay an affinity partner a small royalty for the right to sell a custom-designed credit card to its members. Group members use the card for the benefit of the group and also because some groups pay MBNA's annual fee for them. Stephen Szekely, a vice president at consulting firm Payment Systems, believes that MBNA cuts more favorable affiliate deals than competitors because it gets more of the affiliate organization's members to sign up for a card.

MBNA's ability to convert thousands of affiliate members into credit card holders is exemplified in the work it has done for Penn

State. By 1993, for example, MBNA had signed up eighty thousand card accounts for alumni of Pennsylvania State University, a relationship that began in 1989. According to Cawley, Penn State used another bank for three years prior to signing up with MBNA. This bank had a mere fifteen thousand accounts. MBNA achieved superior results through person-to-person selling. It rented booths at annual conventions and sent sales representatives to picnics and other gatherings. It expected its salespeople to attend eleven hundred such events in 1993, personally handing out card applications.

Beyond its strengths in marketing and sales, MBNA drew on still other capabilities to sustain its market leadership. It controlled marketing costs; it had a low rate of customer attrition; and it kept its staff happy so that they provided good customer service. Its in-house advertising staff was unusually productive, mailing 70 million direct-mail marketing pieces in 1993, while making 10 million phone calls through its telemarketing unit. In 1993 all MBNA cards carried an annual fee and an average annual percentage rate of 17.3 percent. Nevertheless, MBNA's customer attrition rate was 6 percent, half of the industry average. Cawley said that customers keep MBNA cards because they generally carry higher credit limits than competitive cards offer. Finally, by providing better customer service than do competitors, MBNA keeps more customers happy. All its employees attend a "customer college" when they start work to learn how to serve customers well. Signs and slogans reinforce the value of service and teamwork. And morale is surprisingly high.[11] Happy MBNA employees make for happy MBNA customers.

Four years later, the company had applied its diverse capabilities to new markets. The result was impressive growth coming from the value that the new markets placed on MBNA's capabilities. According to *U.S. Banker,* the company was able to generate significant growth in three markets that valued its skills. According to Cawley, these three businesses fit with MBNA's criteria for picking new businesses: the product can be delivered through the mail and serviced by telephone.[12]

MBNA's first new market was outside the United States. In 1997 it did business in the United Kingdom, had received approval to operate in Ireland, and was marketing in Canada. Cawley noted that MBNA's international business generated $2 billion of profitable receivables operating out of a fully chartered bank in Chester, England. By 2002, Cawley anticipated that the business in the United Kingdom, Ireland, and Canada could grow to between $5 billion and $7 billion in loans.

MBNA's second new business was consumer finance. In 1995 it placed its consumer finance operation into a separate division that by 1997 had generated $4 billion worth of unsecured installment loans, home equity loans, and second-mortgage loans. Cawley expected that business to grow to between $10 billion and $12 billion by 2002.

MBNA's third growth market was insurance. By 1997, MBNA was licensed to provide insurance in thirty-eight states, and by the end of 1997 it was licensed in fifty states. It operated an insurance agency in partnership with TIG, which performed insurance underwriting; MBNA provided all other insurance services. In 1997 Cawley anticipated $100 million in premiums, growing to exceed $1 billion by 2002. MBNA sold credit life insurance and automobile insurance. Cawley believed that the overlap in capabilities required to sell and service credit cards and insurance helped make insurance a profitable business for MBNA. For example, when consumers telephoned its customer satisfaction department, 30 percent agreed to receive a quote from its insurance division if the customer service agent prompted them. Cawley noted that with 20 million credit card customers, he anticipated that he could sell approximately 6 million insurance policies.

By 2002 Cawley anticipated that these three new markets would make up 30 percent of MBNA's pretax income.

In addition to growth from these new markets, Cawley still saw significant growth potential from affinity sales. According to Cawley, in 1997 55 percent of all U.S. physicians carried MBNA's card, representing another 45 percent who did not and might potentially do so. Furthermore, 25 percent of nurses, 36 percent of lawyers, 27 percent of engineers, and 60 percent of dentists carried the MBNA card, leaving significant swaths of the market open for potential growth. Cawley noted that MBNA's business was diversified into ten market sectors, each with marketing and advertising departments that address those sectors, such as sports marketing, professional marketing, and colleges and universities. In each of these sectors, MBNA was growing faster in 1997 than in 1996.[13]

MBNA's remarkable success reveals general principles about the value of building diverse capabilities. First, these capabilities help the company do a better job than competitors at meeting customer needs. MBNA's skill at marketing to affinity groups and their members helps the affinity groups attract and retain members by offering a service whose benefit to the affinity group and its members exceeds its cost. MBNA's credit culture helps limit its population of cardholders to individuals who are willing to pay a higher interest rate in exchange for a bigger credit limit. Its ability to deliver excellent customer service helps MBNA retain a higher proportion of the most desirable customers by minimizing their dissatisfaction with the company and reducing the moments of frustration that might cause them to leave. Building diverse capabilities helps aspiring market leaders because it helps them outperform competitors at meeting customer needs.

Second, building diverse capabilities is most effective if these are difficult for competitors to copy. Competitors persistently had trouble doing as good a job as MBNA at affiliate marketing, credit analysis, pricing, and customer service. MBNA's competitive superiority emerged from the detailed business processes that it had developed to enable its thousands of employees to perform these activities consistently. It was careful to reveal to competitors neither the details of these processes nor the underlying technology that enabled its employees to perform these activities consistently. The details of the processes and the enabling technologies—such as its systems for targeting direct-marketing strategies to maximize yield or its technologies to help customers resolve service problems most efficiently—constituted enormous barriers to replication for competitors. It was almost impossible for competitors to learn all the details of MBNA's processes and to build the processes and technologies needed to produce competitive outcomes for customers.

Finally, MBNA was able to apply its diverse capabilities to other markets. It identified attractive markets in which its core capabilities would enable it to generate new revenues and profits. Just as important, MBNA stayed away from markets that did not satisfy its criteria. As a result, it upped its odds of earning an attractive return from new market entry. Furthermore, its success in building profitable positions in these new markets helped diversify MBNA's profit. By minimizing the company's dependence on any single business segment, management was able to protect MBNA shareholders from risks such as the loss of market share to new competitors or a sudden decline in growth.

Sustain Competitive Superiority

If market leaders do not stay ahead of competitors scrambling to catch up, then they lose their leadership. In this context, a company's strategy can be thought of as a city built on the ruins of previous generations. A company will develop an initial strategy to get itself off the ground. With the advent of competitive challenges, advances in technology, and changing customer needs, the company's initial strategy ceases to work. So the company develops a new strategy built on the foundation of the ruins of the old one. The company continues the elements of the old strategy that work and experiments to find new strategy elements that help it compete in the new environment. After a while, the new strategy begins to lose its power, and the cycle begins anew.

Although a founding entrepreneur is likely to be able to put in place the initial strategy, subsequent generations of strategy must emerge from ideas generated, in part, by the people that the entrepreneur hires. As a company becomes bigger, the founding entrepreneur reaches the limit of his or her ability to collect and analyze—without the help of others—the huge quantities of data needed to recast the firm's strategy. To sustain competitive superiority, the role of the founding entrepreneur must shift from that of chief strategist to organization builder.

The entrepreneur must build an organization that can do a better job than competitors at meeting the evolving needs of customers. Such an organization must attract people who do the company's jobs as well—or better—than the founding entrepreneur could do them. To sustain competitive superiority, the entrepreneur must build an organization that can come up with ever improved notions of how to win customers, coupled with the drive and ability to turn those ideas into the daily actions of tens of thousands of employees.

Executives seeking to sustain competitive superiority may use the following tactics:

• *Hire employees who can make improvements that create customer value.* With customer needs, competitor strategies, and technologies changing rapidly, a company that keeps doing what it was doing in the past is likely to fall behind. To stay in the lead, it needs to hire people who can analyze these changes and develop new products and processes that continue to keep the company in the lead. To hire such employees, executives should use their most innovative employees as recruiters and develop interview questions and situations that test potential employees for their skills at solving unstructured problems in creative ways.

• *Create an environment that encourages these employees to take the initiative.* Having hired such employees, companies must take care to create a work environment that encourages them to take the initiative to identify the right problems to be solved and to conceive and execute effective solutions.

• *Gather feedback from customers to find out which initiatives worked.* Although the financial impact of product and process innovations is generally an effective measure of these employees' success, gathering feedback from customers to evaluate which innovations did the best job of satisfying customer needs in a competitively superior manner is also useful.

• *Reward the employees who implemented the winning initiatives.* Companies should reward employees who implement winning initiatives in ways that will motivate these employees to create further such innovations and will also encourage other employees to replicate what the winners did to earn their rewards.

Southwest Airlines exemplifies such an organization. As noted earlier, Southwest is the only airline that can boast thirty years of consistently profitable operation. It also leads in customer satisfaction, on-time performance, and cost-effectiveness. According to *Air Transport World,* by 2001 Southwest had won five Air Transport World awards, notably Airline of the Year in 1991, when it reported a profit unlike most all of its peers that year, and a Twenty Years of Excellence Award in 1993 for being the best short-haul airline. In May 1988 Southwest won its first Triple Crown—best on-time performance, best baggage handling, and fewest customer complaints—based on the U.S. Department of Transportation's monthly airline performance report. Between 1988 and 2001, Southwest captured over thirty monthly Triple Crowns and five annual Crowns. It also ranked first for four consecutive years for fewest customer complaints.[14]

Southwest epitomizes the principle of winning through multiple means. It wins by performing most airline activities—choosing airports and airplane models, hiring employees with certain personalities and providing them compensation, and maintaining its fleet—in a unique way. We will explore the specific advantages of Southwest's unique approach to performing each of these activities, but note that Southwest does all these things in order to survive and prosper in an intensely competitive environment. Because the airline fought numerous battles against competitors who tried to put it out of business many times, it came up with ways of operating that satisfied two tests. First, Southwest's procedures were very difficult for competitors to copy because copying them would undermine the competitor's basic mode of operating. Second, the procedures created significantly superior value for customers in the form of cheaper flights that were more pleasant, that is, on time and fun.

One of the most important advantages Southwest enjoys is that it operates a one-hop configuration, whereas its largest competitors use a hub and spoke configuration. The hub and spoke operation funnels large numbers of travelers to a big airport, such as Dallas/Fort Worth, where the travelers must wait—often for hours—until enough passengers arrive from other destinations to fill up the plane that will take them to their final destination. Hub and spoke airlines have higher costs because they have too many planes sitting on the runway for too long waiting for paying passengers to fill them. Southwest's one-hop approach eliminates the problem of empty planes because Southwest keeps its planes flying as often as possible, turning them at the gate in as little as twenty minutes. Although this one-hop configuration with shorter waiting times appealed initially to business travelers, it has since broadened to the growing proportion of travelers looking for a cheap way to get to their destination on time.

Unlike its peers, Southwest flies only one airplane model, the Boeing 737. This strategy makes employee training less expensive for Southwest because training pilots, maintenance staff, and flight attendants for only one plane model is cheaper than for the several that its competitors fly. Furthermore, the cost of maintaining and repairing one type of airplane is far less than that for multiple models. In 2001 the average age of Southwest's entire fleet was a relatively young 8.2 years. Its average trip length was a competitively short 492 miles; each Southwest aircraft flew about eight flights or twelve hours each day, very high use for a short-haul airplane.[15]

Southwest's high rate of airplane use contributed to a virtuous cycle relating to its low fares. By keeping its planes flying more than competitors, Southwest needed to fill up its planes each day with more passengers. It accomplished this by charging lower fares and delivering great customer service. In order to make a profit charging lower fares, Southwest had lower costs. In addition to the lower training and maintenance costs mentioned earlier, the airline saved money in four ways: (1) minimizing paper tickets (in 2000 30 percent of its revenue, $1.7 billion, was booked online), (2) not serving meals on planes (instead serving 90.9 million bags of peanuts and 7.3 million bags of raisins each year), and (3) flying out of smaller airports than its peers, and (4) eliminating assigned seats. The result of the low costs was that Southwest made a profit on lower fares. It invested the profits in new locations that attracted more flyers, which led to lower unit costs that Southwest could pass on to customers by further lowering fares.

The company also invested in capabilities that improved its customer's flying experience. It flew over one hundred Boeing 737-700s, which provided customers with more seat room (the space between seats, or seat pitch, ranged from thirty-three to thirty-four inches), no cabin dividers, and more overhead bin space.[16] Southwest also made flying fun. According to Southwest passenger Nancy Huseman, Southwest employees have the freedom and the personalities to make their flights a uniquely fun and comforting experience. In May 2002 Huseman chaperoned a group of students from Souhegan High School in New Hampshire to a Destination Imagination (a program to encourage teams of student to solve problems creatively) event in Knoxville, Tennessee. The group of high school juniors and seniors flew Southwest out of Manchester, New Hampshire. One of the students, Sam, an experienced flyer, asked the Southwest flight attendant if he could make the flight announcement about buckling seatbelts. The flight attendant denied Sam's request, instead offering to let Sam serve peanuts to the passengers.[17]

Sam took the microphone and joked to the passengers that they were fortunate to have VIPs serving their peanuts. He proceeded to read the ingredients on the back of the peanut package while his classmates served peanuts to the passengers. The passengers were delighted with Sam's antics and genuinely appreciated what he and his classmates were doing. At the end of the flight, the flight attendants told Sam and his classmates how well mannered they were and how much they appreciated their enthusiasm. The captain gave the students flight wings, and the flight attendants took photos of the students with the captains. As passengers left the plane, the flight attendants sang a song thanking the passengers for flying Southwest. As Huseman pointed out, only people with special personalities could have done what the Southwest flight attendants had done to make the flight so fun and so comforting.

Southwest's competitive advantages are no secret. In order to stay ahead of competitors, the organization works relentlessly to sustain its leadership. According to Donna Conover, executive vice president of customer service, Southwest thinks of itself as a customer service business that happens to be in the airline industry. Although this concept sounds simple, it has important implications for Southwest's ability to sustain its competitive advantages. It gives every employee a chance to take on more responsibility to solve problems that may impede Southwest's pursuit of excellence.[18]

By unlocking each employee's potential to make it a better company, Southwest enjoys significant advantages over competitors, whose employees feel like off-the-shelf parts in a machine. Southwest employees feel as though they are part of a family, and they feel a personal responsibility for improving Southwest's well-being. By contrast, employees in other airlines feel as though management views them as costs to be managed. Employees tend to project the feelings they get from management onto customers, so Southwest customers feel that they are part of a warm family, while competitors' customers do not.

Conover's own experience suggests how Southwest gives its employees a chance to take on greater responsibility for the company's well-being. She started out as a reservations agent in 1977 and subsequently moved into training employees in technical and cultural topics. In 1986 Conover took on responsibility for implementing a new reservation system. In 1994 Southwest faced a huge challenge to its market position when major reservation systems decided to start charging a fee of one dollar per transaction to list Southwest flights on travel agents' reservation systems. Because Southwest could not afford to pay this fee, it was in danger of being pulled off the travel agents' systems, which could have seriously reduced Southwest's revenue.

Herb Kelleher, then Southwest chairman and CEO, asked a team on which Conover participated to build Southwest's first ticketless reservation system. In May 1994 the team took on the challenge, meeting in a hotel conference room for four days to design the system. By July 1994, Conover and the team had developed the system that allowed customers buy tickets online with their credit cards. The system worked well, and its timely introduction helped to avert what could have been an unpleasant outcome for Southwest. In many companies, Conover believes, such a team would have been paralyzed with bureaucracy and would not have developed such a workable solution so quickly.

Southwest's constant focus on keeping costs low benefits its employees. Although participating in Southwest's profit-sharing plan helps motivate employees to take cost-saving initiatives, the Southwest family feeling seems to play an even more important role. Southwest employees, 85 percent of whom belong to unions, feel a personal stake in the airline's continued survival. As a result, Southwest keeps a tight rein on spending, resisting the urge that some of its peers feel to spend money on stadiums and perks that do not add value to customers. Furthermore, when Southwest experiences a financial pinch, employees pitch in. In 1990 and 1991, fuel prices skyrocketed as a result of political tensions in Middle Eastern oil-pro-ducing regions. In response to this threat, Southwest employees vol-unteered to participate in a program called Fuel from the Heart, in which employees bought airplane fuel for Southwest flights through payroll deduction.

Ultimately, Southwest is able to sustain its competitive advantages because it encourages its people at all levels to challenge ideas. In most organizations people who reach a high level develop egos that make them feel that no one at lower rungs in the organization should challenge them. Southwest screens out people with egos early in the hiring process. One oft-cited story describes a candidate for a pilot's job at Southwest who was encouraged to call Southwest to reserve a flight to the job inter-view. The pilot candidate was so rude to the reservations agent that the agent notified her manager, who passed along the information to the per-son who was scheduled to interview the candidate. When the candidate arrived for the interview, he was told that Southwest did not need his services as a result of his rudeness to the reservation agent.

In 2002 openness to challenging ideas led Southwest to yet another innovation that would keep it ahead of competitors. Since September 11, 2001, passengers have to spend additional time in lines to clear secu-rity. Southwest developed a kiosk system that allows passengers quicker access to baggage tags and boarding passes. Southwest got input for the kiosk design from five groups of people: airport customer service, infor-mation technology, customers, ground operations, and executives. These groups' input led the kiosk designers to leave out bells and whistles, lim-iting the kiosk attendant's function to taking customer's tickets and issu-ing boarding passes and baggage tags. Southwest intends to use whatever savings result from the kiosks to assess its ability to accomplish more with the same number of people, rather than laying off people.[19]

Southwest illustrates general principles for sustaining competitive superiority. First, it demonstrates that although the harder-edged parts of a company's competitive arsenal are important, people are often the most powerful competitive weapon. As we saw earlier, Southwest enjoyed considerable cost advantages that enabled it to profit while charging customers low fares. Most of these advantages have been well publicized, however, and therefore Southwest's ability to stay ahead of its competitors must be attributable to other factors that are either less well understood or simply far more difficult for competitors to copy. At Southwest this factor is its people, who are able to develop creative, practical solutions to problems that might otherwise impede the air-line's ability to deliver excellent service.

Second, sustaining competitive advantage can depend heavily on "egoless" (or teamwork) management. As we noted, egoless management can be particularly powerful from a competitive perspective because it is so difficult for most companies to copy. It multiplies the opportunities for new ideas to emerge from employees at all levels. Furthermore, it permits good ideas that may emerge from senior executives to be improved manifold as employees refine them and take ownership of them as they do their jobs. Thus, egoless management vastly extends an organization's creative problem-solving skills, widening the advantage between a market leader and its peers.

Finally, Southwest's ability to sustain its competitive advantages rests heavily on its speedy response to problems and opportunities. As we saw in the case of Southwest's development of a ticketless reservation system in 1994 and again in the flight attendant's quick thinking during the Destination Imagination flight, Southwest can react fast when speed makes a big difference. Its ability to react quickly reflects the tremendous emphasis that the company places on freedom and responsibility. Following a very careful process of hiring, Southwest gives its people the freedom to be themselves in their jobs as long as they use that freedom responsibly. This freedom reduces the amount of bureaucracy the company needs to come up with ideas and put them into practice. As a consequence, Southwest people can embrace new challenges, develop solutions to them, and enlist their colleagues to use these solutions in their jobs. Because it tends to respond faster than competitors to similar challenges, Southwest sustains its competitive advantages.

TURNAROUND AT J. C. PENNEY

Winning through multiple means is particularly difficult for an established company that has seen its performance slump for years. Generally, an established company can survive for years without a burning desire to win. Although its shareholders may be frustrated with management's indifference to creating value for shareholders and customers, shareholders often can do little to infuse the management team with a passion for winning. As a result, spurring the board to do something generally takes some sort of crisis. And this something usually involves putting in place new management that can revive the company.

Although bringing in new management invariably involves significant risk, it also represents the best hope for transforming a laggard company into a winner. A new CEO has the freedom to take a fresh look at the company and to make changes without being fettered by long-standing relationships with managers and suppliers. In order to make progress, the CEO must first take a hard look at the company from the perspective of customers. What aspects of the company most frustrate the customers? What products generate the most volume and the most profit? Which ones are the biggest money losers? What changes in the company's strategy can help build momentum for change by getting quick results and convincing the workforce that the company has a good future? Which managers and employees are likely to become part of the solution? Which are not?

J. C. Penney has grappled with these issues since its best year in 1994. By 2000 the company's six-year slide triggered the hiring of Allen Questrom, who led Federated Department Stores out of bankruptcy. Despite the problems described in Chapter Three, by 2002 Questrom's strategy for turning around J. C. Penney had generated some positive results. For the six months ending July 2002, for example, the retailer posted a 1 percent increase in sales to $15 billion and a profit of $66 million compared to a loss of $28 million year earlier. According to *HFN: The Weekly Newspaper for the Home Furnishing Network,* an important part of J. C. Penney's turnaround initiatives related to a fundamental shift in its relationships with suppliers. In May 2001 the company hosted one thousand people representing 65 percent of its merchandise purchases, to whom it presented its new strategy toward suppliers. J. C. Penney announced its intention to seek a first look at new products, shorten delivery times, and cut sharper deals with its suppliers.[20]

The company's new strategy focused on identifying the critical few items that its customers expected it to sell and cutting out the remaining dross. The strategy consisted of initiatives within its functions intended to enhance customer satisfaction and to lower costs, including the following:

- *Get first access to popular new merchandise.* J. C. Penney asked suppliers to give it a chance to sell—before its peers—new items in popular colors in order to fulfill its customers' expectations. Vanessa Castagna, executive vice president and chief operating officer, offered suppliers incentives to do so. Specifically, Penney offered to respond faster to vendors, improve the way it displayed product categories in which it led (for example, sheets and towels), and spend money on promotion and advertising.
- *Reengineer merchandising.* In addition to hiring Questrom as CEO, the retailer replaced half of its merchandising staff. It also replaced a decentralized buying and forecasting system with a

centralized one, emphasizing the most popular assortments of items and cutting back on less popular ones. For example, in 2001 the company reduced the number of styles by half. As a result, J. C. Penney hoped to free capital for spending on the most popular items.

• *Restore dominance in main categories.* The company sought to make itself a destination store for merchandise most wanted by its customers, such as bed and bath products and national brands such as KitchenAid and Royal Velvet. According to Mike Taxter, senior vice president and director of J. C. Penney Stores, customer research showed that Penney's customers expected but were not getting a far faster process of finding what they wanted to buy and checking out. In response, the company changed the way it displayed merchandise in its stores, grouping its clothing by category (for example, shirts, pants, and towels) so that customers would be able to find what they were looking for faster. It also streamlined the ways that it displays merchandise. Charles Foughty, Penney's vice president and director of store environment, reclassified thirteen different prototype floor plans into six groups. Each group had its own fixed square footage for every merchandise category. The result was modular merchandising and standard fixture packages for different-sized stores.

• *Place checkout centrally.* According to *Chain Store Age,* Penney's central checkout plan put the checkout stations (where customers pay for merchandise) throughout a store near the central aisle and exits. By June 2002, J. C. Penney had tested the central checkout concept in fourteen stores, and the results were so good that the company invested $50 million to roll out the central-checkout design to all its stores by the end of the third quarter of 2002. Because of the faster customer checkout times, test stores generated 2.7 percent higher sales and 0.6 percent lower salaries relative to the company average. Furthermore, J. C. Penney received very positive customer feedback to centralized checkout.[21]

• *Enhance logistics.* J. C. Penney also took steps to shorten the time to replenish its inventory. For example, in its fine-jewelry department, replenishment time dropped from twenty days to six, as a result of a new logistics infrastructure that included new store support centers. According to Beryl Raff, senior vice president and general merchandising manager of fine jewelry, more efficient logistics and marketing helped attract an important group of J. C. Penney customers—brides preparing for their weddings.[22]

• *Reduce price of merchandise.* With a reputation for being too lenient in structuring deals with suppliers, J. C. Penney intended to purchase centrally, thereby using its size to negotiate tougher deals with suppliers—a goal that would be unwelcome to its suppliers although potentially profitable for its shareholders.[23]

Penney's turnaround strategy may work; however, as of this writing the results are inconclusive. In the two years following Questrom's first day as CEO in September 2000, Penney's stock appreciated 42 percent compared to a 45 percent decline in the Standard & Poor 500 during the same period. After taking big write-offs in 2000, resulting in a $705 million loss for the year, J. C. Penney eked out a $98 million profit in 2001. Nevertheless, its initiatives are promising because they appear to be generating tangible cost savings and measurable improvements in customer satisfaction.

MANAGEMENT LEVERS

J. C. Penney's turnaround initiatives suggest that aspiring market leaders can take practical steps to win through multiple means. Although simple in concept, these steps require sustained effort to make them work effectively, particularly in a large organization with a tradition of lethargic adaptation to change. J. C. Penney's turnaround applies the principle of winning through multiple means that we examined above. Specifically, the source of the company's improvement initiatives was customer research. This research revealed important opportunities for improvement both in merchandising and store operations. The retailer's management also realized that given the challenge of obtaining additional financing, it was essential for J. C. Penney to use cost savings to finance its turnaround. Having identified opportunities for improvement, the company made improvements in all its activities that were tightly linked to its efforts to raise customer satisfaction and cut costs.

J. C. Penney's turnaround suggests that executives aspiring to win through multiple means can use the following management levers:

• *Identify unmet customer needs.* For executives leading a turnaround, the primary focus of understanding the customer should be finding out specific expectations of customers that the company is not meeting. In the case of J. C. Penney, customers wanted to find the merchandise far more quickly and then check out fast. Such insights are valuable because they can galvanize a large organization to change in a way that is both pervasive and will ultimately enhance the company's competitive position.

- *Upgrade activities to satisfy these needs.* In general, an executive seeking to turn a company around should build diverse capabilities that satisfy unmet customer needs. At J. C. Penney, the goal of streamlining the customer shopping experience led to changes in the mix of merchandise, the way the merchandise was displayed, and the process of checking out of the store. These changes in diverse activities actually strengthened the company's competitive position because they gave customers what they wanted.

- *Self-finance through cost cuts.* Generally, executives leading a turnaround will have a very difficult time obtaining external financing. As a result, the company will need to finance investments in enhanced capabilities needed to achieve the turnaround through internally generated profits. In the short run, such profits tend to come from cost reductions. So executives must identify cost reductions that will at a minimum not degrade customer satisfaction. J. C. Penney's efforts to use its purchasing volume to negotiate better deals with suppliers, its streamlining of inventory replenishment, its efforts to cut unpopular merchandise, and its initiatives to speed up customer checkout all led to cost savings that helped finance further improvement initiatives.

Winning through multiple means is a continuous process. Executives leading turnarounds must cycle through the three steps outlined in this chapter on an ongoing basis. In order to enhance its competitive position, a company must seek out new customer feedback to identify further opportunities for improvement. For a turnaround executive, such continuous improvement may ultimately lead to achieving competitive parity and, if persistent, competitive advantage.

VALUE QUOTIENT

Tactical-level analysis can help executives pinpoint opportunities for improvement. If you perceive that your organization can improve in the way it applies the principle "Win through multiple means," such analysis can help identify how best to improve the way your organization performs targeted activities.

Exhibit 7.1 can help you calculate your company's Value Quotient through two levels of analysis. The first level of analysis is binary, meaning that you can use the worksheet as a checklist to determine whether or not your company performs the specific tactics on the list. If your company does not perform any of the tactics within a specific activity, then it should consider initiating such tactics. The second level of analysis is analog, meaning that the worksheet can help pinpoint opportunities to improve how well your company performs a specific tactic that it has already been performing. To raise your company's score on a particular tactic, you may wish to initiate an in-depth process to change the way your organization performs the tactic along the lines developed in Chapter Nine.

To conduct the binary and analog levels of analysis, your company should gather data through interviews with employees, customers,

Win Through Multiple Means: Activity and Tactics	Score
Understand the customer	
☐ Assemble representative customers within the relevant market segments.	____
☐ Ask the customers to list and rank the criteria they use to consider purchases among competing products.	____
☐ Ask them to articulate how well the company's products satisfy the customer purchase criteria relative to competitors'.	____
Build diverse capabilities	
☐ Understand the incumbent's strengths and weaknesses in meeting customer needs.	____
☐ Assess how well the company performs the activities needed to outperform competitors in satisfying unmet customer needs.	____
☐ Close the capability gap by hiring, acquiring, or partnering.	____
☐ Make the capabilities difficult for competitors to copy.	____
Sustain competitive superiority	
☐ Hire employees who can make improvements that create customer value.	____
☐ Create an environment that encourages these employees to take the initiative.	____
☐ Gather feedback from customers to find out which initiatives worked.	____
☐ Reward the employees who implemented the winning initiatives.	____
Total	____

Exhibit 7.1.   Value Quotient Worksheet: Win Through Multiple Means.
Key: 5 = excellent; 4 = very good; 3 = good; 2 = fair; 1 = poor; 0 = not applicable.

suppliers, analysts, and shareholders. Ideally, your company should use objective third parties to identify an appropriate sample of interviewees, develop interview guides, conduct the interviews, and analyze the results. The outcomes of collecting and analyzing the data will be specific scores for each tactic. Although assigning these scores requires judgment, they should be calibrated by comparing the scores with the Value Leaders and other best-of-breed competitors.

Scores for each tactic range from excellent (five) to poor (one). If an organization does not perform the tactic at all, it receives a score of zero. To calculate the activity scores, the analyst can average the scores for the tactics supporting that activity and round the average to the nearest whole number. To illustrate how a score might be assigned for a specific tactic, consider the tactic "Understand the incumbent's strengths and weaknesses in meeting customer needs." If your company has not conducted any competitor analysis, it would be scored zero. On the other hand, if your company has recently completed a detailed analysis of, say, over one hundred customer interviews that ranked the incumbent's performance relative to the top ten customer purchase criteria, then it would receive a score of five.

CONCLUSION

Winning through multiple means is a crucial principle of value leadership. Winning inspires employees to work toward a timeless goal of sustaining market leadership. Winning in the present is no guarantee of future market leadership. In order to sustain such leadership, companies need to keep an open channel of communication with customers so that they can close gaps that may emerge between customer expectations and what the company is actually delivering. Aspiring market leaders must also recognize that incumbents and new competitors scramble to take their customers and that market leaders must respond to the challenge. To protect their businesses, market leaders must craft a customer value proposition based on several capabilities that are difficult for competitors to copy. In addition, market leaders must find new markets in which their capabilities will yield competitive advantage. Only through such relentless self-improvement can market leaders sustain their competitive superiority.

CHAPTER EIGHT

Doing Good Matters

(Give to Your Community)

—ᴥ—

Giving to your community means transferring corporate resources to society. Companies give products and services, cash, or time to a range of communities, from the ones in which they operate and in which their employees live to remote countries with big problems whose solutions challenge executives' entrepreneurial abilities. The principle "Give to your community" requires executives to forge delicate balances. They must balance the interests of shareholders who claim all the company's profits against those of some consumers and social advocates who want to use corporate profits to fund their pet causes. Shareholders may feel that it is presumptuous of executives to decide how shareholders should contribute to charity. Social advocates believe that society provides the oxygen that companies inhale to generate their profits and therefore corporations have a vital interest in giving back to society. Most companies resolve this balance by giving to their communities in ways that they believe will enhance their reputations among their customers and regulators.

LINK WITH VALUE LEADERSHIP

"Give to your community" is a crucial principle of Value Leadership. Companies that contribute to the communities in which they operate display a commitment to others that makes potential employees and customers feel better about the companies. Such companies also generate pride among employees who, although often lacking the financial stature to make significant charitable contributions, derive an inherent satisfaction from working for an employer that is perceived as a good corporate citizen. As we will explore further in this chapter, such companies reinforce employee pride by letting the employees determine which charitable causes will receive corporate contributions. Companies benefit from the resulting increase in employee loyalty, which leads to less voluntary turnover. Some of the wealthiest companies, such as Microsoft, Merck, and Johnson & Johnson, can use their cash to spur positive social change on a scale that defies the power of governments. Such change can benefit the lives of millions of people, and it also enhances the reputations of the companies that spur the change and satisfy executives' drive to make a difference.

ECONOMIC BENEFITS

Although giving to the community enhances a company's reputation, the economic benefits are inconclusive. According to the *Wall Street Journal,* corporate philanthropy can be fraught with peril. Giving away popular products can generate consumer goodwill, but if the company touts its generosity in advertising, consumers can be annoyed. On the other hand, if a company does not advertise what it gives to a cause, consumers can criticize it unfairly for not contributing. Nevertheless, companies can enhance their reputations by giving to the community. For example, Value Leaders Johnson & Johnson, Wal-Mart, and Microsoft were ranked first, third, and seventh, respectively, in social responsibility in an October 2001 Harris Interactive survey of 21,630 consumers.[1]

The benefits to a firm's reputation seem to emerge from a well-conceived strategy of what a firm contributes, whom the firm contributes to, and how it communicates that contribution. According to the *Sarasota Herald-Tribune,* consumer reactions to corporate contributions vary depending on what the companies give. Such gifts also enhance society's perception of a company. In a 1998 survey of one thousand people, conducted by Hill and Knowlton and Yankelovich Partners, 43 percent of those polled said donating products or services impressed them most; employee volunteerism followed with 37 percent; and large cash donations impressed most only 12 percent of those polled. The tax benefits of giving products or services are better for public companies than private ones. Publicly traded companies that give away their products get tax deductions equal to their cost plus half the markup price; private ones receive tax breaks that match only their cost.[2] These findings suggest some of the parameters that executives must consider in striking the appropriate balance between corporate obligations to shareholders and society.

CASES

Despite the subtleties of giving to the community, the cumulative benefits of such giving outweigh its costs. This chapter bolsters this assertion with stories of how Merck and Microsoft are using their products, money, and influence to create a new infrastructure in Botswana to prevent the spread of AIDS. The chapter draws general inferences from the Botswana AIDS initiative for executives seeking to use their resources to implement solutions to massive societal problems that have defied governmental intervention. The chapter continues with the story of how Southwest Airlines enables its employees to choose and participate in charitable causes that they find meaningful, drawing general prescriptions for how companies can enhance employee loyalty by letting them decide how best to give to their communities. The chapter continues with case studies of how Wal-Mart and Microsoft engage in grassroots giving at the community level, in part to maintain political support and to overcome nascent opposition to their presence in those communities. It discusses how Microsoft and Merck applied their brains, money, and ambition in efforts to change society by struggling to control the spread of AIDS in Botswana and vaccinating millions of children in countries like Mozambique. The chapter concludes with a case study of how Johnson & Johnson worked to transform its foundation from a donor of free drugs to a force for implementing solutions to broad societal challenges.

ACTIVITY ANALYSIS

Giving to your community works best if it makes both the donor and recipient communities better off. Several of the cases we'll explore in this chapter suggest that a fairly small number of specific matches between donor and recipient seem to generate a positive outcome for both parties. Given the pitfalls alluded to earlier, executives seeking to benefit from giving to their community may wish to consider these specific configurations as a way to gain the benefits while avoiding the risks. In particular, three key activities match donors and recipients in a mutually beneficial way:

- **Inspire employees.** When companies support charitable causes that employees find meaningful, the recipients gain committed support while the companies enhance loyalty by letting employees choose a charity in whose cause they believe.

- **Enrich the community.** By making carefully selected contributions to key community leaders and local causes, companies can overcome resistance to the opening of a local operation or sustain support for its expansion. While the community benefits from such contributions, the company creates an environment that is more receptive to its business objectives.

- **Attack big societal problems.** A handful of companies have the wealth and the management will to address societal problems that go beyond the areas where the companies hire and sell. These companies use their products, cash, and political influence to implement systemic solutions to diseases that affect millions of people, such as river blindness or AIDS. The recipient's benefit is clear, and the companies benefit through an enhanced global reputation and the executives' satisfaction of exercising a unique form of power to better society.

Inspire Employees

Inspiring employees by giving them the opportunity to participate in charities of their choosing is a powerful way to give to your community. The best employees are passionate about their work. In order to create an environment that fuels the passion of such employees, executives should let them choose community causes with which they feel a strong connection. Companies benefit when they create an environment that lets the best employees engage personally in their work for the company and for the community. Simply knowing that an employer is willing to support an employee's devotion to a cause that the employee finds meaningful is likely to increase that employee's loyalty and commitment to the company.

The way a company treats its employees tends to trickle down to its customers as well. According to *PR Week US*, consumers perceive that employee participation in charitable causes is the most impressive indicator of the sincerity of a company's commitment to social responsibility. Hill & Knowlton's 2001 Corporate Citizen Watch found that only 33 percent of consumers polled said they were "very impressed" when a CEO talked about a company's social involvement; however, nearly 60 percent were "very impressed" by employees volunteering their time to charitable causes.[3] This positive consumer perception may translate into greater customer loyalty, which can lead to higher profitability.

Executives seeking to enhance customer loyalty—and therefore customer profitability—should look for ways to increase employee loyalty. Establishing clear values and hiring employees who embody these values can go a long way to securing such loyalty. So does rewarding employees who go the extra mile for the customer. However, companies that compete on the basis of customer service have an important opportunity for inspiring their employees—and thereby increasing their loyalty.

Service-oriented people are rare. Such people derive energy and affirmation from helping other people. If managers offer these employees a chance to choose how to serve others outside of work, these employees jump at the opportunity. Matching employees who like to give of themselves with people in need makes both parties better off. While the charities appreciate cash contributions from these firms and others, they generally find that the service orientation of such companies lends a unique dimension. Rather than giving cash and distancing themselves personally, these companies' employees give cash and get personally involved, establishing relationships with people in need, without demanding public relations (PR) in return. Such companies depend so heavily on keeping their employees satisfied that employee satisfaction with the experience is sufficient recompense.

Executives seeking to inspire employees by giving to the community can follow these tactics:

• *Create a central point in the company for corporate giving, generally reporting to the CEO.* For a company to do an effective job of giving to the community, it must have a central organizational locus reporting to the CEO. This corporate-giving organization will serve as a central point for employee and community requests for corporate resources. By aligning this organization with the CEO, it can more effectively achieve the CEO's objectives.

• *Separate corporate giving from PR and marketing to clarify its purpose and defuse community and employee cynicism.* Critics commonly dismiss corporate giving as a means of garnering positive press. One way to defuse some of that criticism is for the company to locate its corporate-giving organization outside the marketing department.

• *Create a program that lets employees recommend causes that inspire them.* One powerful way to think of corporate giving is as a benefit that makes employees feel a greater sense of belonging to the organization. When employees see that their employer often is willing to invest corporate resources in causes that employees find meaningful, the employees feel an even closer bond to their employer.

• *Invest executive time and money to support the employee-recommended causes.* When senior executives participate in the causes that employees find meaningful, companies have an opportunity to reinforce deeply the corporate sense of identification with the employee-selected causes. Senior executive participation also makes the initiating employees feel that the company values their initiative.

• *Communicate the success of such programs to all employees to encourage greater participation.* Because employees value peer recognition, companies can strongly encourage employee-initiated corporate giving by communicating the most successful such programs across the company. The peer recognition makes the employees who initiated the giving feel good, and it encourages other employees to follow their lead.

• *Give employees time off work to contribute to the company's charity of choice, for example, one day every six or twelve months.* Executives can further reinforce the importance of employee giving by offering employees regular time off to contribute time to charities of employees' choosing.

Southwest Airlines uses many of these tactics to create an environment that inspires employees through corporate giving. According to Barbara McDermott, the executive director of Dallas's Ronald McDonald House (RMH), Southwest Airlines is full of people—from flight attendants to accountants—who get real satisfaction from helping people in need.[4]

RMH is a home away from home for families with seriously ill children. Dick East is a Southwest pilot whose daughter died of leukemia.

East was touched by RMH's mission, and when East joined Southwest as a pilot in 1981, he urged the airline to get involved with RMH.

Southwest's chairman, Herb Kelleher, demonstrated that he genuinely cared, was genuinely community-minded himself, and ran Southwest as a community-minded organization. In fact, Southwest agreed to participate; on its first day of involvement with RMH, Kelleher appeared at RMH at 4:30 P.M. When Kelleher arrived, he asked East how he could help. East suggested that Kelleher could serve refreshments to the families. Kelleher did so willingly for over an hour, carrying beverages from the ice chest to the family members.

Since then, Southwest's involvement with RMH has extended nationwide. According to McDermott, Southwest's involvement with her agency is unique. Whereas other RMH sponsors may look for a quid pro quo (in the form of writing press releases, displaying the sponsor's corporate logo, and featuring the sponsor on the RMH Web site), Southwest employees have a waiting list to serve dinner and lunch to RMH families because the employees find the service rewarding.

Since beginning its involvement with RMHs, Southwest has contributed over $4 million to the houses around the United States through the proceeds of a golf tournament it sponsors, the LUV Classic.

McDermott believes that Southwest's service-oriented people match well with RMH's needy visitors. She noticed that Southwest employees, from flight attendants to accountants, are hired due to their genuine interest in serving people. When Southwest employees serve meals at RMH, they make it fun for the children by doing face painting, playing games, or putting a Southwest hat on the children's heads and letting them cook. By contrast, some of the other sponsors' employees are a bit uncomfortable interacting with sick children or those from different socioeconomic backgrounds, so they are somewhat reticent to interact with them.

Southwest responds to RMH's urgent needs quickly and without bureaucracy. When RMH first received computers, it needed training, so Southwest invited RMH staff to the airline's computer-training classes. Southwest also donates flights to families that need to fly in an emergency situation related to RMH.[5]

Southwest's involvement with RMH is among the most compelling results of a formal process for managing its giving to the community. According to Tracie Martin, Southwest's manager of civic and charitable contributions, charitable contributions have always been part of Southwest's corporate philosophy. However, as Southwest grew, the volume of Southwest's charitable requests increased. As a result, Martin developed a more formal process to manage them. She noted that unlike most companies, where her department would report to the PR or communications offices, she reports to the chairman. This reporting relationship underscores an important philosophical difference between Southwest and other companies: Southwest views its civic and charitable contributions not as a way to enhance (or sanitize) its reputation but as a way to reward employees. By separating the organizational locus of responsibility for civic and charitable contributions from its marketing unit, Southwest underlines the importance of this value.[6]

Rather, Southwest sees civic and charitable contributions as a way to reward its employees. Martin said that the airline is open to anybody who calls to make a request, and it reviews the requests carefully. She receives many calls from employees seeking support for fundraisers and help with formal charities such as the American Cancer Society and the March of Dimes. She also gets calls from individuals seeking help with medical problems, beauty contests seeking money, 10K runs looking for sponsors, and teams raising money to climb Mount Everest.

Southwest screens these requests based on its local budgets. Specifically, it establishes budgets for contributions to a local community based on the number of passengers originating there. Martin asks callers to put their requests in writing. During her tenure of almost twenty years, she has developed a good gut feeling regarding the legitimacy of their requests. As Martin asks for increasingly detailed levels of documentation for, say, a caller's medical problem, it quickly becomes clear whether the request is legitimate. Those making illegitimate requests tend to stall when asked to provide documentation, plead more strenuously for their case, and then ultimately disappear when it becomes clear that Southwest will not fund their request. Ultimately, Martin decides whether or not to fund a request based on three tests:

- Can Southwest afford to fund the request?
- Does it want to affiliate itself with the cause?
- Does it believe that funding the request is the right thing to do?

As noted earlier, the airline's involvement with RMH emerged from an employee's request that clearly passed these three tests.

Southwest benefits from funding employee-led charitable initiatives because employees are so thrilled to make them happen. Some flight crews stay overnight at RMHs and report that they love interacting with the families, according to Martin, introducing themselves, serving them pizza, and listening to what's on their mind. The flight crews develop close relationships with families, which can be emotionally challenging when family members do not survive their illness. Nevertheless, Southwest crews forge lifelong relationships with the families, which they find immensely rewarding.

Martin spends a significant amount of time promoting her department to Southwest's thirty-five thousand employees. Her objective is to make them aware of the opportunities available for employees looking to make a contribution to the community. She notes that when employees come to work, they do not necessarily have philanthropy on their mind. When they discover that Southwest makes philanthropy available to them, they experience a sense of awakening. Employees are inspired by the discovery that they can extend their natural service orientation to the community. Martin's efforts to create this sense of discovery have generated a significant response, including requests from employees to help a terminally ill neighbor financially or to donate travel so that their families can get together. Southwest's participation in such causes gives employees a chance to feel recipients' gratitude, and employees love knowing that their company makes such help available.

Southwest argues that getting PR is not the primary focus of its civic and charitable contributions. As McDermott confirmed, the airline takes a different approach than some other companies. It does not require that Southwest's logo appear on T-shirts for fundraisers. Martin would hate to represent yet another airline insisting on exclusivity in exchange for its sponsorship of a charitable organization. Southwest does not mind if its name is number two or number three in marketing materials for a charitable event.

Martin offered other companies four pieces of advice on how to manage civic and charitable giving. First, she suggested that they listen to every request that comes in and resist the urge to categorize them. She believes that if a company only limits itself to contributing to education and the arts, then it loses large segments of society and risks making people feel slighted. Second, she recommends that a company not take on too many requests initially, making sure that it develops the systems to support the grant evaluation process. She also notes that it is often easier for Southwest to manage requests for airline tickets and cash because the amount being contributed is relatively small and does not necessarily require such extensive review. Third, she suggests that Southwest has found it useful to send people out into the community to meet and share mutually beneficial ideas with charitable organizations open-mindedly rather than sending out people with predetermined objectives. Finally, she found that as Southwest's involvement in civic and charitable contributions expanded, her organization became more specialized in terms of the causes it funded and the infrastructure needed to support those causes.[7]

Southwest's ability to inspire employees by letting them get involved in giving to the community reveals three general lessons. First, executives must recognize the benefits of hiring and retaining employees with a bias for service. In industries where service is a key source of competitive advantage, attracting and retaining such people is a matter of survival. In industries where service is a secondary source of advantage, attracting and retaining service-oriented people can still be an important source of competitive differentiation.

Second, executives must enable such employees to discover opportunities for philanthropy. In companies where power flows only from the top down, CEOs decide which philanthropic causes receive corporate attention and resources. Such companies are unlikely to let employees direct the companies' charitable actions. Nevertheless, if executives seek to benefit employees in giving to the community, it is essential that employees play a central role in directing how the company gives to the community. As the Southwest case illustrates, employee leadership of corporate giving can inspire them.

Finally, executives should support employee initiatives by supporting an organization to manage philanthropy and by giving their own time to the initiatives. As the Southwest case illustrates, when senior executives support causes that inspire employees, the executives send a very powerful message. Executives tell employees that corporate philanthropy is an important place for leaders—and by extension their people—to spend time and money. Executives also convey to employees the power of a leadership style that seeks to create a work environment that encourages employees to suggest new ideas and carry them out. Finally, executives let employees know that the highest calling of all people in an organization—from the chairman on down—is to deliver great service with enthusiasm.

Enrich the Community

Some companies, particularly those that operate in communities with few large employers, must overcome local opposition by giving to the communities. These companies face particularly high levels of local suspicion because such communities are not accustomed to managing the changes that a new employer brings to an area. Despite these companies' tangible contributions of products, cash, and time to local causes, the extent of local opposition to their presence suggests that such giving to the community is intended to create a situation in which community leaders make a political judgment that the benefits that the company brings to constituents—and in some cases their own political campaigns—overwhelms the strength of local opponents. In this sense giving to the community reflects the extent to which the company takes on the guise of a community political force whose survival depends on its ability to defeat local opponents of change.

Companies seeking to enrich the community must be able to analyze and satisfy the needs of the local communities in which they operate. To do so, they must identify the most influential members of a local community, understand their perception of local needs, and give the right mix of products, cash, or time to satisfy the local needs. The right mix of corporate giving varies for each community. Some mayors or governors will admit a new business into the community if the business contributes to their reelection campaign or a favorite local charity. Once companies overcome initial resistance to their presence in a community, they generally seek to sustain local goodwill in several ways. Most importantly, they offer jobs with good pay and benefits to local citizens. They also help with municipal improvements such as road-widening projects, utility enhancements, and library modernization, all while adding to the local tax base. Furthermore, some companies let their local employees work on charitable causes that they find meaningful as a way of further planting their roots in the local community.

Although the following tactics are primarily useful for helping executives seeking to operate in a new community, they can be applied in a modified way to help executives who are seeking to enrich the communities in which they currently operate:

• *Establish an organization within the company that specializes in serving local communities.* If a company depends heavily for its growth on the favor of those in its local communities, then it can benefit by establishing an organization that focuses on generating that favor. As such a company attempts to conduct business in new communities, such an organization can become a valuable repository of corporate best practices and people with growing expertise in gaining community favor.

• *Assign people from that organization to identify local movers and shakers.* When a company seeks a chance to do business in a new community, it should assign its specialists in local community relations to identify and meet the most influential community members.

• *Meet with these influential people and listen to their description of community needs, potential objections to the company, and ways that the company can overcome these objections.* Company representatives should listen to the concerns of these local leaders in order to evaluate how best to address them.

• *Assess whether the benefits of operating in the community exceed the costs of overcoming these objections.* In some cases the objections may be so strong that the company may decide not to pursue further efforts to enter the new market. Skilled community relations staff should be able to identify creative ways to overcome such objections over time.

• *Deliver the right mix of cash, products, and time to satisfy the local movers and shakers, enabling the company to operate in the community.* In many cases each individual local leader seeks a unique bundle of value to overcome objections and take a neutral or—at best—favorable attitude towards the company's potential entry into the community. In general, community leaders will be amenable to the company's entry into the community if they perceive that tax revenues and total community employment will rise without too much additional disruption from traffic and displacement of local businesses.

• *Maintain contact with leaders and remain responsive to their needs in order to continue to enrich the community.* Companies should recognize that over time the community's attitudes will change and that there may be opportunities for further expansion. Companies may also find that new problems arise in their relationships with local communities. As a result, companies should maintain communication with key members of the community to head off problems before they become difficult to solve.

Microsoft's initiatives to enrich California's Silicon Valley followed many of these tactics. Although Microsoft is headquartered near

Seattle, Washington, by 2001 it employed fifteen hundred workers in Silicon Valley. These employees managed Microsoft WebTV Networks and MSN Hotmail. Microsoft had many critics in Silicon Valley, many of whom were intense competitors such as Sun Microsystems. These competitors viewed Microsoft's local philanthropy as a Trojan horse that would create a softer image for Microsoft that would enable it to hire the area's best engineers. According to *Knight Ridder Tribune Business News,* in 1999 Microsoft created a positive buzz by donating $20 million in Silicon Valley: roughly $1.67 million was in cash and $19.7 million in software to local charities.[8]

The reaction to Microsoft's donations to local charities generated much positive feedback. For example, Hewlett-Packard (HP), a Microsoft partner, congratulated Microsoft's help in meeting a great local need. Local charities, such as United Way Silicon Valley, also benefited from a 1999 contribution of $5 million from Microsoft chairman Bill Gates. In 2001 Microsoft contributed $15 million in software to San Francisco–based Compumentor, which provides technical help to other nonprofit organizations.

The company made smaller cash donations to a variety of local charities. Specifically, it gave $25,000 in cash to public television station KTEH in San Jose, the Digital Clubhouse Network in Sunnyvale, and the Emergency Housing Consortium in San Jose. Silicon Valley chapters of the Boys & Girls Clubs benefited from the company's $100 million cash and software grant to establish Club Tech, a nationwide program of technology centers.

Microsoft also generated substantial contributions for United Way Silicon Valley. In 2001 Microsoft's Mountain View campus gave $500,000 in employee contributions and matching funds to the agency, about double the 2000 amount. Its 2001 contribution made the company a top contributor to United Way along with leading valley corporate givers such as HP, IBM, and Intel—each of which contributed at least $500,000 in their 2000 workplace campaigns. Greg Larson, CEO of United Way Silicon Valley, was effusive in his praise, noting that the level of growth of Microsoft's contributions was "phenomenal." Larson also pointed out that Microsoft was active in the leadership of United Way Silicon Valley's campaign and in its board.[9]

Digital Clubhouse Network, which provided technology centers for low-income communities, was also impressed with Microsoft's charitable contributions. Warren Hegg, the group's executive director and founder, described Microsoft as a massive company and "world leader." Hegg was impressed that such a company would take time with his "tiny operation." Digital Clubhouse Network received $45,000 in cash and $100,000 in software from Microsoft. After making these contributions, the company exceeded Hegg's expectations by calling Hegg regularly to see how things were running. Although he acknowledged that Microsoft may have followed through because the company knew it was being watched, he wished most companies took such a personal or professional view of their charitable giving.[10]

Critics argued that Microsoft's participation in such philanthropy had hidden motives. They suggested that Gates was trying to soften criticism that he took too long to become philanthropic, that Microsoft was giving away mostly software rather than cash, and that its local gifts amounted to branding behind enemy lines. Many in Silicon Valley suggested that Microsoft used its market influence to scare or crush potential competitors. These critics' voices seemed powerful when their companies were performing better, but following the bursting of the dot-com bubble, as jobs in Silicon Valley became scarce, Microsoft's relative business success helped dampen some of the job losses from these formerly more successful critics. Even when the critics were more powerful, it is clear that Microsoft's strategy was far better for the community and for Microsoft than doing nothing would have been.

Bruce Brooks, director of Microsoft community affairs, countered these critics. He suggested that Microsoft's goal was not short-term PR; rather, the company was trying to be seen as a leader in corporate philanthropy. According to Brooks, Microsoft contributed $34 million in cash and $200 million in software during fiscal year 2000, and Silicon Valley was and would continue to be an important part of Microsoft's organization. Brooks argued that Microsoft gave away software because software was the company's area of expertise, and therefore it was the best way for Microsoft to help nonprofit organizations and low-income communities benefit from the information age. Brooks concluded that his organization's job was to find ways to make sure Microsoft played "constructive roles" in the communities where Microsoft employees lived.[11]

Microsoft's efforts to enrich the Silicon Valley community reflect a sophisticated understanding of the challenges of moving corporate operations into a new region, particularly one that contains opponents. These efforts underscore the lurking dangers of giving to the community when executives are seeking to enter from outside and take some ownership. This example illustrates that critics can carp about even the most seemingly well-intentioned contributions. It also points out how important good word-of-mouth reactions from the "right" charitable organizations are to overcoming local suspicion of outsiders. Because Bill Gates's mother, to whom he was reportedly close, had been very active in United Way in Seattle, Gates was inclined to support United Way himself. Undoubtedly, Greg Larson's positive reaction to Microsoft's involvement in United Way Silicon Valley helped assuage local community leaders. By 2001, Microsoft's efforts to generate positive feelings in Silicon Valley appeared to be generating many of the results it sought.

Unlike Microsoft, Wal-Mart's continued growth depended heavily on its ability to repeat the process of enriching local communities in hundreds of new locations around the world every year. As Wal-Mart opened new stores to sustain its extraordinary growth rate as the world's largest company, it had developed the process of enriching the community into something of a science, overcoming often very vocal and sometimes well-organized opposition. Although measuring the depth of such opposition is difficult, it often finds visible expression in the newspapers of communities where Wal-Mart sought to locate a new store.

Two examples of such community opposition offer insight into the nature of such opposition. Lancaster, Pennsylvania, viewed Wal-Mart's effort to open a store there as a pitted battle between the locals' love for their community and Wal-Mart's greed. According to the *Lancaster New Era,* Wal-Mart's arsenal for overcoming local opposition was extensive and sophisticated. Dawn Rapchinski Ephrata, a community opponent of Wal-Mart, argued that the retailer battled local volunteers with paid advertising consultants. She contended that for every dollar of profit from businesses based in the area, employees and suppliers spent four or five additional dollars on products and services in the local community, while Wal-Mart's profits were sent back to Wal-Mart headquarters each night. She said that for every dollar of tax revenue that Wal-Mart generated, it would use three dollars of municipal services. Finally, she argued that for every job Wal-Mart created, the community would lose one and a half jobs from existing businesses.[12]

To bolster her case against the retailer, Rapchinski Ephrata quoted a group called the Council of Canadians. This group alleged that Wal-Mart's success is based on "misleading advertising, predatory pricing, violating competition law, keeping wages down and coercive sourcing from suppliers." The council further contended that Wal-Mart subsidized short-term losses in one area with higher prices in other stores. Rapchinski Ephrata also suggested that more than one hundred citizen groups opposed Wal-Mart in the United States and other countries.[13]

By 2002, it was clear that her campaign against the retailer had failed: Wal-Mart was operating at 2034 Lincoln Highway East in Lancaster, Pennsylvania. The company succeeded in overcoming objections by acceding to community requests to improve traffic flow into the store. For example, according to the *Lancaster New Era,* Wal-Mart offered a revised proposal for its store that provided separate traffic patterns for supply trucks, customers, and employees. The company also suggested planting trees to buffer the rear property line.[14] Ultimately, residents who objected to Wal-Mart were outvoted by those who believed Wal-Mart's presence would offer jobs and greater shopping convenience.

Although Rapchinski Ephrata's argument against Wal-Mart was one-sided and ultimately unsuccessful, a fly-on-the-wall look at an Albuquerque, New Mexico, debate on opening a Wal-Mart Supercenter reveals that in some communities the arguments against a new Wal-Mart can prevail. According to the *Albuquerque Journal,* in April 2002 the Corrales village council unanimously approved a resolution opposing construction of a Wal-Mart Supercenter in Corrales, due to worries about drainage of oil from its parking lot into local sewers, increased crime such as stealing from cash registers or holding up customers in the parking lot, noise and light pollution, and increased traffic through town. For Wal-Mart opponents the resolution was popular, but it was only symbolic because the village council had no direct control over the land in question. Most meeting attendees opposed the retailer and proposed numerous efforts to block its determination to build there. Interestingly, one speaker, Bob Borman, suggested that a Wal-Mart might increase sales at the arts shops and pricey restaurants in town. However, Borman's comment made most residents snicker, with some believing it "a stretch" that Wal-Mart's bargain-hunting customers would also spend their scarce resources on arts and crafts or a special meal at an upscale restaurant.[15]

In the face of such local opposition, Wal-Mart has nevertheless prevailed. On balance, the company's efforts to overcome community opposition succeed because Wal-Mart enriches the communities in which it operates by following an approach that is deeply rooted in its culture. According to *Chain Drug Review,* Wal-Mart's grassroots approach to involving itself in its communities gained formal recognition in 1979 with the opening of the Wal-Mart Foundation. That year, Wal-Mart distributed $200,000 in scholarships nationwide, reflecting an emphasis on education that remained important through 2002. In 2001 Wal-Mart spent $12.3 million in educational causes, part of a record $196 million in contributions it made that year.[16]

Educational contributions are part of an annual process at Wal-Mart. For example, every Wal-Mart store and Sam's Club unit awards a $1,000 Sam Walton scholarship to a local high school senior each year. The company also recognizes the importance of teachers. Each store and club selects an outstanding local teacher and issues a $500 grant to that teacher's school. Every year, the retailer selects a teacher of the year for each state, and in 2001 for the first time, it chose a national winner.

Children's welfare and safety outside of school is also an important focus for Wal-Mart. The company developed its Code Adam program, for example, in response to the hundreds of abductions of children committed each year. And like many programs at Wal-Mart, it began with the initiative of one individual at one store. Now, if a child is reported missing in a Wal-Mart store, an employee takes a description of the child and issues an alert. The alert causes all exits to be monitored and all employees not operating registers to search all areas of the store, including rest rooms and dressing rooms. According to *USA Today,* Wal-Mart posts missing kids' pictures on thirty-one hundred bulletin boards in its stores and has been credited with locating seventy-two missing children since 1996.[17]

The company encourages store employees and managers to develop new community programs. For example, the 2002 fires in Arizona and Colorado prompted associates to help the affected communities. Wal-Mart employees in Arizona gave $250,000 in merchandise, phone cards, and disaster-relief funds to affected communities; its Colorado employees donated $120,000. According to Wal-Mart president and CEO Lee Scott, the company's giving program is driven by its employees at the grassroots level. Its employees decide which programs to participate in based on the causes that they believe are of greatest interest and will best serve the local community. Scott believes that these employees know what is best for their customers and their communities.[18]

The overall scope of Wal-Mart's giving to the community is extensive. According to *PR Newswire,* Wal-Mart and Sam's Clubs employees at thirty-two hundred stores awarded 115,000 grants during 2001. The $196 million in grants were distributed to seventy thousand local charities and causes. Between 1997 and 2001, the company's annual giving increased at an average of 23 percent. These donations reflected

Sam Walton's philosophy that stores should be a "pillar of the local community as well as a pillar of commerce."[19]

Wal-Mart's 2001 giving focused on local communities, emphasizing themes of concern to its employees, such as education and children. For example, the company offered $3 million to community organizations at store grand openings. It gave many of these funds to elementary and secondary schools, homeless shelters, food banks, youth centers, and libraries during grand opening ceremonies for three hundred new Wal-Mart locations. Wal-Mart and Sam's Clubs employees raised $18 million in 2001 for the United Way. Salvation Army estimates its kettles at the front of Wal-Mart and Sam's Clubs collected $14 million. Wal-Mart employees raised $5.4 million during Wal-Mart's annual charity appeal on the Friday morning after Thanksgiving. The retailer also contributed $12.2 million to educational causes during 2001 and $31.7 million to 170 children's hospitals across the country and in Canada that year through the Children's Miracle Network.[20]

The ways that Wal-Mart and Microsoft have enriched local communities suggest general principles. First, executives must recognize that expanding a company's operations into a new community is not likely to generate unalloyed enthusiasm. Executives who anticipate opposition and develop plans to overcome it are more likely to succeed. Second, it is often effective for companies to encourage their employees to contribute to local causes that they find meaningful. Because companies entering a new community will be looking to hire and gain customers from the local community, these new entrants are more likely to gain community loyalty if they let their local employees do the giving. Third, executives should realize that the company must enrich the community strategically. In other words executives should target the recipients of the company's giving as well as the specific causes of interest to these recipients in order to maximize the perceived benefit within the community. In general, communities seem to perceive greater benefits from many smaller contributions than from one very large check. A single large check tends to make those who did not receive the check confused about why that person or organization received the check and not them. Many smaller checks tend to satisfy more people and confuse fewer. Fourth, executives must create ongoing processes to sustain community enrichment. If companies slack off once they have overcome initial resistance to their operation in a community, they are likely to lose the support of their employees and their customers who reside there.

Attack Big Societal Problems

Some companies give to the community because they aspire to change society. In many cases the companies themselves may be formally left out of such ambitious change efforts. Rather, company founders and their foundations take a lead role in such change initiatives, often targeting societal problems affecting millions of people that have resisted the efforts of governments to solve them. In this sense companies seeking to attack big societal problems exercise a unique form of institutional power, a metagovernment that focuses on solving large-scale societal problems and that operates somewhat independently of the governments responsible for the countries in which these problems occur. Although participation in such metagovernmental activities creates a general aura of goodwill around the companies that initiate them, the ultimate benefit of such activities is the personal satisfaction that they provide to the executives who direct them.

Successful company founders often have ample self-confidence, believing that their success in business presents challenges and opportunities. One challenge may be a desire to sanitize the fearsome reputations that may have accompanied their success. With the right amount of money, brainpower, and ambition, such entrepreneurs can find themselves in a position to achieve success on a far larger and socially more significant scale. Ultimately, an entrepreneur's motivation for changing society may be both to sanitize a reputation for ruthlessness and to enjoy the exercise of power as a de facto head of a metagovernment established to solve a big societal problem.

While avoiding explicit discussion of the matter, corporate initiatives to solve large-scale societal problems can strongly influence public perception. If a company that is otherwise perceived as dominant in its industry uses the wealth resulting from that dominance to solve a problem that the general public agrees is significant, this use of corporate wealth can dampen negative public perceptions. If such initiatives actually produce tangible solutions to the problems, they are most likely to create a positive perceptual halo around the company, which can help increase customer and employee loyalty to the company. Such initiatives can backfire, however, if they do not produce the anticipated benefits, leaving the company open to criticism that could sour public perception.

Executives seeking to attack big societal problems may employ the following tactics:

• *Identify big societal problems that fit the company's interests.* Unless corporate executives have a passionate interest in the importance of the problem they seek to address, they will not be able to sustain the allocation of money and executive time needed to solve the problem. Therefore, executives seeking to attack big societal problems must be confident that the problems have deep meaning to them and to society.

• *Screen problems based on their ability to be solved through the right combination of foundation money and partner capabilities.* Ambition alone does not represent a sufficient criterion for picking a problem to solve. Executives must balance their ambitions with a sober assessment of whether they have—or can partner to obtain—the capabilities needed to make a significant dent in the problem.

• *Develop strategies to solve the selected problems through detailed analysis.* Executives should analyze whether they can assemble the capabilities needed to achieve their ambitions before announcing which problem they will attempt to solve. Furthermore, they should apply their executive abilities to develop a robust plan to overcome the barriers to success and be willing to apply the time and resources necessary to carry the plan to fruition.

• *Establish relationships with the right governmental, corporate, and service partners.* In many cases big societal problems can be solved only by leading a team of alliance partners with the needed skills. Therefore, companies that have demonstrated an ability to lead industry alliances are more likely than their peers to manage such alliances successfully.

• *Set specific goals and monitor results against goals, modifying strategies as needed.* Just as executives set and monitor the achievement of business objectives, they should apply the same logic to their efforts to solve big societal problems. Although executives may need to be creative in developing meaningful measures of success, they must develop and monitor such measures persistently in order to motivate people to achieve the desired outcomes.

Microsoft and Merck have followed several of these tactics in their efforts to change society. Bill Gates hoped to apply his brains, ambition, and money to solve societal problems to which he believed he could bring a unique approach. According to the *Economist,* Gates kicked off this approach with the 1998 announcement that he would contribute $100 million to vaccinate children in the developing world. Gates made this donation through the Program for Appropriate Technology in Health (http://www.path.org), a Seattle-based nonprofit organization that works with governments and non-governmental organizations to help improve the health of women and children by exchanging knowledge and technology on how best to reduce the spread of communicable diseases, and it had two unique features. First, vaccines, the quickest way to save lives around the world, represented a much wider cause than enhancing Microsoft's reputation. Gates intended his donation to support four expensive new vaccines for hepatitis B and the rotavirus infection, which killed 2.5 million children a year in poor countries.[21]

Most of Gates's money went into ways to make the drugs more available in the third world. Some vaccines took fifteen years to reach poorer countries, and many such countries continued to suffer from inadequate drug-distribution systems. Some governments in Asia and Africa even failed to admit that their citizens had even contracted the diseases in the first place.

When Gates announced his donation, the biggest impediment to implementing a vaccination program was the pricing structure of the vaccines. U.S. drug companies resisted the notion of selling medicines at a lower price in poorer countries. These companies were worried about a political backlash in Washington because the U.S. government was a major vaccine buyer. Drug companies also had a difficult time interacting with the idealistic staffers at United Nations (UN) agencies and funds, which were the main buyers of vaccines for the third world. Initially, the UN staffers demanded that drug companies give away their vaccines without regard to the business implications for the drug companies. Although UN agencies eventually did a better job of attracting companies such as Merck in the mid-1990s, driving effective cooperation between companies, UN agencies, governments, and financial sources such as the World Bank remained a significant challenge.

This challenge required Gates's brains and money, representing the second reason why his donation was interesting. Gates argued that vaccine prices should come down because his contribution would generate greater volume. He compared the economics of vaccines with software: in both industries the cost of the first copy is very high, whereas subsequent copies cost very little to produce. Gates also felt that he would want to get involved in discussions between the private and public sectors. His goals and ideas for achieving them represented his initial foray into his philanthropic strategy—somewhat reminiscent of Microsoft's strategy for new product development. Although the first version did not set the world on fire, Gates learned from that version's shortcomings and eventually developed a strategy that worked very effectively.

By 1998, Gates had begun to settle into a process for managing his philanthropic efforts. He spent five hours a week on philanthropy, ranking medicine as his second-biggest interest after information technology; and at a 1998 meeting of vaccine experts at his house, he asked his guests probing questions about the business and technology involved so that he could develop effective vaccination strategies.[22]

By 2002, Gates's philanthropic efforts had become more formalized through the Bill & Melinda Gates Foundation. Led by Bill Gates's father, William H. Gates Sr., and Patty Stonesifer, the foundation had a $24 billion endowment. According to the *Bulletin of the World Health Organization,* in April 2001 the foundation had generated significant benefits. Specifically, it had helped to arrange for vaccines to arrive in Mozambique, the first of several dozen countries that previously lacked access to children's vaccines. Gates Sr. pointed out that this was one of the foundation's first grants, $750 million, which went to the Global Fund for Children's Vaccines. According to him, children in developing countries often waited ten to fifteen years before they could have access to the same vaccines that children in the United States received. Through a concerted effort by governments and organizations to make access to vaccines a priority, the foundation and its partners anticipated saving three million children each year.[23]

Merck's efforts to inhibit the spread of AIDS emerges from its deeply held corporate belief in the idea that Merck's purpose is to help relieve suffering. Unfortunately, Merck's efforts to solve the AIDS problem in Botswana has met with mixed success. According to the *Wall Street Journal Europe,* Merck's $100 million, five-year campaign to fight AIDS in Botswana has achieved some success due to the partnerships that the company forged with government and nonprofit agencies.[24] The $100 million represents the combined contributions of Merck ($50 million) and the Bill & Melinda Gates Foundation ($50 million).[25, 26] In 2001 29 percent of Botswana's adult population was infected with the AIDS virus, HIV. Merck believed that AIDS drugs such as its own Crixivan did little good in Africa because they were not offered as part of a systematic treatment program. In Merck's view African health care was not comprehensive and infectious diseases such as tuberculosis and pneumonia, to which AIDS-weakened individuals were particularly vulnerable, were common medical problems.

Merck's analysis led it to conclude that the only way to solve Botswana's AIDS problem would be to fix its health care system. The magnitude of this goal made it essential for Merck to find partners. Merck succeeded: partnering with the Bill and Melinda Gates Foundation, which pledged $50 million, and with the Harvard AIDS Institute, which conducted research on the prevention of mother-to-child AIDS transmission, on the design and development of an HIV-1C vaccine and on the susceptibility and resistance to antiretroviral drugs. Merck also attracted other companies, such as Unilever PLC, which contributed distribution capabilities and shaped AIDS-awareness marketing initiatives.

Merck officials met with Botswana's president, Festus Mogae, in July 2000 to emphasize the company's desire to solve the problems jointly with Botswana's health agencies. Dr. Banu Khan, Botswana's national AIDS coordinator, pointed out that the problem would not be solved unless an ample supply of antiretroviral drugs were made available to citizens in the context of a comprehensive health care system. The partners planned to build such a system, including a Botswana-wide HIV training program for doctors, nurses, and counselors, as well as diagnostic labs in remote areas of Botswana.[27]

The initial results of this program were disappointing, according to the *Financial Times*. In September 2002, for example, President Festus Mogae said Botswana did not have the skills required to care for the vast majority of its estimated three hundred thousand HIV-AIDS sufferers. Private contributions and the health budget covered only a fraction of the target population. The rollout of the Merck-led program, first announced in August 2001, had been slower than expected, with only about two thousand people enrolled by September 2002. The initial partners—Merck, the Gates Foundation, the Harvard AIDS Institute, and Unilever—did not achieve significant results. In an effort to achieve better results, Ray Gilmartin, Merck's CEO, sought help from a "larger coalition," consisting of UN agencies, pharmaceutical companies, large employers, and governments.[28, 29]

Merck's efforts to resolve the AIDS problem in Botswana highlight some of the challenges and opportunities facing executives seeking to change society. Clearly, Merck did not believe that it could solve the problem of AIDS in Botswana without help. Two years after announcing its initiative, Merck had fallen short and was seeking to bring in more partners to help achieve its goal. The company had underestimated the challenge of motivating its initial partners. Its decision to take on partners in the first place may have reflected a somewhat lukewarm commitment to the cause. Its partners may have underestimated how difficult it was to achieve the desired results. Economic conditions may have deteriorated in the United States and other key markets in which the partners operated, replacing the sense of urgency these partners initially felt for the cause with concern for resuscitating their companies' earnings growth.

The experiences of Microsoft and Merck highlight general principles about corporate efforts to give to the community by attacking big societal problems. First, initiatives to attack big societal problems are generally not directly related to companies' day-to-day business. Microsoft's involvement in the vaccine program was clearly disconnected from its main business of selling software. Unlike philanthropy targeted at inspiring employees or enriching the community, attacking big societal problems is intended to generate longer-term benefits such as helping the company deal with government officials and attracting talented employees who savor the idea that their employer has such broad influence on society. Although the Merck efforts to battle AIDS likely involved using its drugs, the donation of the drugs and the risks that the program in Botswana might not achieve the desired results both suggested that Merck's business would not benefit from the program.

Second, attacking broad societal problems may achieve significant results. Microsoft's efforts to increase childhood vaccines seemed to generate results because they were more carefully targeted at countries and at delivery mechanisms that did not require as much complex coordination. Furthermore, because Microsoft's donations came from a well-funded and well-organized foundation, the vaccination project had clear accountability for achieving results. This contrasts with Merck's approach, in which accountability for achieving specific outcomes appeared more diffuse. With respect to its efforts in Botswana, Merck likely did not allocate enough resources—money and management commitment—to attracting the right set of partners and motivating them to generate results.

Third, attacking big societal problems can create a metagovernment. This metagovernment augments the functioning of a local government without supplanting its role or diminishing the power of a political leader. When the metagovernment achieves results, such as saving lives through vaccination or other medical means, it can benefit the citizens and political leadership. Ultimately, the entrepreneur who contributes brains, ambition, and money gets rewarded through the satisfaction of making the world a better place for millions of people. Indirectly, this accomplishment enhances the company's reputation with customers, regulators, and employees.

TRANSFORMING THE ROBERT WOOD JOHNSON FOUNDATION

Giving to your community, if done persistently, requires changes in strategy based on what works and what does not. A basic management axiom is that what gets measured gets done. And its corollary, that what does not get measured, does not get done, is equally important. These axioms often apply to corporate giving. Executives must decide how to measure the effects of their contributions to the community. And having decided how to measure these effects, executives must have the courage and wisdom to change their corporate-giving strategies if the results fall short. Executives can transfer some of the performance management techniques from the world of for-profit industry to their nonprofit activities.

Attacking big societal problems is important because the company's effort, if executed well, can create a multiplier effect that ricochets through the world and makes the company stronger. Attacking big societal problems keeps a company's executives in contact with world leaders, giving these executives a chance to apply their skills and the corporation's money, know-how, and technology to problems that resist governmental solutions. Attacking big societal problems stretches the imagination of a company and inspires employees who take pride in working for an organization that makes the world better. And attacking big societal problems benefits the individuals who are most damaged by these problems.

All these factors came into play as Johnson & Johnson considered making changes in its philanthropic foundation. According to *Health-Week,* the Robert Wood Johnson was the largest health care philanthropy in the United States in 1988. Although the foundation had a reputation for improving access to primary care, a 1987 review led to setting three new goals:

- Helping people most vulnerable to disease, such as children and the elderly

- Helping solve specific diseases, such as AIDS and mental illness

- Addressing broad national health issues, such as the financing of health care and inequities in the health care system[30]

Robert Wood Johnson, heir to Johnson & Johnson, began the philanthropy in 1936 as a local foundation in the company's headquarters town, New Brunswick, New Jersey. When Johnson died in 1968, he left his estate to the foundation, which became a national philanthropy in 1972. Between 1972 and 1987, the foundation distributed $826 million.

Dr. Leighton Cluff joined the foundation in 1976 as executive vice president and became president in 1986. According to Cluff, the foundation conducted surveys that revealed a significant improvement in access to general medical care for the American people between 1972 and 1986. When Cluff took over the foundation, he and its board of trustees asked whether the foundation should reexamine its mission to include a larger number of health problems. In 1987 the foundation's board of trustees and staff analyzed what the foundation had done in the past, what it had learned, and what it wanted to do differently in the future. They also asked "distinguished Americans" what they viewed as the health problems for the next decade.[31] This analysis led the foundation to identify its three new goals of helping people most vulnerable to disease, helping solve specific diseases, and addressing broad national issues.

In the area of the vulnerable populations, for example, the foundation decided that it should pay attention to health problems of troubled youth, such as substance abuse, teenage pregnancy, destructive behavior, suicide, and homicide. The foundation decided that it would mobilize the community to deal with the causes of substance abuse rather than merely focus on primary care services. For example, it decided that the way to deal with substance abuse was to supplement primary care services by mobilizing community action among hospitals, physicians, nurses, health departments, business leaders, union leaders, and religious communities. Although the foundation maintained its focus on health care, it realized that social intervention might be required to deal with health problems.

The foundation also decided to make itself a focal point for funding programs to treat specific diseases such as AIDS. In this case the foundation began soliciting proposals in February 1987 for programs dealing with the prevention of AIDS, as well as the development of in-hospital service programs, nursing home service programs, or primary care service programs. The foundation received 1,026 proposals from forty-nine states requesting $535 million in funds. Although it could not fund all these requests, it generated interest from state and federal governments and other foundations to help fund parts of the programs that it could not fund itself.

Under Cluff's direction, the foundation began funding programs targeted at social change. For example, Cluff drove the financing of a program to improve the capacity of pastors, priests, and ministers to help patients with AIDS. He also helped finance church groups interested in using the church to help prevent AIDS. Overall, he anticipated that between 1988 and 1991, the foundation would spend $50 million in AIDS-related programs, an amount representing half of the foundation's payout requirement during that period. (A foundation that wants to retain its tax-exempt status must pay out a certain proportion of its assets to grant recipients; this is its payout requirement.)

Cluff also focused the foundation on addressing ethical dilemmas related to health care. Specifically, he wanted to address the problem that 37 million Americans lack health insurance and therefore do not have ready access to care. He wanted to focus the nation on the issue of racial inequality in health care coverage and medical care; for example, black men in the United States with coronary artery disease are far less likely to have coronary bypass surgery or coronary angioplasty than are white men with the same disease, and the death rate in infants of black women far exceeded that of white women.

To address these issues, the foundation gave grants to eight states seeking to encourage the state, city, county, and private sectors to cooperate on the development of long-term care insurance programs, particularly for elderly disabled people who require nursing home care. The foundation tended to fund grants that transcended a specific state. For example, in 1988 it supported a program through the Mississippi legislature to examine the state's Medicaid eligibility program because Mississippi had a poor Medicaid program. The foundation believed that solving this state's problem would generate useful ideas that could help other states facing similar challenges. Ordinarily, the foundation would not have supported that program unless all of the Southern states were trying to find ways to improve their Medicaid programs.

Cluff's goal was for others to copy the foundation's most successful programs. As he pointed out, roughly 20 percent to 30 percent of the grants the foundation supports fail. In his view this failure rate suggested that the foundation was taking sufficient risk. Cluff believes that charitable work shares some characteristics of business development: if a charitable organization is not taking enough risks, then it is not trying out ideas with sufficient potential to make a significant difference in the community. Although venture capitalists do not expect all their portfolio companies to succeed, they expect the ones that do succeed to win big, thereby offsetting the lost investment from the ones that failed. A similar dynamic applies to the foundation's work. In general, the foundation has a much higher success rate than a venture capitalist, who expects only 10 percent of investments to pay off significantly.

On the other hand, Cluff mentioned two programs whose success caused others to replicate them. The foundation was an earlier supporter of the development of the emergency medical response system to develop regionalized emergency response systems around the country. It encouraged the establishment of the 911 emergency number. The federal government subsequently invested to develop those programs. Another program in the mid-1980s helped church congregations and health providers train volunteers to provide home services to elderly and disabled people. The foundation initially funded twenty-five such projects; by 1988, 350 existed in the United States.[32]

The foundation helps Johnson & Johnson's business. First, its recent focus on improving the health care system helps to expand the market for its products. With more and better managed health care providers and payers, the foundation increases the number of organizations that can purchase Johnson & Johnson products. Second, by improving the health of citizens in communities with traditionally poor health care systems, the foundation frees up resources that their local governments can spend on economic development. This local economic development can bring in employers who can also become customers of Johnson & Johnson products. Finally, the work of the foundation signals that Johnson & Johnson's long-term interests are aligned with those of the communities in which it operates. This creates a positive reputation for Johnson & Johnson among politicians, regulators, employees, and customers.

MANAGEMENT LEVERS

The Johnson & Johnson case reveals the importance of managing the change process well. Cluff's appointment as president of the foundation led to a broad rethinking of how best to achieve its goals. Cluff worked well with the foundation's stakeholders—including the board, staff, and "distinguished Americans"—to review its performance and aspirations. He established a clear set of new goals and altered the foundation's strategy in order to achieve them. Specifically, Cluff funded programs intended to mobilize the community to address the underlying causes of medical problems in the targeted demographic groups, diseases, and social issues related to the foundation's new goals.

Cluff's success in transforming the Robert Wood Johnson Foundation suggests four management levers for executives seeking to change the way their companies give to their communities:

• *Agree on common values.* Generally, a company will not reexamine its fundamental values unless it acquires a new CEO to turn it around. In any case companies should agree on their shared values, articulate those values clearly, and communicate them persistently. As a result, the way that a company gives to its community should flow from the shared values.

• *Set goals reflecting capabilities and aspirations.* Having agreed on common values, executives must build a consensus on how best to realize those values. The process of building such a consensus starts with seeking out the views of key stakeholders. Then executives must assess which charitable activities will best fit with the company's capabilities and values. Ultimately, executives should articulate the most appropriate targets of opportunity in the form of shared goals.

• *Change strategies to reflect new goals.* Once executives have agreed on a set of shared goals, they should assess which strategies will work most effectively to achieve the goals. Executives should study charitable organizations and companies with similar goals and assess which strategies work and which do not. Finally, executives should develop strategies and put in place processes to implement them.

• *Evaluate results and adjust strategy accordingly.* Executives should decide how best to measure their charitable initiatives, track the measures, and make people in their organizations accountable for them. Executives can then assess which strategies work and which don't, thus helping executives to adjust their strategies to align more closely with the goals.

VALUE QUOTIENT

Tactical-level analysis can help executives pinpoint opportunities for improvement. If you perceive that your organization can improve in the way it applies the principle "Give to your community," such analysis can help identify how best to improve the way your organization performs targeted activities.

Exhibit 8.1 can help you calculate your company's Value Quotient through two levels of analysis. The first level of analysis is binary, meaning that you can use the worksheet as a checklist to determine whether or not your company performs the specific tactics on the list. If your company does not perform any of the tactics within a specific activity, then it should consider initiating such tactics. The second level of analysis is analog, meaning that the worksheet can help pinpoint opportunities to improve how well your company performs a specific tactic that it has already been performing. To raise your company's score on a particular tactic, you may wish to initiate an in-depth process to change the way your organization performs the tactic along the lines developed in Chapter Nine.

To conduct the binary and analog levels of analysis, your company should gather data through interviews with employees, customers, analysts, and shareholders. Ideally, your company should use objective third parties to identify an appropriate sample of interviewees, develop interview guides, conduct the interviews, and analyze the results. The outcomes of collecting and analyzing the data will be specific scores for each tactic. Although assigning these scores requires judgment, they should be calibrated by comparing the scores with the Value Leaders and other best-of-breed competitors.

Scores for each tactic range from excellent (five) to poor (one). If an organization does not perform the tactic at all, it receives a score of zero. To calculate the activity scores, the analyst can average the scores for the tactics supporting that activity and round the average to the nearest whole number. To illustrate how a score might be assigned for a specific tactic, consider the tactic "Create a central point in the organization for corporate giving, generally reporting to the CEO." If your company does not have any formal approach to corporate giving, it would receive a score of zero. On the other hand, if for the last ten years your company has operated a central organization, distinct from the marketing organization, responsible for corporate giving and reporting to the CEO, then your company would receive a score of five.

In assigning scores, it helps to first assess whether or not your organization performs the tactic, and if so compare your organization to one of the examples discussed in the chapter. For example, in scoring your company on the tactic of creating a central point in the organization for corporate giving, give your company a score of zero if it does not have such an organization. If it does have such an

Give to Your Community: Activity and Tactics	Score

Inspire employees

☐ Create a central point in the organization for corporate giving, generally reporting to the CEO. _____

☐ Separate corporate giving from public relations and marketing to clarify its purpose and defuse community and employee cynicism. _____

☐ Create a program that lets employees recommend causes that inspire them. _____

☐ Invest executive time and money to support the employee-recommended causes. _____

☐ Communicate the success of such programs to all employees to encourage greater participation. _____

☐ Give employees time off work to contribute to the company's charity of choice, for example, one day every six or twelve months. _____

Enrich the community

☐ Establish an organization within the company that specializes in serving local communities. _____

☐ Assign people from that organization to identify local movers and shakers. _____

☐ Meet with these influential people and listen to their description of community needs, potential objections to the company, and ways that the company can overcome these objections. _____

☐ Assess whether the benefits of operating in the community exceed the costs of overcoming these objections. _____

☐ Deliver the right mix of cash, products, and time to satisfy the local movers and shakers, enabling the company to operate in the community. _____

☐ Maintain contact with leaders and remain responsive to their needs in order to continue to enrich the community. _____

Attack big societal problems

☐ Identify big societal problems that fit the company's interests. _____

☐ Screen problems based on their ability to be solved through the right combination of foundation money and partner capabilities. _____

☐ Develop strategies to solve the selected problems through detailed analysis. _____

☐ Establish relationships with the right governmental, corporate, and service partners. _____

☐ Set specific goals and monitor results against goals, modifying strategies as needed. _____

Total _____

Exhibit 8.1. Value Quotient Worksheet: Give to Your Community.

Key: 5 = excellent; 4 = very good; 3 = good; 2 = fair; 1 = poor; 0 = not applicable.

organization, give your company five points if its organization is as effective as Southwest's, based both on its popularity with employees and with the charitable organizations it serves. Adjust your company's score downward if its central charitable organization performs less effectively than Southwest's.

CONCLUSION

Giving to your community is an essential principle of Value Leadership. Giving to your community inspires employees, enriches the locations in which your company operates, and solves big societal problems. How well your company adopts this principle can influence how fast your company grows, how productive and loyal your employees are, and ultimately how much profit your company returns to shareholders.

CHAPTER NINE

Actions Speak Louder Than Words

(Instill Value Leadership in Executives, Investors, and Policymakers)

H ow can executives, investors, and policymakers benefit from Value Leadership? Before addressing this question, let's review why it is worth striving for. As we noted at the beginning of this book, Value Leadership means that superior profits flow to companies that outperform competitors in creating value for employees, customers, and communities. To bring Value Leadership to life, we identified companies whose past track record suggests that they embody Value Leadership. We found that these Value Leaders outperformed their peers in terms of higher stock price appreciation, faster growth, and wider profit margins.

VALUE LEADERSHIP FOR EXECUTIVES

As we discussed in Chapter One, executives may decide that the most effective way to use Value Leadership is to focus on making improvements in specific principles where this book's Value Quotient (VQ) worksheets identified the greatest opportunities for improvement. As they do before implementing any change initiative, executives should weigh the benefits and the costs before starting. Executives must begin with a clear understanding of how these benefits are likely to manifest themselves within their own companies. And the costs of such change initiatives could be considerable—particularly in terms of the executive time required to lead the change process.

Once executives have concluded that the benefits of Value Leadership exceed its costs, they should take the following steps:

- Create a Value Leadership change team
- Educate the team on Value Leadership
- Conduct interviews to develop the company's VQ
- Pinpoint Value Leadership principles that the company can follow more closely
- Analyze practices that affect the company's ability to apply these principles
- Develop improvement initiatives
- Implement improvement initiatives
- Evaluate improvement initiatives' effectiveness through a new VQ analysis

Create a Value Leadership Change Team

A Value Leadership change team is a group of senior executives whose mission is to create shareholder value by making the company's employees, customers, and communities better off. In light of the importance of this mission, the Value Leadership change team should include executives with the power to make the changes needed to achieve the mission. Different companies could decide to include different team members; however, here is a suggested list of members:

- CEO
- CFO
- Selected business unit executives
- Selected functional executives such as sales, marketing, manufacturing
- Key staff executives from, say, human resources and information technology departments

In composing the team, the CEO should balance the need for including those with the power to act with the need to let the team operate efficiently. One way to achieve this balance might be to cast a broad net for inclusion in the team at the beginning of the process but to allow participants' roles to change during the process. For example, the team could include a steering committee of the most senior executives who set the team's mission, objectives, and key project milestones. A team of operating executives could spend more time on the project conducting the analysis and producing the deliverables. Participation in the project could offer a unique management development opportunity for these operating executives.

Educate the Team on Value Leadership

To motivate the change team, the CEO must generate enthusiasm for Value Leadership. To accomplish this the CEO should sponsor a seminar on Value Leadership designed to accomplish the following objectives:

- Define Value Leadership.
- Explain why Value Leadership is important.
- Describe the benefits of Value Leadership.
- Highlight the principles and activities that let companies apply Value Leadership.
- Present case studies of Value Leaders and peers.
- Conduct workshops that highlight the potential benefits of Value Leadership to the company.

The seminar should convince top executives that the concept of Value Leadership is worth an investment of their time. More specifically, it should generate interest in using tools such as the VQ to help the company pinpoint opportunities for improvement.

Conduct Interviews to Develop the Company's VQ

The VQ can be a valuable tool for assessing opportunities for improvement within an organization. The value of the VQ depends on the quality of the data used to calculate it. Therefore, the team should conduct extensive interviews with the company's stakeholders. To generate an objective perspective on the results, it may make sense for the team to engage a third party to conduct the interviews. As we noted in Chapter One, the interview guides should vary depending on the person being interviewed, with the focus on Value Leadership topics with which the interviewee is likely to have the most experience.

The interviews should provide insights into how the company's stakeholders perceive its use of Value Leadership. As Table 9.1 suggests, different stakeholders could be interviewed for topics on which they are likely to have the most knowledge.

The team should analyze the interviews and develop the company's VQ, using the VQ template presented in Chapter One. As noted there, the team should focus on each activity and determine whether the company performs the activity. If not, the team should give the company a score of zero on that activity. If the company does perform the activity, the team must make a judgment about how well it does so. In order to make the qualitative assessment, the team can benchmark the company's performance of the activity against other companies. The Appendix summarizes the VQs of the eight Value Leaders and those of the eight peer companies. The team should score the company's activities by comparing the results of the interviews with these sixteen companies.

As an example of how to apply the scores, let's review the logic behind the Synopsys VQ of 87 percent from Table 1.2. In the principle "Value human relationships," Synopsys earned sixty points, the highest possible score. Its top score resulted from the company's excellent

Stakeholder	Value Leadership Principle
CEO	All Value Leadership principles.
CFO	All Value Leadership principles with focus on "Fulfill your commitments."
Customers	Focus on "Value human relationships," "Foster teamwork," "Experiment frugally," "Fight complacency," and "Win through multiple means."
Employees	Focus on "Value human relationships," "Foster teamwork," "Experiment frugally," "Fight complacency," "Win through multiple means," and "Give to your community."
Communities	Focus on "Give to your community."
Investors	Focus on "Win through multiple means," "Fulfill your commitments," and "Fight complacency."
Partners	Focus on "Foster teamwork," "Win through multiple means," "Fulfill your commitments," and "Fight complacency."

Table 9.1.   Value Quotient Interview Topics by Stakeholder.

performance of all four of the key activities that support the principle. For the activity "Adhere to core values," Synopsys received the highest possible score of five because the interviews revealed that the company's core values emerged from a careful effort to synthesize what its founding team considered most important. Synopsys articulated these values clearly, communicated them through multiple means, and used them to make decisions about who to hire and promote, who to fire, and even which companies to acquire. Synopsys earned an excellent score for the activity "Adhere to core values" because the interviews revealed that it commits to its values and then fulfills this commitment through its actions.

If Synopsys clearly articulated its core values and frequently acted according to the values, it might have received a good score. If it articulated its core values but only occasionally acted according to them, it would receive a fair score. And if it articulated its core values but did not act accordingly or if it did not articulate its core values at all, it would receive a score of zero.

Pinpoint Value Leadership Principles That the Company Can Follow More Closely

Once the VQ is complete, the team can identify which Value Leadership principles the company follows closely and which it follows more loosely. The team may decide that the company should focus its attention on tightening up the company's conformance with the two or three principles for which the company has the lowest VQ scores or which have the potential for making the greatest impact on stakeholders.

Analyze Practices That Affect the Company's Ability to Apply These Principles

The team should then develop a case for changing the practices that affect the company's use of these principles. It should identify what practices need to change and assess the costs and benefits of such changes. To that end the team should first analyze the practices that affect the firm's VQ score for that principle. For example, if the company decides to value human relationships, then it should map out how it performs the four activities that underlie the principle. To do so, the team should conduct interviews with the appropriate stakeholders to assess how the company currently performs the activities.

As Table 9.2 suggests, the stakeholders interviewed might vary depending on the principle.

Although the specific topics of the interviews should vary depending on the principle and the interviewee, the stakeholder interviews should focus on the following general topics:

- The overall level of satisfaction with the company's practices and recent trends
- Specific sources of dissatisfaction with the company
- Specific competitors who do a better job than the company
- Specific competitor practices that provide greater satisfaction
- Ideas for improving the company's performance

In seeking ideas for improvement, the team might also consider using process mapping as a tool to identify the specific steps that the company follows to perform these activities. *Process mapping* details the specific activities making up a business process, such as fulfilling a customer order, and the flow of information among the activities. Process mapping might be particularly helpful for activities linked to the sources of dissatisfaction identified in the interview process. For example, if the team was working on improving how well the company values human relationships, it might interview employees. If these interviews revealed that employees felt that the company's process of evaluating and rewarding employees was arbitrary, then the team might consider mapping the process of how the company makes its employee evaluation decisions. Such mapping might identify clear opportunities for improving the process by highlighting problems,

Principle	Stakeholders to Interview
Value human relationships	Employees and customers
Foster teamwork	Employees, customers, and suppliers
Experiment frugally	Employees, customers, and suppliers
Fulfill your commitments	Employees, customers, suppliers, and investors
Fight complacency	Employees, customers, and investors
Win through multiple means	Employees, customers, and investors
Give to your community	Employees and communities

Table 9.2.   Stakeholders to Interview for Each Principle.

say, in the communication between a department manager and the human resources department.

The team might also consider conducting a quantitative analysis to help model the economic impact of adopting the principles under review. As Table 9.3 indicates, the specific quantitative measures vary by principle. If the team's analysis confirms the relationships described earlier, it can offer compelling evidence of the benefits of following the principle more closely. For example, if the firm is trying to fight complacency, then it should analyze trends in market share, return on equity, productivity, balance sheet strength, earnings growth, and shareholder return. The relationships described in Table 9.3 suggest that the company's trends in all these areas should have gotten worse as the company's use of the principle loosened. Conversely, this quantitative analysis can help the team estimate how much the company's economic performance might improve if the company followed the principle more tightly.

Develop Improvement Initiatives

The team needs to take the three strands of analysis—stakeholder interviews, process mapping, and quantitative analysis—and decide what to do. Specifically, it should review the analysis and then brainstorm possible ways to get the company to follow the principles under review more closely. Initially, the team should try to develop a large number (about fifty) of potential improvement initiatives. Next, the team should develop criteria for ranking the initiatives. Such criteria might include the following:

- Time to results
- Financial cost to implement
- Soft costs to implement (for example, amount of cultural change required)
- Impact on shareholders (for example, market share growth and earning per share growth)
- Impact on customers (customer satisfaction, customer retention, market share growth, and average revenue per customer)
- Impact on employees (for example, retention and stated job satisfaction through surveys)

Principle	Link with Criteria for Quantitative Value Leader Selection
Value human relationships	**Return on equity:** Less turnover lowers costs, increases return on equity. **Productivity:** Employees treated well produce more. **Earnings growth:** High productivity accelerates earnings growth. **Shareholder return:** Earnings growth increases stock price.
Foster teamwork	**Market share:** Teamwork helps increase customer value and market share. **Return on equity:** Teamwork increases productivity and return on equity. **Productivity:** Teamwork increases productivity. **Earnings growth:** High productivity accelerates earnings growth. **Shareholder return:** Earnings growth increases stock price.
Experiment frugally	**Market share:** New product success increases market share. **Return on equity:** Profitable growth increases return on equity. **Productivity:** New product success enhances revenue per employee. **Balance sheet strength:** New product success strengthens cash. **Earnings growth:** New product success accelerates earnings growth. **Shareholder return:** Earnings growth increases stock price.
Fulfill your commitments	**Return on equity:** Lower litigation costs increase return on equity. **Productivity:** Employees treated honestly are happier and thus produce more. **Earnings growth:** High productivity accelerates earnings growth. **Shareholder return:** Earnings growth increases stock price.
Fight complacency	**Market share:** Self-renewal drives market share improvement. **Return on equity:** Self-renewal drives earnings, increases return on equity. **Productivity:** Self-renewal enhances productivity. **Balance sheet strength:** Self-renewal increases cash generation. **Earnings growth:** High productivity accelerates earnings growth. **Shareholder return:** Earnings growth increases stock price.
Win through multiple means	**Market share:** Winning is market share leadership. **Return on equity:** Winning increases pricing power, return on equity. **Productivity:** Winning can lead to higher productivity. **Balance sheet strength:** Winning can increase cash generation. **Earnings growth:** Winning accelerates earnings growth. **Shareholder return:** Winning increases stock price.
Give to your community	**Market share:** Giving to community may attract more local customers. **Return on equity:** Growth increases return on equity. **Productivity:** Employees who give are happier and produce more. **Balance sheet strength:** Growth can increase cash. **Earnings growth:** Giving to community supports earnings growth. **Shareholder return:** Earnings growth increases stock price.

Table 9.3.   Quantitative Measures of Value Leadership Principles.

The team should score each idea on each criterion and calculate an overall score for each improvement initiative. It should then rank the initiatives by the overall score and decide how many of the top five or ten the company can realistically achieve. As a general rule, the team should select some initiatives that are likely to generate quick results, thereby reinforcing confidence in the change process. For initiatives likely to require greater investment, the team should develop a detailed budget that estimates the amount and timing of any investment as well as the benefits likely to flow from them. If the company has created a steering committee for the project, the team should present its recommendations to the committee before proceeding.

After gathering input from the steering committee, the team should develop detailed implementation plans for the selected initiatives. The implementation plans should include the following elements:

- Initiative definition
- Expected benefits of the initiative
- Executive(s) accountable for implementation
- Action steps, completion dates, accountable managers, deliverables
- Initiative cash flows

Implement Improvement Initiatives

Although each implementation is different, the team should proceed with an understanding of these seven principles of change management:

- The CEO must communicate the importance of the change and reinforce the message with his or her own actions.
- The team must recognize that people are likely to resist the change, often through passive-aggressive behavior (for example, people may say they agree and then stall when it comes to taking action).
- Resistance to change may be overcome by providing a forum in which people can express their anxieties about the change and come to see how they might benefit from it.

- Transforming employees' anxiety to enthusiasm demands frequent give-and-take with employees and potentially other stakeholders.

- If the change involves new ways for people to do their work, the people must have a clear idea of specifically how their jobs will change and why that change is beneficial.

- If executives want to change the way people work, they must change the compensation system to reward the new way of working.

- Sequencing of initiatives matters, as alluded to earlier. The team should work to obtain quick wins because they help maintain executives' support for further initiatives.

If the company implements the change initiatives, the ultimate test of their success is whether customers, employees, communities, and shareholders are better off. Often, there is a time lag between the improved value to stakeholders and higher returns for shareholders. In the medium term, changes in the way the company works may make employees more productive and customers more satisfied. Over the longer term, these changes will lead to higher revenues, profits, and shareholder value.

Evaluate Improvement Initiatives' Effectiveness Through a New VQ Analysis

A basic axiom of management is that what gets measured gets done. In order to embed the concept of Value Leadership into a company and to test whether the improvement initiatives have generated the desired results, the team should conduct new VQ analyses every six months after the company has implemented the initiatives. Such analyses will, we hope, confirm that the company is improving. If not, the team should analyze why not and take corrective action. If new opportunities for improvement emerge, the team should evaluate them and develop new improvement initiatives.

VALUE LEADERSHIP FOR INVESTORS

Value Leadership is useful for investors in any market. In up markets investors can profit by purchasing shares in Value Leader companies because they are likely to generate higher profits and earn higher returns for investors. In down markets investors can identify companies that do not embody Value Leadership. Investors can profit by selling short these companies' shares, which are likely to drop more than the market averages.

Profiting in Up Markets

The more information investors have about the companies in which they invest, the less risk they undertake before committing their capital to a stock. In a rising market, such risks may appear not worth considering because the greatest perceived risk may be in not getting the maximum investment returns possible. It is precisely during such periods that investors should conduct detailed analysis to avoid purchasing shares at the top of an investment bubble, which could collapse to zero when market trends reverse.

Investors should seek out companies that best satisfy the quantitative indicators used to select Value Leaders. As noted in the Introduction, these factors include the following:

- Market share
- Ten-year average return on equity
- Revenues and profits per employee
- Balance sheet strength
- Ten-year earnings growth
- Ten-year shareholder return

Because these measures are relatively easy for investors to track, they do not necessarily provide investors with an opportunity to earn higher than average returns. Nevertheless, investors should screen potential investments based on how well a company meets these criteria relative to others in their industry. A set of companies that beats its competitors on these six measures may make a good candidate for stock purchase.

Investors who want to increase their odds of finding good stocks to buy in an up market should consider conducting research to gain insight into the extent to which the companies embody Value Leadership. For example, after conducting the quantitative screening described earlier, investors may wish to develop a VQ analysis of the companies that pass that initial screen. A small investor might be able to gather the data needed to conduct such an analysis through a combination of searching online databases and interviews with customers, employees, and possibly even executives of the company. Larger investors would likely have an advantage in terms of gaining access to top executives as well as all the sources mentioned for the small investor.

Investors could then consider investing in the companies with strong performance on the quantitative indicators and a high VQ. Once investors had purchased shares in such companies, they could conduct periodic VQ analyses on the companies in which they invested to identify a trend. If the VQ performance was improving or remaining high, the trend might suggest that the investor should continue to hold shares of the stock. If the VQ was declining, the trend might suggest that the company's financial performance was likely to deteriorate in the future. Because there is likely to be a lag between the time that the VQ trend turns down and the time that the company's financial performance deteriorates, the VQ could be a valuable early warning indicator for investors to sell a stock.

Profiting in Down Markets

As we saw in Chapter One, investors had significant opportunities to profit from the bear market that began in March 2000. Among the companies whose stock prices plunged were many whose management did not embrace Value Leadership. One of the most useful ways for investors to identify this lack of commitment to Value Leadership came in the form of financial reporting that did not reflect the company's true economic performance. In short, companies whose stock prices dropped precipitously violated the principle "Fulfill your commitments."

As the examples in Chapter One illustrate, companies' violation of this principle manifested itself in different ways. Williams Communications Group's management insisted that it would not file for bankruptcy despite rapidly deteriorating financial performance, right up until the day it actually filed Chapter 11 in April 2002. AOL Time Warner's management allegedly engaged in various fraudulent transactions that had the effect of overstating revenues. And its management also repeated overly optimistic forecasts of its financial performance both to justify the merger of AOL and Time Warner and to inflate its stock price while some members of management sold shares.

Investors can profit from the failure of companies to adopt Value Leadership, particularly in a down market. As we noted in the Introduction, it is often most difficult for executives to employ Value Leadership during an up market. When economic tides are rising, stock prices also tend to surge. The surging stock prices reward any management behavior that can keep them surging. During the boom years from 1995 to 2000, for example, managers overlooked Value Leadership as a costly anachronism. Instead, they manufactured financial statements that would create the perception that their companies were meeting performance expectations that were in fact beyond the capabilities of the underlying economic reality of the business.

When the markets started to fall, managers were out of sync with the change in the market. A few managers continued to act as though they could restore their deflated stock prices by continuing to manipulate reported financial results. These managers—perhaps unwittingly—created investment opportunities for investors willing to study their financial statements. In many cases these financial statements provided clues of underlying gaps between what the managers were saying publicly about their businesses and their actual economic performance.

Many books have been written about how to analyze financial statements to look for such gaps. In up markets many individual investors buy specific stocks based on what they see on TV or what someone tells them at a cocktail party. In down markets many investors get out of stocks altogether or simply ignore the stocks in which they've invested. Few take the time to read published financial statements. Available at no cost on the U.S. Securities and Exchange Commission (SEC) Web site (http://www.sec.gov/cgi-bin/srch-edgar), these statements are a treasure trove of details that can help investors pinpoint gaps between what management says about the company and its underlying economic reality. Although managers can manipulate these financial statements, a careful reader can identify weak signals of future trouble that could create opportunities for short sellers.

Although a comprehensive list is beyond the scope of this book, here are some of the analyses used to pinpoint the specific opportunities detailed in Chapter One.

Compare earnings press releases and conference call statements with financial statements companies file with the SEC. Investors with Internet access can listen to conference calls between company managers and analysts that deal with past results and future expectations.

Sometimes, the tone of these conference calls is far more optimistic than reported financial results. For example, Williams Communications Group's executives made optimistic statements about the company's ability to avoid bankruptcy virtually up until the day it filed Chapter 11. A review of Williams's financial statements revealed that its net loss had doubled and that it was involved in a dispute with its banks for violating a term of its loan agreement not to purchase its debt on the open market. Ultimately, the company's auditor could not certify its financial statements because of this dispute. The auditor's "going concern" letter was itself a violation of Williams's bank agreement. The bank demanded repayment of the company's multibillion debt load, and Williams responded by filing Chapter 11.

Although this analysis may appear too technical for the small investor, all this information was available in public documents. Company filings with the SEC were accessible on its Web site. Many investors do not read these documents. Instead, they rely on recommendations from their stockbrokers or someone they met at a party. Many investors said that they trusted Williams's executives because they met them at church on Sundays and because Williams was such a prominent member of the local community. These investors may have reasoned that such prominent local executives would not risk the local shunning they would receive if they lost money for investors. The company's bankruptcy helped these investors realize that their trust was misplaced.

Analyze goodwill, net loss, debt, and cash trends. Companies that have grown by making acquisitions tend to accumulate huge amounts of goodwill on their balance sheets. *Goodwill* is the difference between the price an acquirer pays and the book value of the acquired company. Accounting rules require companies to adjust downward the goodwill on their balance sheets if its market value declines. Although such write-offs are noncash charges, they generally result in the reporting of huge net losses that reduce the company's shareholders' equity.

If such companies carry heavy debt loads, the resulting decline in shareholders' equity can increase the company's debt-to-equity ratio. In many cases banks require borrowers to maintain a debt-to-equity ratio below a specific threshold, so such dramatic increases can cause borrowers to default on their credit agreements, requiring immediate repayment of their loans.

At the same time, investors should examine whether a company's cash balances are dwindling. Although companies often point out that the write-off of goodwill is a noncash charge, investors should also examine trends in the company's cash balances. If the company's cash balances are dropping fast, investors may be able to estimate how much time will elapse before the company runs out of cash by dividing the cash on the balance sheet by the company's net loss. For example, a company losing $400 million a quarter with $200 million in cash may have six weeks before it runs out of cash unless it can raise cash quickly from some other source, such as borrowing more money or selling assets.

Look for opaque reporting of liabilities. Some companies use accounting rules regarding the reporting of unconsolidated subsidiaries and lawsuits to confuse investors about their true liabilities. Companies might create off-balance sheet subsidiaries that borrow money that gets siphoned to the company. Yet for accounting purposes, the debt does not get reported to investors on the company's balance sheet. Or companies might downplay in their financial statements the financial impact of a lawsuit filed against it, only to surprise investors with a far worse impact than that previously reported.

El Paso Corporation offers a useful example of both approaches to hiding liabilities. Its annual report listed thirty-three pages of subsidiaries, only a fraction of whose financial results were reported. When a reporter at TheStreet.com asked management questions regarding how much money these subsidiaries had borrowed and how much of their debt had been reported, El Paso did not answer clearly.[1] A review of its financial statements revealed that El Paso operated a subsidiary that had been part of Enron, so El Paso filed to change its name so that investors would "forget" El Paso's Enron associations. Furthermore, El Paso was facing a legal judgment from one of its government regulators, the Federal Energy Regulatory Commission (FERC), which in September 2002 charged El Paso with withholding natural gas from California in order to charge artificially high prices. This "surprise" legal judgment threatened to cost El Paso over a billion dollars.

Uncovering such gaps between financial reporting and economic reality can involve complex analysis. Nevertheless, the underlying impetus for the gap is a management team that violates the concept of Value Leadership. In an ideal world, such a gap would not exist. In the real world, investors can profit from the gap by shorting the stocks of companies that create the gap. The stock market offers discerning investors a chance to profit from bringing the stock prices of companies that violate the concept of Value Leadership into line with their underlying economic reality.

VALUE LEADERSHIP FOR POLICYMAKERS

As we discussed in the Introduction, the premise of this book is that restoring confidence in U.S. capitalism depends on companies, not on government. The daily operations of capitalism are far too complex for the government to regulate all its machinations effectively. Even if our government could pass laws and regulations designed to force companies to adopt Value Leadership, the government could not afford enough corporate police to monitor whether every corporate act complied with these regulations. To restore confidence in U.S. capitalism and sustain that confidence through future economic cycles, harnessing the natural competitiveness of executives is likely to be far more effective and efficient. If executives begin to believe that Value Leadership will give their companies a competitive advantage, they will use it.

Nevertheless, policymakers can create a context that favors the emergence of Value Leadership. Capitalism depends for its efficient operation on trust. Specifically, employees need to trust their employers; customers must trust suppliers; investors must trust the analysts, brokers, and executives who sell them investments and manage the companies that underlie these investments. Without trust, capitalist actors must verify the truth of every statement they make in every commercial interaction. Given the trillions of commercial interactions among all these actors, such a system of verification would be extremely expensive and would slam the brakes on the pace of business.

The saga that began with the bankruptcy of Enron and continued by exposing the corruption of stock analysts has shattered this trust. The current legal and regulatory structure of U.S. capitalism is fraught with trust-eroding conflicts of interest. These conflicts create financial inducements that keep key actors in the capitalist system from adopting Value Leadership. As Table 9.4 suggests, these key actors face formidable conflicts of interest that impede Value Leadership.

A common thread in these conflicts is that key actors receive financial inducements to use their positions as protectors of the public interest to make decisions that abuse that trust. For example, investment banks felt it was important for analysts to promote their clients' stocks. Meanwhile, the investing public trusted the integrity of analyst reports. Specifically, if an analyst rated a stock a "buy," that rating was valuable, and the investing public was likely to buy the stock in response to the analyst's rating. To the extent that the public

Actor	Conflicts and Potential Solutions
Accountants	**Conflicts:** Paid by company to audit while ostensibly protecting interests of nonpaying investors, collect high consulting fees from clients they are auditing. **Potential solution:** Separate consulting from auditing, find a noncorporate source to pay audit fees.
Investment bankers	**Conflicts:** Competing for 7% underwriting fees while acting as enforcer of underwriting standards, offering initial public offering shares to potential clients as inducement. **Potential solution:** Institute SEC tests for adherence to underwriting standards, such as three quarters of profitable growth, before permitting initial public offering.
Lenders	**Conflicts:** Competing for up-front loan fees that lenders syndicate to other banks, diminishing incentive to scrutinize credit quality. **Potential solution:** Withhold portion of lender bonuses until customers pay back debt.
Analysts	**Conflicts:** Receive portion of investment-banking revenues to promote client companies while supposedly picking stocks that are likely to go up. **Potential solution:** Separate analysts from investment banks and pay based on accuracy of forecasts and performance of stock recommendations.
Media	**Conflicts:** Need to attract advertising from companies while reporting accurately on company's activities. **Potential solution:** Raise subscription rates and minimize advertising; promote investigative reporting in place of hyping latest hot trend.
Regulators	**Conflicts:** Receiving contributions from companies against whose malfeasance they are supposed to protect the general public. **Potential solution:** Eliminate political contributions to regulators by those being regulated.
Executives	**Conflicts:** CEO's stock and options may lead to decisions that increase the value of CEO compensation in the short term while reducing the long-term value of the company. **Potential solution:** Stop heads-I-win, tails-you-lose executive compensation practices and replace with a greater proportion of compensation that declines if the company's financial performance and stock market value declines.
Politicians	**Conflicts:** Receiving cash from companies against whose malfeasance they are supposed to protect the general public. **Potential solution:** Replace political contributions by corporations with tax deductions for free media coverage.

Table 9.4.   Conflicts of Interest and Potential Solutions.

responded this way, the public relied on the analyst to pick its investments. Nevertheless, because the public was not paying directly for the analyst's recommendations, the market was signaling that these recommendations were worth what the public was paying for them—nothing.

A key weakness in the system is important participants' reliance on cross-subsidies. As we just noted, investors do not purchase analysts' research reports directly. Rather, analysts' salaries are subsidized through a combination of revenues from corporate and retail customers. Most politicians do not finance their own political campaigns, relying instead on contributions from companies and individuals.

Analysts and politicians both rely on public trust. Analysts' ability to influence investors depends on the public's belief in the objectivity of their analyses. Politicians' ability to get votes depends in part on whether the public trusts them to look out for its interests. Yet analysts' and politicians' ability to act in the public interest is constrained by the cross-subsidies. Analysts get paid more if they help increase the size of the pool from which their compensation is drawn. Sometimes this has meant that analyst reports are written to increase investment banking revenues, yielding higher analyst compensation, even if the reports are not objective. Similarly, politicians who depend on corporate contributions to finance their campaigns may perform the functions that corporate donors intended them to perform while avoiding criticism for taking an action that might not be in the broader public interest.

To the extent that capitalist cross-subsidized actors can't pay their own way, they may not be able to earn the public's trust. There is a chance that investors will not part with their cash to buy shares of companies until these conflicts are eliminated. The potential solutions described in Table 9.4 are intended to minimize or eliminate these conflicts. However, the forces opposing such solutions are formidable. Politicians need money to win elections, and companies want to use their cash to curry favor with politicians. Unless politicians can find another way to finance their campaigns, the current system will prevail. Analysts need to generate investment-banking revenue to fund their compensation because investors do not consider their analyses worth paying for. The media needs to curry favor with advertisers to pay for its salaries and cover its costs because the general public is not willing to pay enough for the content itself to offset the cost of producing it.

Given the power of the interests supporting the status quo, it is unlikely that these conflicts will be eliminated. Therefore, more progress may be made in encouraging government to nudge accounting, the language of business, in a direction that more accurately reflects companies' underlying economic reality. As we noted earlier, when economic booms reach their peak, some companies yield to the temptation to stretch the truth in order to keep their stock prices rising. The latest boom-and-bust cycle is no exception. In the aftermath our system faces an inability to trust the most basic performance statistics on which investment decisions should be made.

Maybe accounting rules make it acceptable to count revenues that involve limited cash receipts. And some companies went beyond acceptable practices to report growth that was an economic fiction in order to boost stock prices and make sales commissions.

In 2002 many examples of this emerged to public view. Here are three:

> Global Crossing bought worthless network capacity from EPIK, an Orlando, Florida, company, while selling Global Crossing network capacity to EPIK. Global Crossing's accountants booked the EPIK purchase as a capital expenditure and the sale to EPIK as revenue. Because capital expenditures don't affect results that Wall Street scrutinized most closely, Global Crossing was able to use these kinds of transactions to boost revenue artificially.[2]

> Qwest, a service provider, sold $450 million of telecom equipment to privately held KMC Telecom Holdings while Qwest agreed to pay hundreds of millions to KMC for telecom services. Qwest made a profit on the equipment sales and was able to boost its reported revenues—transactions that have not been disclosed in regulatory findings.[3]

> EMC, a maker of data storage equipment, shipped excess product inventory to resellers such as Unisys to avoid having to report the inventory on its own books. An internal investigation found certain workers in EMC's professional-service division in Chicago had forged work orders in order to meet their mandated quotas.[4]

These examples are just a fraction of the examples of accounting being used to create a fiction intended to disguise economic reality. In order to restore credibility to our financial system, we need to find a way to reconnect reported financial statements with economic reality.

One way to do this would be to go back to cash accounting. *Cash accounting* means recording a sale as the amount of cash that a customer receives when the customer receives the cash. Cash accounting means recording an expense as the amount of cash that a company disburses to a supplier or employee when that cash is disbursed. Small businesses with no interest in accessing the public markets find it more realistic and cost-effective to use cash accounting. Cash accounting does not require the hiring of expensive accountants to research and resolve complex matters of accounting policy.

Larger businesses or those with aspirations to access the public markets use accrual accounting because it is the standard approach for public companies. Many vested interests support the use of accrual accounting. For example, by allowing financial statements to get away from cash accounting, we have allowed lobbyists to argue for generally accepted accounting principles (GAAP), which detach financial reporting from economic reality. The examples we have offered are fairly complex. The point of these examples is that companies use GAAP to report revenues that exceed the cash received from the "acceptable" transactions. What is acceptable is not necessarily accurate.

A statement of cash flows in publicly reported financial statements does not reflect cash accounting. A quick peek at such cash flow statements reveals that the cash flow from operations starts with the reported net income or loss, a calculation that is based on the various accounting conventions exemplified by Global Crossing, Qwest, and EMC.

Although unscrupulous executives could manipulate any form of accounting, cash accounting could be audited by comparing a company's financial reports against bank records. As long as the auditors were compensated for the quality of their audits rather than their ability to sell consulting services, the system of cash accounting could help restore confidence to our financial markets.

Under accrual accounting, income is counted when the sale occurs, and expenses are counted when a company receives goods or services rather than when a check arrives or leaves a bank account. Accrual accounting allows companies to count revenues before they receive cash and to defer expenses even though cash has gone out the door. For example, by capitalizing its expenses, bankrupt WorldCom was able to keep expenses off its income statement and therefore falsely report profits.

The concept of accrual accounting is at the core of very complex accounting policies that give accountants leeway to essentially make up numbers to satisfy investors and lenders. Here are some other examples:

> Energy traders use market-to-market accounting for long-term energy contracts, which allow traders to forecast the value of long-term contracts and inflate their revenues well in excess of the cash they actually receive from those contracts during the period in which they report those revenues. Furthermore, energy traders counted as revenues the dollar value of the energy they were trading rather than the amount of cash they received as a result of the trades, a much smaller figure. Traders received bonuses based on the bigger numbers, so they had every incentive to overstate how much they made.

> Telecommunications companies engaged in capacity swaps, in which they recognized revenues for trading unused transmission capacity between telecom providers even though no cash had actually changed hands. Global Crossing, Qwest, and WorldCom all allegedly conducted such cash-free transactions to boost reported revenue.

> Companies that have made huge acquisitions, such as AOL Time Warner and WorldCom, must write off the value of the goodwill and intangible assets they receive when they paid more than book value for a company. In 2002, for example, AOL took a $54 billion write-off, although the basis for the amount of the write-off was based on complex value estimates that it did not disclose. And in 2003 AOL took a further $45 billion goodwill write-off.

Accrual accounting leaves plenty of room for such gaps to emerge between economic reality and what companies report in filings to the SEC. And exposing accounting scandals such as those at WorldCom or Enron does not happen through regular financial reporting; it happens when disgruntled former insiders leak documents or new CEOs conduct special investigations. Given the complexity of accrual-accounting procedures and the incentives to abuse them, investors have little reason to have confidence in reported numbers.

A potential solution is to scrap accrual accounting and go to cash-basis accounting. Here, a company would report as revenues the amount of cash that went into its bank account during the period when it received that cash. Similarly, it would count expenses during the period when cash left its bank account.

Although a determined executive could game such a system, cash-basis accounting would leave fewer avenues for deceiving investors and lenders and would go a long way toward restoring trust in our capital markets.

Policymakers must weigh the benefits of restoring the public's trust in capitalism against the costs of changing a conflicted set of incentives on which their power depends. If the costs of lost public trust become high enough, then the public might hold policymakers accountable for not eliminating the conflicts that sap that trust. At the other extreme, if the stock market rises for an extended period of time, the public's concern about these conflicts could be washed away in a soothing bath of equity wealth—at least until the next market decline. Perhaps the most likely outcome is that marginal reforms to the system of conflicts will be enacted as a way of lancing the boil of public anger. Such reforms might create a more suitable, if not ideal, context in which companies can adapt to Value Leadership.

CONCLUSION

Value Leadership is a powerful concept because it goes to the heart of capitalism. Its critics argue that capitalism succeeds because bosses exploit workers. Value Leadership suggests that capitalism succeeds because it makes workers, customers, and communities better off. Value Leadership works most effectively in the context of trust. When that context is shattered, trust must be rebuilt slowly—by a series of commitments backed up by actions that fulfill these commitments. Executives have the power to rebuild and sustain that trust. Value Leadership is a concept that rewards executives—in their role as shareholders—for creating competitively superior value for their company's employees, customers, and communities.

Selection and Value Quotient Analysis of Value Leaders

T his Appendix contains details of the research that underlies the key concepts presented in this book. It is organized into two sections:

- Selection of Value Leaders
- Value Quotient Analyses of Value Leaders

SELECTION OF VALUE LEADERS

As noted in the Introduction, we selected the Value Leaders based on eleven criteria. This section presents the results of applying those criteria to the eight Value Leaders. Tables A.1 through A.8 outline each company's performance on Value Leader selection criteria.

Table A.1.   Value Leader Selection-Criteria Performance: Synopsys.

Market share: 35% share of Field programmable gate arrays tools (2001), 27.6% of silicon intellectual property market (2001)
Ten-year average return on equity: 14.2% vs. 6% for technical and system software industry
Revenue per employee: $242,000 vs. $169,000 for technical and system software industry
Balance sheet strength: Debt-equity of 0 vs. 0.13 for technical and system software industry
Ten-year earnings growth: Not available
Ten-year shareholder return: +150% vs. +105% for S&P 500 (11/92 to 11/02)

Financial reporting quality: Conservative revenue accounting
Few legal problems: Cadence intellectual property litigation managed through insurance policy
High employee satisfaction: 30% of executive time devoted to retention-related activities
Excellent customer service: Measures and gets high scores on customer satisfaction
High peer respect: Not available

Sources: eeTimes, MSN Moneycentral, Synopsys 10-K, author interviews.

Table A.2.   Value Leader Selection-Criteria Performance: Southwest Airlines.

Market share: Fourth-largest U.S. carrier based on domestic passengers boarded
Ten-year average return on equity: 14.66% vs. 10.3% for regional airline industry
Profit per employee: $8,000 vs. $4,000 for regional airline industry
Balance sheet strength: Debt-equity of 0.38 vs. 0.78 for regional airline industry
Five-year earnings growth: 2.54% vs. −7.24% for regional airline industry
Ten-year shareholder return: +320% vs. +105% for S&P 500 (11/92 to 11/02)

Financial reporting quality: Conservative accounting
Few legal problems: No significant legal contingencies
High employee satisfaction: Ranked in 100 best companies to work for in United States (2000) by *Fortune*
Excellent customer service: Highest airline customer-satisfaction index (74) in 2002
High peer respect: Second most admired by *Fortune,* 2002 and 2003

Sources: Fortune, MSN Moneycentral, Southwest Airlines 10-K, author interviews.

Table A.3.   Value Leader Selection-Criteria Performance: J. M. Smucker.

Market share: Leading share of jam and jelly market
Two-year average return on equity: 11.9% vs. 10.4% for processed and packaged goods industry
Profit per employee: $17,000 vs. $6,000 for processed and packaged goods industry
Balance sheet strength: Debt-equity of 0.13 vs. 0.58 for processed and packaged goods industry
One-year earnings growth: 14.7% vs. 9.4% for processed and packaged goods industry
One-year shareholder return: +10% vs. −20% for S&P 500 (11/01 to 11/02)

Financial reporting quality: Conservative revenue accounting
Few legal problems: No material legal matters
High employee satisfaction: Ranked 8th best to work for in 2003 according to *Fortune*
Excellent customer service: Happy employees deliver good customer service
High peer respect: Respected in local community

Sources: Fortune, Business Week, MSN Moneycentral, Smucker 10-K.

Table A.4.   Value Leader Selection-Criteria Performance: Johnson & Johnson.

Market share: 75% of sales from businesses with number 1 or number 2 global market share
Ten-year average return on equity: 26.9% vs. 29.1% for major drug manufacturers
Revenue per employee: $347,000 vs. $344,000 for major drug manufacturers
Balance sheet strength: Debt-equity of 0.10 vs. 0.26 for major drug manufacturers
Five-year earnings growth: 12.51% vs. 6.14% for major drug manufacturers
Ten-year shareholder return: +370% vs. +105% for S&P 500 (11/92 to 11/02)

Financial reporting quality: Conservative accounting policies
Moderate legal problems: Product liability, patent infringement, and environmental cases
High employee satisfaction: Ranked 98th on *Fortune*'s list of America's best companies to work for (2002)
Excellent customer service: Ranked 3rd in industry on quality of products or services (2002)
High peer respect: Ranked 6th on *Fortune*'s list of America's most admired companies (2003)

Sources: Fortune, fool.com, MSN Moneycentral, Johnson & Johnson 10-K.

Table A.5.   Value Leader Selection-Criteria Performance: Microsoft.

Market share: World's largest software company
Ten-year average return on equity: 26.07% vs. 12.4% for application software industry
Revenue per employee: $594,000 vs. $276,000 for application software industry
Balance sheet strength: Debt-equity of 0.00 vs. 0.05 for application software industry
Five-year earnings growth: 14.97% vs. −5.77% for S&P 500
Ten-year shareholder return: +810% vs. +105% for S&P 500 (11/92 to 11/02)

Financial reporting quality: Revenue accounting becoming more conservative
Moderate legal problems: Resolving antitrust matters
High employee satisfaction: Ranked 28th on *Fortune*'s list of America's best companies to work for (2002)
Excellent customer service: Ranked 3rd in industry on quality of products or services (2002)
High peer respect: Ranked 4th on *Fortune*'s list of America's most admired companies (2002), 7th in 2003

Sources: Fortune, MSN Moneycentral.

Table A.6.   Value Leader Selection-Criteria Performance: MBNA.

Market share: Largest issuer of affinity cards
Ten-year average return on equity: 26.78% vs. 15.2% for regional mid-Atlantic banks
Revenue per employee: $378,000 vs. $286,000 for regional mid-Atlantic banks
Balance sheet strength: Debt-equity of 1.02 vs. 0.94 for regional mid-Atlantic banks
Five-year earnings growth: 23.33% vs. −2.12% for regional mid-Atlantic banks
Ten-year shareholder return: +900% vs. +105% for S&P 500 (11/92 to 11/02)

Financial reporting quality: Conservative revenue accounting
Moderate legal problems: $18 million settlement of deceptive advertising lawsuit (11/01)
High employee satisfaction: Ranked 22nd on *Fortune*'s list of America's best companies to work for (2003)
Excellent customer service: High satisfaction yields 97% profitable customer retention
High peer respect: Ranked 190th on *Fortune*'s list of America's most admired companies (2002)

Sources: Fortune, MSN Moneycentral, MBNA 10-K.

Table A.7. Value Leader Selection-Criteria Performance: Wal-Mart.

Market share: World's number 1 retailer, with more than 4,500 stores
Ten-year average return on equity: 20.28% vs. 15.6% for discount and variety stores
Revenue per employee: $167,000 vs. $176,000 for discount and variety stores
Balance sheet strength: Debt-equity of 0.52 vs. 0.54 for discount and variety stores
Ten-year earnings growth: 16.38% vs. 0.80% for discount and variety stores
Ten-year shareholder return: +240% vs. +105% for S&P 500 (11/92 to 11/02)

Financial reporting quality: Conservative accounting policies
Moderate legal problems: 4,851 lawsuits in 2000 for discrimination, unpaid overtime, and so on
High employee satisfaction: Ranked 94th on *Fortune*'s list of America's best companies to work for (2002)
Fair customer service: Ranked 5th in customer satisfaction in July 2002
High peer respect: Ranked 1st on *Fortune*'s list of America's most admired companies (2003)

Sources: *Fortune*, MSN Moneycentral, *Consumer Reports* (July 2002).

Table A.8. Value Leader Selection-Criteria Performance: Goldman Sachs.

Market share: Global mergers and acquisitions leader in 2001
Two-year average return on equity: 19.33% vs. 16.9% for investment brokerage, national industry
Revenue per employee: $1,000,000 vs. $638,000 for investment brokerage, national industry
Balance sheet strength: Debt-equity of 2.0 vs. 2.74 for investment brokerage, national industry
One-year earnings growth: –8.7% vs. –23.2% for investment brokerage, national industry
Ten-year shareholder return: 0% vs. –35% for S&P 500 (11/99 to 11/02)

Financial reporting quality: Conservative accounting
Low legal problems: Legal proceedings not material
High employee satisfaction: Ranked 35th on *Fortune*'s list of America's best companies to work for (2003)
Excellent customer service: Committed to anticipating client needs
High peer respect: Ranked 54th on *Fortune*'s list of America's most admired companies (2002)

Sources: *Fortune*, MSN Moneycentral, Goldman Sachs 10-K.

VALUE QUOTIENT ANALYSES OF VALUE LEADERS

This section presents a Value Quotient (VQ) interview guide in Exhibit A.1. Details of the analyses used to arrive at VQs for seven Value Leaders appear in Tables A.9 through A.15; details for the eighth Value Leader, Synopsys, appear in Table 1.2 (Chapter One).

Exhibit A.1.   Value Quotient Interview Guide.

CEO Background
- What was your background prior to working at your company?
- Why did you join your company?

Value Human Relationships
- What are your company's core values?
- How were these values developed?
- How widely and how frequently are these values communicated within your company?
- How do these values influence the way employees are hired, evaluated, and rewarded?

Foster Teamwork
- How does your company encourage teamwork among different departments within your company?
- How does your company manage partnerships within its industry?
- What steps, if any, is your company taking to enhance teamwork?
- How does your company use its performance measurement and compensation systems to influence manager and employee behavior?

Fulfill Your Commitments
- Does your company have specific policies regarding integrity?
- How does your company's hiring and promotion process enforce such policies?
- How conservative are your company's accounting policies?
- Have questions been raised about your company's financial reporting?
- Have employees, customers, or communities sued your company alleging unfair treatment?

Experiment Frugally
- How does your company develop new products and services?
- How does your company measure the effectiveness of its new product development process?

Fight Complacency
- Is your company worried about becoming complacent? If so, how does your company fight complacency?
- What performance measurement and reward processes encourage your company's self-renewal?
- Why does your company make acquisitions, and how does it manage their financial risks and integration issues?
- How is your company developing its next generation of managers and executives? How confident is your company of its executive bench strength?

Win Through Multiple Means
- What capabilities contribute most to your company's market leadership?
- How does your company keep competitors from copying these capabilities? How, in general, does your company keep ahead of its competitors?
- What are the most significant risks facing your company, and what processes manage these risks?

Give to Your Community
- How does your company give to its communities?
- Why is such giving important?

Table A.9.   Value Quotient Analysis: Southwest Airlines.

Principle	Activity: Evaluation	Score
Value human relationships	**Commit to core values:** Core values permeate all activities.	5
	Hire for values: Hiring screens strictly for attitude.	5
	Balance performance measurement: Balances results and values.	5
	Reward employees intelligently: Money for results, praise for values.	5
	Weighted total (sum times 3)	60
Foster teamwork	**Train teams:** Management training programs build teams.	5
	Rotate jobs: High-potential employees choose rotations.	5
	Make team decisions: Teams motivated to learn and improve.	5
	Reward team behavior: Rewards team behavior through profit sharing.	5
	Weighted total (sum times 3)	60
Experiment frugally	**Grow organically:** New market entry based on careful analysis.	5
	Manage development risk: Market entry risks analyzed in detail.	5
	Partner internally: Use of teams in service enhancements.	5
	Partner externally: Tailors services to customer wants.	4
	Weighted total (sum times 3)	56
Fulfill your commitments	**Hire and promote honest people:** Integrity tested by interviews.	5
	Account honestly: Conservative accounting and financial policies.	5
	Treat employees, customers, and communities fairly: Top-down concern for fair treatment.	5
	Weighted total (sum times 4)	60

(Continues)

Table A.9.   Continued.

Principle	Activity: Evaluation	Score
Fight complacency	**Plan CEO succession:** Promoted long-time employee to president.	4
	Sustain a healthy paranoia: Fighting for survival since founding.	5
	Attack new markets: Strategy yields best industry profit record.	<u>5</u>
	Weighted total (sum times 4)	56
Win through multiple means	**Understand the customer:** Deep understanding of customer.	5
	Build diverse capabilities: Ultimate example of diverse capabilities.	5
	Sustain competitive superiority: Best industry results.	<u>5</u>
	Weighted total (sum times 4)	60
Give to your community	**Inspire employees:** Ronald McDonald House (RMH) story demonstrates high inspiration.	5
	Enrich the community: RMH and free flights enrich community.	4
	Attack big societal problems: RMH solves part of a societal problem.	<u>3</u>
	Weighted total (sum times 4)	48
Value Quotient	(Sum divided by 420)	95%

Key: 5 = excellent; 4 = very good; 3 = good; 2 = fair; 1 = poor. Weighted scores for each principle are calculated by multiplying the activity scores by 3 for four-activity principles and by 4 for three-activity principles.

Table A.10.   Value Quotient Analysis: J. M. Smucker.

Principle	Activity: Evaluation	Score
Value human relationships	**Commit to core values:** Multiple generations of family values.	5
	Hire for values: Tight culture screens for values.	5
	Balance performance measurement: Balances results and values.	5
	Reward employees intelligently: Profit sharing, praise for values.	<u>5</u>
	Weighted total (sum times 3)	60
Foster teamwork	**Train teams:** Employee training builds teams.	5
	Rotate jobs: Job rotations keep employees motivated.	5
	Make team decisions: Listens to all employees.	5
	Reward team behavior: Rewards results and values behavior.	<u>5</u>
	Weighted total (sum times 3)	60

Principle	Activity: Evaluation	Score
Experiment frugally	**Grow organically:** Jif and Crisco acquisitions built capabilities.	4
	Manage development risk: Project Appleseed screened risky projects.	4
	Partner internally: Used teams in Project Appleseed.	3
	Partner externally: Partner with food service for Uncrustables.	<u>3</u>
	Weighted total (sum times 3)	42
Fulfill your commitments	**Hire and promote honest people:** Integrity tested by interviews.	5
	Account honestly: Conservative accounting.	5
	Treat employees, customers, and communities fairly: Lauded for fair treatment of stakeholders.	<u>5</u>
	Weighted total (sum times 4)	60
Fight complacency	**Plan CEO succession:** Promoted family members with long tenure.	4
	Sustain a healthy paranoia: Ambition and tradition drive company.	4
	Attack new markets: Acquisitions have improved results.	<u>5</u>
	Weighted total (sum times 4)	52
Win through multiple means	**Understand the customer:** Deep understanding of customers.	5
	Build diverse capabilities: Acquisitions add to capabilities.	4
	Sustain competitive superiority: Ambition keeps standards high.	<u>4</u>
	Weighted total (sum times 4)	52
Give to your community	**Inspire employees:** Employees share management respect outside.	5
	Enrich the community: Heartland Education Community is enriching.	5
	Attack big societal problems: Attacks local problems well.	<u>3</u>
	Weighted total (sum times 4)	52
Value Quotient	(Sum divided by 420)	90%

Key: 5 = excellent; 4 = very good; 3 = good; 2 = fair; 1 = poor. Weighted scores for each principle are calculated by multiplying the activity scores by 3 for four-activity principles and by 4 for three-activity principles.

Table A.11.   Value Quotient Analysis: Johnson & Johnson.

Principle	Activity: Evaluation	Score
Value human relationships	**Commit to core values:** Employees buy into credo.	5
	Hire for values: Screens potential employees for values.	5
	Balance performance measurement: Balances work and life.	5
	Reward employees intelligently: Money for results, praise for values.	5
	Weighted total (sum times 3)	60
Foster teamwork	**Train teams:** Leadership development program builds teams.	3
	Rotate jobs: Individual and manager pick next jobs.	3
	Make team decisions: Kaizen method at Critikon uses teamwork.	5
	Reward team behavior: Kaizen method at Critikon rewards teams.	5
	Weighted total (sum times 3)	48
Experiment frugally	**Grow organically:** Builds off marketing strengths.	4
	Manage development risk: R&D productivity has improved.	4
	Partner internally: Significant internal partnering for new products.	5
	Partner externally: Excellent partnerships with big buyers.	5
	Weighted total (sum times 3)	54
Fulfill your commitments	**Hire and promote honest people:** Tylenol response proves honesty.	5
	Account honestly: Conservative accounting.	5
	Treat employees, customers, and communities fairly: Lives credo for all stakeholders.	5
	Weighted total (sum times 4)	60
Fight complacency	**Plan CEO succession:** Promoted long-time employee to CEO.	5
	Sustain a healthy paranoia: Focused on market leadership.	5
	Attack new markets: Acquisition strategy has been very effective.	5
	Weighted total (sum times 4)	60
Win through multiple means	**Understand the customer:** Works closely with customers.	5
	Build diverse capabilities: Acquisitions add to capabilities.	3
	Sustain competitive superiority: Ambition raises performance bar.	5
	Weighted total (sum times 4)	52

Principle	Activity: Evaluation	Score
Give to your community	**Inspire employees:** Credo and reputation inspire employees.	5
	Enrich the community: Strong community involvement.	5
	Attack big societal problems: Foundation has addressed many big problems.	<u>5</u>
	Weighted total (sum times 4)	60
Value Quotient	(Sum divided by 420)	94%

Key: 5 = excellent; 4 = very good; 3 = good; 2 = fair; 1 = poor. Weighted scores for each principle are calculated by multiplying the activity scores by 3 for four-activity principles and by 4 for three-activity principles.

Table A.12.   Value Quotient Analysis: Microsoft.

Principle	Activity: Evaluation	Score
Value human relationships	**Commit to core values:** Values high intellect and energy.	5
	Hire for values: Unique interviews screen for reasoning under stress.	5
	Balance performance measurement: Evolving balance between results and values.	4
	Reward employees intelligently: Drives productivity with cash and options.	<u>5</u>
	Weighted total (sum times 3)	57
Foster teamwork	**Train teams:** Emphasis on technical training.	3
	Rotate jobs: Technical and management career ladders.	4
	Make team decisions: Use of teams in product development.	4
	Reward team behavior: Rewards results and moving to values.	<u>3</u>
	Weighted total (sum times 3)	42
Experiment frugally	**Grow organically:** Builds off marketing and coding strengths.	5
	Manage development risk: Development process manages risk.	5
	Partner internally: Core product development teams work well.	5
	Partner externally: Attempting to improve partner relationships.	<u>3</u>
	Weighted total (sum times 3)	54

(Continues)

Table A.12.   Continued.

Principle	Activity: Evaluation	Score
Fulfill your commitments	**Hire and promote honest people:** Evolving focus on integrity.	3
	Account honestly: Increased emphasis on conservative accounting.	3
	Treat employees, customers, and communities fairly: Improving fairness of treating customers.	<u>4</u>
	Weighted total (sum times 4)	40
Fight complacency	**Plan CEO succession:** New CEO strong but change incomplete.	4
	Sustain a healthy paranoia: Paranoia and self-criticism dominate.	5
	Attack new markets: Attacks with new product versions.	<u>5</u>
	Weighted total (sum times 4)	56
Win through multiple means	**Understand the customer:** In-depth knowledge of customers.	5
	Build diverse capabilities: Effective at hiring to build new capabilities.	5
	Sustain competitive superiority: Ambition raises performance bar.	<u>5</u>
	Weighted total (sum times 4)	60
Give to your community	**Inspire employees:** Encourages United Way participation.	5
	Enrich the community: Gives extensively to local communities.	5
	Attack big societal problems: Ambitious vaccine and AIDS initiatives.	<u>5</u>
	Weighted total (sum times 4)	60
Value Quotient	(Sum divided by 420)	88%

Key: 5 = excellent; 4 = very good; 3 = good; 2 = fair; 1 = poor. Weighted scores for each principle are calculated by multiplying the activity scores by 3 for four-activity principles and by 4 for three-activity principles.

Table A.13.   Value Quotient Analysis: MBNA.

Principle	Activity: Evaluation	Score
Value human relationships	**Commit to core values:** Cultlike conformity to values and style.	5
	Hire for values: Disciplined hiring process.	5
	Balance performance measurement: Balances results and values.	5
	Reward employees intelligently: Money for results, praise for values.	<u>5</u>
	Weighted total (sum times 3)	60

Principle	Activity: Evaluation	Score
Foster teamwork	**Train teams:** Offers training to develop team skills.	4
	Rotate jobs: Provides self-directed job rotation.	4
	Make team decisions: Use of teams in service and product development.	4
	Reward team behavior: Rewards results and values behavior.	<u>5</u>
	Weighted total (sum times 3)	51
Experiment frugally	**Grow organically:** Expands only where capabilities are competitive.	5
	Manage development risk: Development risk tightly controlled.	5
	Partner internally: Core product development teams work well.	5
	Partner externally: Effective partnering with affiliate groups.	<u>5</u>
	Weighted total (sum times 3)	60
Fulfill your commitments	**Hire and promote honest people:** Integrity tested by interviews.	4
	Account honestly: Conservative revenue accounting.	4
	Treat employees, customers, and communities fairly: Treats all stakeholders fairly.	<u>4</u>
	Weighted total (sum times 4)	48
Fight complacency	**Plan CEO succession:** Cawley successor not clear.	3
	Sustain a healthy paranoia: Obsessive focus on winning.	5
	Attack new markets: Prudently attacks new markets.	<u>5</u>
	Weighted total (sum times 4)	52
Win through multiple means	**Understand the customer:** Very in-depth knowledge of customer.	5
	Build diverse capabilities: Carefully adds to capabilities.	5
	Sustain competitive superiority: Extremely competitive culture.	<u>5</u>
	Weighted total (sum times 4)	60
Give to your community	**Inspire employees:** Encourages employee community involvement.	5
	Enrich the community: Enriches local communities where employees work.	5
	Attack big societal problems: MBNA Foundation works on educational causes.	<u>5</u>
	Weighted total (sum times 4)	60
Value Quotient	(Sum divided by 420)	93%

Key: 5 = excellent; 4 = very good; 3 = good; 2 = fair; 1 = poor. Weighted scores for each principle are calculated by multiplying the activity scores by 3 for four-activity principles and by 4 for three-activity principles.

Table A.14.   Value Quotient Analysis: Wal-Mart.

Principle	Activity: Evaluation	Score
Value human relationships	**Commit to core values:** Wal-Mart cheer epitomizes cultlike culture.	5
	Hire for values: Interviews ensure fit with values.	5
	Balance performance measurement: Stronger emphasis on results.	3
	Reward employees intelligently: Profit sharing, stock ownership, and low wages.	<u>5</u>
	Weighted total (sum times 3)	54
Foster teamwork	**Train teams:** Several effective team-training programs.	5
	Rotate jobs: Systematic development of team skills.	4
	Make team decisions: Teams pull together to improve service.	4
	Reward team behavior: Rewards results and values behavior.	<u>5</u>
	Weighted total (sum times 3)	54
Experiment frugally	**Grow organically:** Used capabilities to expand into new markets.	5
	Manage development risk: Minimized risk by starting small.	5
	Partner internally: Internal teams cut costs.	5
	Partner externally: Strong initiatives to partner with customer.	<u>5</u>
	Weighted total (sum times 3)	60
Fulfill your commitments	**Hire and promote honest people:** Integrity tested by interviews.	4
	Account honestly: Conservative revenue accounting.	4
	Treat employees, customers, and communities fairly: Tough on employees and suppliers, fair to others.	<u>3</u>
	Weighted total (sum times 4)	44
Fight complacency	**Plan CEO succession:** Promoted long-time employee to president.	5
	Sustain a healthy paranoia: Paranoia permeates management.	5
	Attack new markets: Has expanded into new markets with vigor.	<u>5</u>
	Weighted total (sum times 4)	60
Win through multiple means	**Understand the customer:** Customer research leads to deep knowledge.	5
	Build diverse capabilities: Effective development of new capabilities.	5
	Sustain competitive superiority: Ambition raises performance bar.	<u>5</u>
	Weighted total (sum times 4)	60

Principle	Activity: Evaluation	Score
Give to your community	**Inspire employees:** Lets local employees choose charities.	5
	Enrich the community: Enriches local communities.	5
	Attack big societal problems: Moderate improvement of society.	<u>3</u>
	Weighted total (sum times 4)	52
Value Quotient	(Sum divided by 420)	91%

Key: 5 = excellent; 4 = very good; 3 = good; 2 = fair; 1 = poor. Weighted scores for each principle are calculated by multiplying the activity scores by 3 for four-activity principles and by 4 for three-activity principles.

Table A.15. Value Quotient Analysis: Goldman Sachs.

Principle	Activity: Evaluation	Score
Value human relationships	**Commit to core values:** Pop quizzes test knowledge of fourteen core values.	5
	Hire for values: Exhaustive interviews screen for values.	5
	Balance performance measurement: Balances results and values.	5
	Reward employees intelligently: Money for results and values.	<u>5</u>
	Weighted total (sum times 3)	60
Foster teamwork	**Train teams:** Management training program builds teams.	5
	Rotate jobs: Systematic development of team skills.	5
	Make team decisions: Use of teams in sales, deals, and market growth.	5
	Reward team behavior: Rewards results and values behavior.	<u>5</u>
	Weighted total (sum times 3)	60
Experiment frugally	**Grow organically:** Growth builds on strengths.	4
	Manage development risk: Review process cuts risky expansion.	4
	Partner internally: Service development teams work well.	5
	Partner externally: Partners effectively with clients.	<u>5</u>
	Weighted total (sum times 3)	54
Fulfill your commitments	**Hire and promote honest people:** Integrity tested by interviews.	5
	Account honestly: Conservative revenue accounting.	5
	Treat employees, customers, and communities fairly: Rewards role model behavior and hard results.	<u>5</u>
	Weighted total (sum times 4)	60

(Continues)

Table A.15.   Continued.

Principle	Activity: Evaluation	Score
Fight complacency	**Plan CEO succession:** Develops new CEOs from within.	5
	Sustain a healthy paranoia: Acute awareness of competition.	5
	Attack new markets: Expands well into new markets.	<u>5</u>
	Weighted total (sum times 4)	60
Win through multiple means.	**Understand the customer:** Close relationships with clients.	5
	Build diverse capabilities: Selective outside hiring to bolster skills.	5
	Sustain competitive superiority: Relentless focus on winning.	<u>5</u>
	Weighted total (sum times 4)	60
Give to your community	**Inspire employees:** Lets employees devote time to charity.	5
	Enrich the community: Focuses on community education.	5
	Attack big societal problems: Major political involvement of some alumni.	<u>4</u>
	Weighted total (sum times 4)	56
Value Quotient	(Sum divided by 420)	98%

Key: 5 = excellent; 4 = very good; 3 = good; 2 = fair; 1 = poor. Weighted scores for each principle are calculated by multiplying the activity scores by 3 for four-activity principles and by 4 for three-activity principles.

~~~ Notes

Introduction

1. Enron Corporation, *2000 Annual Report* (Houston, Tex.: Enron Corporation, 2000), p. 53.
2. P. Behr and A. Witt, "Ex-Enron Exec Related a Dispute," *Washington Post*, Mar. 19, 2002, p. A01.
3. J. Harwood, "Enron Scandal Taints Business Leaders," *Wall Street Journal*, Apr. 11, 2002, p. D5.
4. Hart-Teeter, "Study #6205," NBC News/*Wall Street Journal*, [http://online. wsj.com/documents/poll-20020613.html], June 2002.
5. N. Maestri, "War Rally Didn't Save Quarter for Stock Traders," Reuters, [http://www.forbes.com/home_europe/newswire/2003/04/01/rtr926532. html], Apr. 1, 2003.
6. "Ouch! Shareholders Lost $2.4 Trillion in 2002," *San Jose Mercury News*, [http://www.siliconvalley.com/mld/siliconvalley/3643410.htm], July 11, 2002.
7. Author interview with J. Bachmann, managing director of Edward Jones, Feb. 5, 2003.
8. Author interview with Bachmann.
9. Jowett translation, "Exploring Plato's Dialogues, *Republic* 29 (514a-521b)," [http://plato.evansville.edu/texts/jowett/republic29.htm], no date.
10. The peer companies (and their Value Leader counterparts) are Cadence Design Systems (Synopsys), J. C. Penney (Wal-Mart), Merrill Lynch (Goldman Sachs), Merck (Johnson & Johnson), Hansen Natural (J. M. Smucker), American Airlines (Southwest Airlines), Computer Associates (Microsoft), and Capital One (MBNA).

Chapter One

1. The returns that bigtipper.com (http://www.bigtipper.com) calculated reflected the percentage change in stock price for all publicly announced buy recommendations on CNBC between the day of the recommendation and the last trading day of the years 1998 and 1999.

    The returns that validea.com (http://www.validea.com) calculated were the returns six months following the day of the recommendation on CNBC, CNN, or CBS MarketWatch in 2000.

2. *Covering a position* refers to selling a stock if the investor has purchased it or buying back the shares if the investor has sold the shares short. In a *short sale,* an investor borrows shares from a broker and sells the shares at the current market price. The investor is betting that the shares will drop in price, after which the investor can profit by buying back the borrowed shares at the lower market price. The investor profits by keeping the difference between the price at the time of the initial sale and the price at the subsequent time of purchase. Short selling is very risky because the investor can bet wrong and the price of the stock can rise instead of falling as the investor hoped. In this case the investor's potential loss is theoretically unlimited.

3. Author e-mail "Recent Calls," July 25, 2002. Investors can use sources such as Yahoo Finance to identify the prices of these stocks on the dates mentioned.

4. Author interview with A. de Geus, chairman and CEO of Synopsys, Sept. 30, 2002.

5. Author interview with B. Henske, former CFO of Synopsys, Sept. 24, 2002.

6. Author interview with de Geus.

7. Author interview with de Geus.

Chapter Two

1. L. Thompson, "Simply Smucker's," *Small Business Network,* Apr. 1, 2001, p. 13.

2. L. Haferd, "Small-Town Ohio to Help J. M. Smucker Co. Celebrate 100th Birthday," *Akron (Ohio) Beacon Journal,* Oct. 23, 1997.

3. J. L. Sullivan, "Putting the Fiz Back In: Passed by Rivals, Hansen Seeks to Regain Soda Niche," *Orange County Business Journal,* May 23, 1994, p. 1.

4. Hansen Natural Corporation, *Hansen's Naturals 2001 Annual Report* (Corona, Calif.: Hansen Natural Corporation, 2001), p. 15.

5. M. Brelis, "Herb's Way—Chairman's Unconventional Business Strategy Has Made Southwest Airlines a Model for Success," *Boston Globe,* Nov. 5, 2000, p. F1.

6. A. Walmsley, "Plane Crazy Southwest Airlines' Herb Kelleher and His Crew Break All the Rules—and Beat the Pants off Their Competitors Doing It," *Globe and Mail,* Nov. 26, 1999, p. 62.

7. Brelis, "Herb's Way."

8. J. Hoffer-Gittell, "Paradox of Coordination and Control," *California Management Review,* Apr. 1, 2000, pp. 101–117.

9. "Goldman Sachs," TheVault.com, [http://www.vault.com/companies/company_main.jsp?co_page=2&product_id=307&ch_id=240&v=2&tab-num=2], no date.

10. "Goldman Sachs," TheVault.com.

11. S. McMurray, "The Team Player," *Fast Company,* June 1996, p. 134.

12. McMurray, "Team Player."

13. "The Merrill Lynch Principles," [http://www.ml.com/about/principles.htm], no date.

14. "Merrill Lynch, 2002 Edition," TheVault.com [http://www.vault.com/bookstore/book_preview.jsp?product_id=311], no date.

15. "Merrill Lynch, 2002 Edition."

16. C. Goforth, "Jam-Maker Smucker Relies on Attitude, Not Incentives, for Happy Workers," *Akron (Ohio) Beacon Journal,* Jan. 23, 2000.

17. "SJM Financial Results Key Ratios," Moneycentral.msn.com, [http://moneycentral.msn.com/investor/invsub/results/compare.asp?Page=ManagementEfficiency&Symbol=SJM], July 5, 2002.

18. "SJM Financial Results Key Ratios."

19. K. L. Alexander, "Cultivating a Culture: Companies See Strong Link Between Worker Attitudes, Profits," *Washington Post,* Apr. 21, 2002, p. H01.

20. Alexander, "Cultivating a Culture."

21. J. Huey, "Outlaw Flyboy CEOs: Two Texas Mavericks Rant About the Wreckage of the U.S. Aviation Industry—and Reveal How They've Managed to Keep Their Companies Above the Miserable Average; Gordon Bethune; Herb Kelleher," *Fortune,* Nov. 13, 2000, p. 237.

22. Huey, "Outlaw Flyboy CEOs."

Chapter Three

1. B. Paik Sunoo, "How Fun Flies at Southwest Airlines," *Personnel Journal,* June 1, 1995, p. 62.

2. Paik Sunoo, "How Fun Flies at Southwest Airlines."

3. AMR Corporation, American Airlines information, [http://www.amrcorp.com], no date.

4. American Customer Satisfaction Index, "First Quarter Scores, May 2002," [http://www.theacsi.org/first_quarter.htm#air], May 2002.

5. C. J. Loomis, "Sam Would Be Proud [Wal-Mart No. 2]: As It Changes CEOs, Mighty Wal-Mart Is Poised to Become No. 1 on the Fortune 500," *Fortune*, Apr. 17, 2000, p. 130.

6. Loomis, "Sam Would Be Proud."

7. D. Moin, "Wal-Mart's New CEO Seen [as] Pivotal in Apparel Strategies," *WWD*, Jan. 18, 2000, p. 2.

8. Moin, "Wal-Mart's New CEO Seen [as] Pivotal in Apparel Strategies."

9. Moin, "Wal-Mart's New CEO Seen [as] Pivotal in Apparel Strategies."

10. T. Arango, "J. C. Penney Denies Rumors of Accounting Irregularities: The Company Rebuts Talk of Alleged Improprieties in Its Eckerd Drugstores' Medicare Accounts," TheStreet.com, [http://www.thestreet.com/stocks/timarango/10007453.html], Jan. 25, 2002.

11. A. M. Raucher, "Dime Store Chains: The Making of Organization Men, 1880–1940," *Business History Review*, Mar. 22, 1991, p. 130.

12. J. Hoffer-Gittell, "Paradox of Coordination and Control," *California Management Review*, Apr. 1, 2000, pp. 101–117.

13. Hoffer-Gittell, "Paradox of Coordination and Control."

14. S. Loeffelholz, "Competitive Anger (American Airlines Management)," *FW*, Jan. 10, 1989, p. 28.

15. Hoffer-Gittell, "Paradox of Coordination and Control."

16. Hoffer-Gittell, "Paradox of Coordination and Control."

17. "No More Star Wars on Wall Street: Egos on Back Seat at Brokerages," *Plain Dealer (Cleveland, Ohio)*, Aug. 21, 1993, p. 7D.

18. C. Chandler, "Goldman's Golden Chance: An IPO or Merger Could Reap Millions for Partners at the Wall Street Titan—but Would It Destroy What Makes Goldman Sachs Goldman Sachs?" *Washington Post*, June 7, 1998, p. H01.

19. Chandler, "Goldman's Golden Chance."

20. S. Swartz and A. Monroe, "Girding for Battle: Goldman Sachs Strives to Adapt to Changes by Wall Street Rivals—It Expands Fast, Risks More and Fixes Weak Spots; Resignations Rise a Bit—But It Will Keep Partnership," *Wall Street Journal*, Oct. 9, 1986.

21. A. Schwimmer and R. Cooper, "The Raid on Merrill Lynch: How Deutsche Bank Did It," *Investment Dealers' Digest*, June 19, 1995, p. 12.

22. Schwimmer and Cooper, "The Raid on Merrill Lynch."

23. C. Tanner and R. Roncarti, "Kaizen Leads to Breakthroughs in Responsive- ness—and the Shingo Prize—at Critikon. (Johnson and Johnson Medical Inc.'s Critikon Vascular Access Facility)," *National Productivity Review,* Sept. 22, 1994, p. 517.

24. Tanner and Roncarti, "Kaizen Leads to Breakthroughs in Responsiveness."

Chapter Four

1. J. Frederick, "Wal-Mart Thrives on Innovation as Pharmacy Superpower," *Drug Store News,* June 12, 2000, p. 6.

2. Frederick, "Wal-Mart Thrives on Innovation as Pharmacy Superpower."

3. G. Jacobson, "The End for Phar-Mor," *Mass Market Retailers,* [http://www. massmarketretailers.com/articles/Pharmor_end.html], no date.

4. Frederick, "Wal-Mart Thrives on Innovation as Pharmacy Superpower."

5. Frederick, "Wal-Mart Thrives on Innovation as Pharmacy Superpower."

6. Frederick, "Wal-Mart Thrives on Innovation as Pharmacy Superpower."

7. L. Holton, "Penney's Ends Its Experiment with Telaction," *Chicago Sun-Times,* Mar. 31, 1989, p. 43.

8. Holton, "Penney's Ends Its Experiment with Telaction."

9. E. Ullman, "When It Comes to Innovation, Microsoft Sure Can Copy It," *Washington Post,* June 11, 2000, p. B02.

10. Ullman, "When It Comes to Innovation."

11. K. MacIver, "CA: The Hidden Dimension," *Computer Business Review,* July 1, 1998, p. 14.

12. MacIver, "CA: The Hidden Dimension."

13. "Computer Associates Reports First Quarter Fiscal Year 2003 Results," *PR Newswire,* [http://news.moneycentral.msn.com/ticker/article.asp? Symbol=US:CA&Feed=PR&Date=20020722&ID=1797893], July 22, 2002.

14. M. Pledger, "Work Force Helped Mold New Smucker Brainstorming Sessions [That] Led to New Products, Marketing," *Plain Dealer (Cleveland, Ohio),* May 23, 1999, p. 1H.

15. Pledger, "Work Force Helped Mold New Smucker Brainstorming Sessions."

16. Pledger, "Work Force Helped Mold New Smucker Brainstorming Sessions."

17. C. Hazard, "Pushing the Limit: Capital One Financial Leads a Marketing Revolution," *Richmond Times-Dispatch,* July 26, 1999, p. D-16.

18. Hazard, "Pushing the Limit."

19. "Capital One Hangs up on Wireless Test," *CardFAX,* Mar. 2, 2001, p. 1.

20. "Merck-Medco Fosters Innovation in Rx Care. Merck-Medco Inc. Strategies Help Keep Drug Cost Growth Low," *Chain Drug Review,* May 21, 2001, p. 1.

21. "Merck-Medco Fosters Innovation in Rx Care."

22. P. S. Cohan, "3M Is an American Multinational but Not a Typical One," Gurusonline, [http://gurusonline.tv/uk/conteudos/tulin.asp], June 2002.

23. Cohan, "3M Is an American Multinational but Not a Typical One."

Chapter Five

1. T. Maxon, "Heir Born: Southwest Airlines' Incoming CEO Earned His Wings Behind the Scenes," *Dallas Morning News,* May 16, 2001, p. 1D.

2. Maxon, "Heir Born."

3. Maxon, "Heir Born."

4. Maxon, "Heir Born."

5. K. Eichenwald, "For WorldCom, Acquisitions Were Behind Its Rise and Fall," *New York Times,* [http://www.nytimes.com/2002/08/08/technology/08TELE.html], Aug. 8, 2002.

6. Eichenwald, "For WorldCom."

7. Eichenwald, "For WorldCom."

8. AOL Time Warner Inc., 10-K filing, [http://www.sec.gov/Archives/edgar/data/1105705/000095014403004064/0000950144-03-004064-index.htm], Mar. 28, 2003, p. F-9.

9. M. Clowes, "Monday Morning: Honest-EPS Stocks Found to Fare Better," *Investment News,* Apr. 29, 2002, p. 2.

10. Clowes, "Monday Morning."

11. R. Buckman, "U.S. Agency Queries Microsoft Accounting—SEC Explores if Earnings Are Understated," *Asian Wall Street Journal,* June 10, 2002, p. 10.

12. Buckman, "U.S. Agency Queries Microsoft Accounting."

13. "SEC to Okay Microsoft Accounting Settlement-Report," *Reuters News,* May 31, 2002.

14. J. Guidera, "Computer Associates Says SEC Widens Accounting Probe," *Dow Jones Business News,* May 15, 2002.

15. Guidera, "Computer Associates Says SEC Widens Accounting Probe."

16. J. Guidera, "Leading the News: Probe of Computer Associates Centers on Firm's Revenue," *Wall Street Journal,* May 20, 2002, p. A3.

17. L. G. Foster, "The Credo Lives On," *Executive Excellence,* May 1, 2000, p. 5.

18. L. K. Trevino, L. P. Hartman, and M. Brown, "Moral Person and Moral Manager: How Executives Develop a Reputation for Ethical Leadership," *California Management Review,* July 1, 2000, pp. 128–142.

19. Foster, "The Credo Lives On."

20. J. Greene, "Ballmer's Microsoft: How CEO Steve Ballmer Is Remaking the Company That Bill Gates Built," *Business Week,* June 17, 2002, p. 66.

21. Greene, "Ballmer's Microsoft."

Chapter Six

1. J. Yardley, "Is Wal-Mart Immortal?" *Chicago Sun Times,* Nov. 22, 1998, p. 20.
2. Yardley, "Is Wal-Mart Immortal?"
3. "Kmart's Antonini Puts His Faith in the 'Big Boxes,'" *Financial Times,* Nov. 17, 1992, p. 26.
4 Yardley, "Is Wal-Mart Immortal?"
5. "Discounting Would Sweep U.S.," *Chain Drug Review,* July 22, 2002, p. 81.
6. "Discounting Would Sweep U.S."
7. C. J. Loomis, "Sam Would Be Proud [Wal-Mart No. 2]: As It Changes CEOs, Mighty Wal-Mart Is Poised to Become No. 1 on the Fortune 500," *Fortune,* Apr. 17, 2000, p. 130.
8. Loomis, "Sam Would Be Proud."
9. M. Nannery, "His Turn, Again," *Chain Store Age,* June 1, 2000, p. 86.
10. Nannery, "His Turn, Again."
11. C. Horyn, "Unabashed Wal-Mart Shopper Speaks," *New York Times,* [http://www.nytimes.com/2002/08/27/fashion/27DRES.html?8hpib], Aug. 27, 2002, p. B8.
12. Horyn, "Unabashed Wal-Mart Shopper Speaks."
13. P. Weever, "The Invader from Wall Street: Remarkable Rise of Goldman Sachs, the Investment Bank," *Sunday Telegraph,* Nov. 17, 1991, p. 37.
14. Weever, "The Invader from Wall Street."
15. C. Pretzlik, "Goldman Banker Who Shook City Heads Back to U.S.," *Financial Times* (FT.com), Apr. 13, 2002.
16. R. Wachman, "Thornton's China Station," *Observer,* [http://www.observer.co.uk/Print/0,3858,4636472,00.html], Mar. 30, 2003.
17. Pretzlik, "Goldman Banker Who Shook City Heads Back to U.S."
18. Z. Moukheiber and R. Langreth, "J&J an Unfinished Symphony: Revamped Labs, New Drugs, Big Plans," *Forbes,* Dec. 10, 2001, p. 62.
19. Moukheiber and Langreth, "J&J an Unfinished Symphony."

Chapter Seven

1. "Goldman Sachs Dominates in Emerging Markets," *Banker,* Aug. 1, 2001, p. 49.
2. "Goldman Sachs Dominates."
3. S. McGee, "Deals and Deal Makers: Goldman Sachs Seeks Junk-Bond Heft," *Wall Street Journal,* Nov. 1, 1999, p. C1.
4. McGee, "Deals and Deal Makers."
5. McGee, "Deals and Deal Makers."

6. R. Peterson, "Debt Deals Push Wall Street Underwriting to New Record," *Thomson Financial,* [http://216.239.35.100/search?q=cache:KDws7–23wp8C:www.tfibcm.com/league/pdfs/SL/4Q2001/Docs/4Q01Global CapitalMarketsPressRelease.PDF+high-yield+underwriting+rank+2002&hl=en&ie=UTF-8], Dec. 31, 2001.

7. A. Raghavan, "Merrill Lynch's Share of IPO Underwriting Market in Steady Decline," *Dow Jones Online News,* Mar. 12, 1998.

8. Raghavan, "Merrill Lynch's Share of IPO Underwriting Market in Steady Decline."

9. Y. D. Kantrow, "MBNA's Lerner & Cawley: Masters of Card Marketing Series: 1," *American Banker,* Mar. 2, 1993, p. 1.

10. Kantrow, "MBNA's Lerner & Cawley."

11. Kantrow, "MBNA's Lerner & Cawley."

12. J. W. Milligan, "Defying Gravity at MBNA," *U.S. Banker,* July 1, 1997, p. 35.

13. Milligan, "Defying Gravity at MBNA."

14. W. A. Schoneberger, "Southwest Airlines Thirtieth Anniversary," *Air Transport World,* June 1, 2001, p. 100.

15. Schoneberger, "Southwest Airlines 30th Anniversary."

16. Schoneberger, "Southwest Airlines 30th Anniversary."

17. Author interview with N. Huseman, Southwest Airlines passenger, Sept. 10, 2002.

18. Author interview with D. Conover, executive vice president customer service, Southwest Airlines, Sept. 4, 2002.

19. Author interview with Conover.

20. B. Thau, "Plano and Simple: J. C. Penney's New Strategy," *HFN: The Weekly Newspaper for the Home Furnishing Network,* May 24, 2001, p. 1.

21. "J. C. Penney One Hundredth Anniversary: Old Vision, New Version," *Chain Store Age,* June 1, 2002, p. 48.

22. "J. C. Penney One Hundredth Anniversary."

23. Thau, "Plano and Simple."

Chapter Eight

1. R. Alsop, "Perils of Corporate Philanthropy: Touting Good Works Offends the Public, but Reticence Is Misperceived as Inaction," *Wall Street Journal,* Jan. 16, 2002, p. B1.

2. M. A. Miille, "Corporate Philanthropy Give[rs] Make More More: A Growing Number of Companies Are Making Regular Donations—of Money and Merchandise—to All Kinds of Charities and Causes," *Sarasota Herald-Tribune,* Dec. 21, 1998, p. 10.

3. S. D. Green, "The Case for Caring," *PR Week US,* Oct. 1, 2001, p. 23.

4. Author interview with B. McDermott, executive director, Ronald McDonald House, Dallas, Texas, Sept. 12, 2002.

5. Author interview with McDermott.

6. Author interview with T. Martin, manager of civic and charitable contributions, Southwest Airlines, Aug. 29, 2002.

7. Author interview with Martin.

8. J. Boudreau, "Microsoft Boosts Philanthropy in Silicon Valley," *Knight Ridder Tribune Business News,* Feb. 16, 2001.

9. Boudreau, "Microsoft Boosts Philanthropy in Silicon Valley."

10. Boudreau, "Microsoft Boosts Philanthropy in Silicon Valley."

11. Boudreau, "Microsoft Boosts Philanthropy in Silicon Valley."

12. D. Rapchinski Ephrata, "Wal-Mart vs. the Community," *Lancaster (Penn.) New Era,* Mar. 3, 1995, p. A-8.

13. Rapchinski Ephrata, "Wal-Mart vs. the Community."

14. D. O'Connor, "Reluctantly, East Lampeter Takes Lead in 'Race' for First Wal-Mart Here," *Lancaster (Penn.) New Era,* Sept. 13, 1994, p. A-1.

15. P. Armijo, "Community Rallies Against Wal-Mart," *Albuquerque Journal,* Apr. 25, 2002, p. 1.

16. "Community Service a Wal-Mart Priority," *Chain Drug Review,* July 22, 2002, p. 82.

17. R. Sharpe, "States Speed Amber Alert Plans," *USA Today,* [http:// www.usatoday.com/news/nation/2002-08-27-amber-alerts_x.htm], Aug. 27, 2002.

18. "Community Service a Wal-Mart Priority."

19. "Wal-Mart and Sam's Club Associates Raise and Contribute a Record $196 Million in 2001," *PR Newswire,* May 30, 2002.

20. "Wal-Mart and Sam's Club Associates."

21. "Philanthropy—Gates the Good," *Economist,* Dec. 5, 1998.

22. "Philanthropy—Gates the Good."

23. B. Whyte, "Wealth for Health—a Gates Perspective," *Bulletin of the World Health Organization,* [http://www.who.int/bulletin/pdf/2001/issue5/ interview.pdf], 2001, *79*(5), 488.

24. D. Woodruff, "World Economic Forum, Davos 2001: Companies Explore Philanthropic Side: Latest Projects Focus on Social Welfare—Firms Rethink Their Role in Society," *Wall Street Journal Europe,* Jan. 29, 2001, p. 32.

25. "The $100 million program, dubbed The African Comprehensive HIV/ AIDS Partnerships (ACHAP) is a collaboration between the Government of Botswana (GOB), the Bill & Melinda Gates Foundation, and Merck to prevent and treat HIV/AIDS in Botswana. ACHAP, established in July 2000, supports the goals of the GOB to decrease HIV incidence and significantly

increase the rate of diagnosis and the treatment of the disease, by rapidly advancing prevention programs, healthcare access, patient management and treatment of HIV/AIDS. The Bill & Melinda Gates Foundation and the Merck Company Foundation have each dedicated $50 million over five years towards the project" (ACHAP Web site, [http://www.achap.org/], no date).

26. "With the ambitious goal of having an AIDS free generation in Botswana by 2016, the Merck-led campaign realized that creating such partnerships were an essential condition for success. Merck's partnership approach in Botswana was based on the company's successful Mectizan program in Africa, Latin America and Yemen, begun in 1987, that serves as a model for how private-public partnerships should be done to have an impact on important issues" (Merck, "The Story of Mectizan," [http://www.merck.com/about/cr/mectizan/home.html], May 2, 2003).

27. Woodruff, "World Economic Forum, Davos 2001."

28. J. Lamont, "Merck Seeks Wider Private-Sector Coalition on AIDS," *Financial Times,* [http://www.businessfightsaids.org/web/html/home_gbcaids_13sept02.html], Sept. 13, 2002.

29. Despite the slower than hoped for progress, ACHAP continued to push forward in 2003. According to the Republic of Botswana, one tangible outcome of ACHAP's efforts was the April 2003 opening of a facility at Botswana's Princess Marina Hospital to expand services to recipients of antiretroviral (ARV) drugs. "ACHAP project leader Dr. Donald de Korte said that this facility would help establish the capacity required to provide ARV therapy to the estimated 110,000 Batswana who need it" ("Health Ministry Receives New ARV Facility for Marina Hospital," Republic of Botswana, [http://www.gov.bw/cgi-bin/news.cgi?d=20030403], April 3, 2003).

30. G. Friedman, "Dr. Leighton Cluff—President, Robert Wood Johnson Foundation," *HealthWeek,* Nov. 28, 1988, p. 24.

31. Friedman, "Dr. Leighton Cluff."

32. Friedman, "Dr. Leighton Cluff."

Chapter Nine

1. M. Davis, "El Paso's Utility Deal Raises Eyebrows," TheStreet.com, [http://www.thestreet.com/stocks/melissadavid/10034166.html], July 26, 2002.

2. D. Berman and D. Solomon, "Questioning the Books: Accounting Questions Surround Telecom Pioneer—Global Crossing Used 'Swaps' to Enhance Its Revenue and It Wasn't the Only One," *Wall Street Journal Europe,* Feb. 14, 2002, p. 9.

3. D. Solomon and S. Liesman, "Deals With KMC Helped Qwest to Improve Its Books," *Wall Street Journal,* Feb. 13, 2002, p. B6.

4. J. Guidera, "EMC Booking of Sales Draws Review by SEC," *Wall Street Journal,* Feb. 13, 2002, p. B6.

⎯∿⎯ Acknowledgments

This book could not have been completed without the help of numerous individuals. Matt Williams, my agent at the Gernert Company, offered tremendously valuable feedback during the initial stages of the project and worked closely with Kathe Sweeney to develop a common agreement on the book's objectives and approach. Kathe Sweeney, business and management editor at Jossey-Bass, expressed a keen interest in this project from the beginning and made significant contributions throughout its development.

During the process of writing the book, I benefited from the insights of several individuals. Tania Yannas, a cofounder of 3PLex, a logistics software company, provided very insightful comments on the initial drafts of each chapter, helping to sharpen my thinking and clarify key points of the book. Tania also provided many useful insights from her experience at Goldman Sachs. Alex Lach, a former colleague at Monitor Company and now a hedge fund manager in Beverly Hills, California, provided many useful insights. And Bruce Henderson, president of Matrix USA, helped me develop the numbering scheme for the Value Quotient.

This book could not have been completed without the insights of executives at Southwest Airlines and Synopsys. Southwest Airlines receives as many as fifty requests a week for authors seeking its input, so Southwest's agreement to participate was an honor. Specifically, my understanding of Value Leadership was far richer as a result of the input of Donna Conover, Tracie Martin, and Beverly Carmichael. The book also benefited from the support of Synopsys senior executives including Aart de Geus, Chi-Foon Chan, and Bob Henske.

Finally, the ideas in the book benefited from my interaction with several leading business journalists. Specifically, I have learned a great deal from my interaction with Amey Stone, David Shook, and Alex

Salkever at BusinessWeek Online, Melissa Davis at TheStreet.com, Justin Fox of *Fortune,* Ianthe Dugan of the *Wall Street Journal,* and Mark Veverka of *Barron's.*

As with all my books, this one could not have been completed without the support of my wife and family, to whom I am deeply grateful.

~~~ The Author

Peter S. Cohan is president of Peter S. Cohan & Associates, a management consulting firm. His strategy consulting practice helps companies in technology-intensive industries to identify, evaluate, and profit from new business opportunities created by changing technology. Services include process facilitation, proprietary research reports, and management development. Clients are global leaders in industries such as telecommunications, computer networking, systems integration, and semiconductors.

Cohan's venture capital business offers entrepreneurs capital and advice. His firm invested in Andromedia, an Internet software company, which was acquired in December 1999 for $440 million in stock by Macromedia (MACR) and SupplierMarket.com, an industrial products Web site, itself acquired in August 2000 by Ariba (ARBA) for $930 million in stock. Cohan serves on the advisory board of Lexar Media (LEXR).

Cohan is also an executive in residence at Babson College in Wellesley, Massachusetts. Since 1981, he has completed over one hundred consulting projects, including the following:

For a major bank, Cohan recommended over $1 billion worth of bank acquisitions and helped sell its credit card portfolio, yielding a $150 million profit.

For the board of directors of a multibillion-dollar insurance company, he evaluated acquisition candidates leading to its purchase of an investment bank.

For a telecommunications firm, he conceptualized a multimedia business partnership and identified and negotiated with partners.

For the board of directors of a major bank, he created a strategic plan, whose implementation helped the bank's stock rise from $3 to over $110 per share.

Cohan is a frequent speaker and TV commentator on high technology. Validea.com calculates a 52 percent six-month return on his 2000 stock picks. Bigtipper.com recognized Cohan as the Top Tipper of 1998 for the 68 percent return of his CNBC stock picks. His 1999 stock picks returned 239 percent. *TeamAsia* called Cohan "one of the top two or three technology strategists in the world." Singapore's *Institute of Advertising* called Cohan "the Peter Drucker of the New Millennium."

Cohan worked at CSC/Index with James A. Champy, coauthor of *Reengineering the Corporation,* and at the Monitor Company, a strategy consulting firm cofounded by Professor Michael E. Porter of the Harvard Business School.

Cohan is the author of six books. His two most recent were *Technology Leaders* and *e-Leaders* (Capstone, 2002). His fourth book, *e-Stocks: Finding the Hidden Blue Chips Among the Internet Impostors* (HarperBusiness, 2001), was praised in *Upside, Publishers Weekly, Library Journal,* and *Booklist. Investors' Business Daily* chose *e-Stocks* as one of its top ten investment books for 2001. The book was published in Italian and Chinese. His third book, *e-Profit: High Payoff Strategies for Capturing the E-Commerce Edge* (AMACOM, April 2000), was an Amazon.com e-commerce best-seller and was praised in MIT's *Sloan Management Review.* Soundview Executive Book Summaries selected *e-Profit* as one of its top thirty business books of 2000, and *Management General* nominated it a top ten business book of 2000.

Cohan's second book is *Net Profit: How to Invest and Compete in the Real World of Internet Business* (Jossey-Bass, 1999). The October 2000 *Economist* best-seller was wholesaler Ingram's second-most requested book of April 1999. The *Washington Post* called *Net Profit* "a savvy, discriminating guide to Internet stocks." The *Industry Standard* wrote "better than any previous book on the subject, [*Net Profit*] maps the true landscape of the Internet economy." *Net Profit* has fourteen five-star customer reviews on Amazon.com and was featured on its New and Notable page. In addition, *Management General* selected *Net Profit* as one of the top three management books of 1999.

Cohan's first book is *The Technology Leaders: How America's Most Profitable High-Tech Companies Innovate Their Way to Success,* published in July 1997. The book, in its second printing, has been published in Japanese, Chinese, Spanish, Portuguese, and Hebrew. *Management General* deemed it one of 1997's top ten management books.

Cohan was a guest of ABC's *Good Morning America,* Bloomberg TV, CNBC, CNBC Asia, CBS MarketWatch, Chicagoland TV News, CNNfn, Fox News Channel's *Forbes on Fox* and *Bulls and Bears,* NPR's *Marketplace Morning Report,* WCIU-TV, ZDTV, PBS, the American Management Association, *Fortune, Business Week,* the *Economist,* the Columbia Senior Executive Program, Stanford University's Industry Thought Leaders seminar, Singapore's National Science and Technology Board and its Institute of Advertising. His conferences have been sponsored by BMC Software, CNBC Asia, Oracle's OAUG, IBM, HP, Nokia, Technologic Partners, Teradyne, SAP, StarHub, Cadence, Cable & Wireless HKT, Development Bank of Singapore, and Verilink. Cohan has written for the *Boston Globe,* the *Industry Standard,* and the *Financial Times,* contributing to its *Handbook of Management* (2001). His online column, Reality Check, appears at gurusonline.tv. He has been quoted in the Associated Press; *Business 2.0; Business Week; Barron's; CBS MarketWatch; Fortune; Le Monde; MSNBC; Newsweek International, Inc.;* the *New York Times;* the *Straits Times;* TheStreet.com; the *Times; Time* magazine; and *USA Today.* He is also featured in *Business Minds: Connect with the World's Greatest Thinkers* (Pearson Educational, 2001) by Brown and Crainer and in *Business: The Ultimate Resource* (Perseus, 2002).

Prior to starting his firm, Cohan worked as an internal consultant in the banking and insurance industries. He received an MBA from the Wharton School, did graduate work in Computer Science at MIT, and earned a B.S. in electrical engineering from Swarthmore College.

~~~ Index